Lecture Notes in Artificial Intelligence   799

Subseries of Lecture Notes in Computer Science
Edited by J. G. Carbonell and J. Siekmann

Lecture Notes in Computer Science
Edited by G. Goos and J. Hartmanis

Munindar P. Singh

Multiagent Systems

A Theoretical Framework for Intentions,
Know-How, and Communications

Foreword by Michael N. Huhns

Springer-Verlag

Berlin Heidelberg New York
London Paris Tokyo
Hong Kong Barcelona
Budapest

Series Editors

Jaime G. Carbonell
School of Computer Science, Carnegie Mellon University
Schenley Park, Pittsburgh, PA 15213-3890, USA

Jörg Siekmann
University of Saarland
German Research Center for Artificial Intelligence (DFKI)
Stuhlsatzenhausweg 3, D-66123 Saarbrücken, Germany

Author

Munindar P. Singh
Information Systems Division, MCC
3500 W. Balcones Center Drive, Austin, TX 78759-5398, USA

CR Subject Classification (1991): I.2.11, C.2.4, D.4.7, F.3.2, I.2

ISBN 3-540-58026-3 Springer-Verlag Berlin Heidelberg New York
ISBN 0-387-58026-3 Springer-Verlag New York Berlin Heidelberg

CIP data applied for

Typesetting: Camera ready by author
SPIN: 10131065   45/3140-543210 - Printed on acid-free paper

To my parents

Foreword

Distributed artificial intelligence (DAI) is a melding of artificial intelligence with distributed computing. From artificial intelligence comes the theory and technology for constructing or analyzing an intelligent system. But where artificial intelligence uses psychology as a source of ideas, inspiration, and metaphor, DAI uses sociology, economics, and management science for inspiration. Where the focus of artificial intelligence is on the individual, the focus of DAI is on the group. Distributed computing provides the computational substrate on which this group focus can occur.

However, DAI is more than just the design of intelligent systems. It also provides insights and understanding about interactions among humans, as they organize themselves into various groups, committees, societies, and economies in order to improve their lives. For example, economists have been studying multiple agents for more than two hundred years, ever since Adam Smith in the eighteenth century, with the goal of being able to understand and predict economies. Economics provides ways to characterize masses of agents, and these are useful for DAI. But in return, DAI provides a means to construct artificial economies that can test economists' theories before, rather than after, they are applied.

Distributed artificial intelligence has become a growing and maturing subfield of computer science. Since the first organized gathering of researchers in DAI at an MIT workshop in 1979, there have been twelve DAI Workshops in the U.S.A., five MAAMAW Workshops in Europe, two CKBS Workshops in England, two MACC Workshops in Japan, and numerous meetings associated with other conferences. A substantial body of results, in the form of theories and working systems, has already been produced. As I write this foreword in late 1993, there are plans underway for five DAI-related colloquia in the next six months and an International Conference the following year. This level of interest around the globe is significant. It is indicative of the importance that DAI has attained in computer science, and of the quality and quantity of research that is being produced by its international research community.

Moreover, DAI is growing, even at a time when AI itself is not. I think there are three major reasons for this: (1) DAI deals with open systems, i.e., systems that are too large or unpredictable to be completely characterized— most real systems are of this type; (2) DAI is the best way to characterize or design distributed computing systems; and (3) DAI provides a natural way to view intelligent systems. I will elaborate on each of these reasons in turn.

First, real systems cannot be meaningfully closed and bounded for analysis purposes. No matter how they are defined, they will always be subject to new information from outside themselves, causing unanticipated outcomes. For example, to analyze fully the operation of a banking system and produce answers to such questions as "How many of the customers will try to access the banking system at the same time, and will the system be able to handle the resulting load?" one must attempt to include all of the people that use the system. This is infeasible. By taking an open systems approach and a social perspective, DAI provides notions of systems of commitment and joint courses of action that permit such questions to be considered naturally.

Second, DAI is the best way to characterize or design distributed computing systems. Information processing is ubiquitous. There are computer processors seemingly everywhere, embedded in all aspects of our environment. My office has five, in such places as my telephone and my clock, and this number does not consider the electrical power system, which probably uses hundreds in getting electricity to my office. The large number of processors and the myriad ways in which they interact makes distributed computing systems the dominant computational paradigm today.

But there is a concomitant complexity in all this processing and interaction that is difficult to manage. One effective way is by considering such distributed computing systems in anthropomorphic terms. For example, it is convenient to think that "my toaster *knows* when the toast is done," and "my coffee pot *knows* when the coffee is ready." When these systems are interconnected so they can interact, then they should also *know* that the coffee and toast should be ready at approximately the same time. In these terms, my kitchen becomes more than just a collection of processors—a distributed computing system—it becomes a *multiagent system*.

Third, DAI also provides a natural way to view intelligent systems. Much of traditional AI has been concerned with how an agent can be constructed to function intelligently, with a single locus of internal reasoning and control implemented in a Von Neumann architecture. But intelligent systems do not function in isolation—they are at the very least a part of the environment in which they operate, and the environment typically contains other such intelligent systems. Thus, it makes sense to view such systems in societal terms.

In support of this view, there is a fundamental principle that I find appealing and applicable here: *cognitive economy*. Cognitive economy is the idea that given several, equally good explanations for a phenomenon, a rational mind will choose the most economical, i.e., the simplest. The simplest explanations are the ones with the most compact representation, or the lowest computational cost to discover and use, or the minimum energy, or the fewest variables or degrees of freedom. Cognitive economy is manifested by an agent choosing the simplest representation that is consistent with its perceptions and knowledge. It is the basis for McCarthy's circumscription and accurately characterizes many aspects of human visual perception.[1]

There are several important ramifications for an agent that adheres to this idea. When applied to an agent's beliefs about its environment, cognitive economy leads an agent to believe in the existence of other agents: characterizing the environment as changing due to the actions of other agents is simpler than trying to cope with a random and unpredictable environment. (This is possibly why, when confronted with a complex and often incomprehensible world, ancient cultures concocted the existence of gods to explain such events as eclipses and the weather. Believing that a god is making it rain is simpler than understanding the physics of cloud formation.) When applied to the unknown internals (whether beliefs, desires, and intentions or states and next-state functions) of other agents, cognitive economy causes an agent to presume that other agents are just like itself, because that is the simplest way to represent them. (This is possibly why hypothesized gods are typically human-like.)

Hence, an agent must construct representations, albeit economical ones, that accurately cover its perceptions of the environment. Representations are simplifications that make certain problems easier to solve, but they must be sufficient for the agent to make realistic predictions about how its actions will change the environment. If an agent had *no* representations, it could still act, but it would be inefficient. For example, it would wander aimlessly if it did not know something about a graph it was traversing to reach a goal. The agent could treat the environment as deterministic and completely under its control—a STRIPS-like approach—but this would be inaccurate and not robust. The agent could model the unpredictability of the environment using statistics, but this would inform the agent only what it should do on the average, not specifically what it should do now. Of the many things that an agent

---

[1] "Rube Goldberg" devices are fascinating for people simply because they violate this principle of cognitive economy.

could choose to represent, agents are among the most important because they purposefully change the environment. It is thus rational for an agent to create and maintain internal representations of other agents; otherwise, it would simply react to the unpredictable (to it) changes in its environment that are caused by the other agents, and its own behavior would be inefficient.

What might be the nature of these representations? Agent architectures based on beliefs, desires, and intentions are common in AI. The beliefs are a representation of the environment, and form the basis upon which the agent chooses its actions. When an agent represents other agents, it must represent what *they* believe, desire, and intend. The other agents have beliefs about (i.e., representations of) this agent, and its beliefs and representations of them, *ad infinitum*. But this must converge, because representations are (by my definition) *simplifications* of the things being represented, and representations of representations of representations ..., soon have no content. A first-order representation for another agent is that it is the same as one's representation for oneself. The representation can then be refined via perception and interaction.

Believing that there are other agents in its environment will cause an agent to act differently, e.g., *benevolently* and *predictably*. First, a benevolent agent might clean up its environment, if it believes that other agents will act similarly, because it knows that it can operate more efficiently in a more orderly environment. For example, it might remove an obstacle that is blocking the path of other agents, under the belief that other agents will also help remove obstacles from its own path.

Second, as stated by Randall Davis, "An agent should act predictably." This implies

- the agent should have a self model with which it is consistent, i.e., its beliefs should be consistent with each other and its actions should be consistent with its beliefs, and

- the agent should have a representation of what other agents believe about it (a representation of their representation of it), and should act in accord with that.

By acting predictably, an agent will reduce conflicts with other agents, thereby increasing not only its own effectiveness, but also the effectiveness of all of the agents. Enabling this behavior is just one of the important capabilities for agents that needs to be researched.

Research Directions

There are two basic ways by which research progress has been made in DAI: (1) by extending single-agent concepts to multiple agents, and (2) by developing uniquely multiagent concepts for which there are no single-agent analogs. Examples of the first are extensions of belief revision and nonmonotonic reasoning to groups of agents, while examples of the second are negotiation, cooperation, content-based communication, and the design of environments in which autonomous and independently-developed agents are guaranteed to interact fairly.

A field is defined by the researchers and practitioners that consider themselves to be working in it, and by the collection of papers, results, and working systems that they produce. A substantial body of results has been produced in DAI, consisting of the proceedings of at least 24 Workshops, held in Europe, Asia, and North America; seven edited collections of DAI papers; numerous research monographs; several special journal issues; and working systems in such areas as manufacturing and process control, scheduling, and decision support. What is missing from all of this is a principled, comprehensive methodology for characterizing and constructing the essential component of a DAI system—an agent's cognitive structure, which determines its behavior and interaction with other agents. This book supplies such a methodology.

This book is also a return to the roots of DAI—the Contract Net— in the following sense. An agent has both knowledge and capabilities. The contract net provided a way for an agent to advertise its capabilities and employ them in assisting other agents. However, much of the work in DAI since the contract net was first described in 1978 has focused on the knowledge of the agents, rather than on their capabilities. This book provides a principled way to represent and discuss the capabilities of agents—not what they think and know, but what they can and will do. From a utilitarian viewpoint, this latter is of *far* greater importance.

For the future, there needs to be experimentation in DAI to validate the theoretical advances exemplified by this monograph. The experiments need to be conducted in both physical and computational environments: there is both difficulty and power in each. But experimentation in small, controlled worlds is not an effective way to establish meaningful relationships between agents and their environment. Such agents would not need or establish the type of relationships required for them to function effectively in real environments, i.e., they would not scale up. Also, the agents themselves need to be long-lived and adaptable. Agents that are restarted each time they are given a problem to solve are not confronting important aspects of autonomy.

There is still no uniquely multiagent aspect to learning. That is, group learning is so far nothing more than replicated individual learning. One promising possibility is based on the observation that an agent does not need to learn or remember something if it can rely on another agent to know or learn it. This affects what an agent chooses to learn, not how it chooses to learn it.

Most importantly, agents must have the ability to acquire and use representations of each other. This is what is needed for negotiation, cooperation, coordination, and multiagent learning. What should be the contents of these representations? This book provides the answer.

Michael N. Huhns

Preface

It is well-known that the future of computing lies in distributed computing. Distributed computing systems are of great significance in a number of current and future applications of computer science. For example, they are central to systems for electronic data interchange, air traffic control, manufacturing automation, computer supported cooperative work, and electronic banking, as well as in robotics and heterogeneous information systems. As the nature of computing comes to be increasingly characterized by networking and resource-integration, distributed computing systems will occur in all key applications.

The expansion and increasing importance of distributed computing presents us with a number of outstanding problems. I introduce these problems in terms of three main desiderata for distributed systems. One, practicable distributed systems must be *heterogeneous*. Reasons for this include the needs to (a) preserve past investment in diverse systems, (b) facilitate introduction of new technology piecemeal, and (c) optimize platform usage by using the most appropriate platform for each task. Two, the components of feasible distributed systems must in general be *locally autonomous*. Reasons for this include the needs to (a) manage security, (b) enable incremental change, and (c) obey legal requirements. Three, deployable distributed systems must behave in a manner that is not just *predictable*, but also *controllable* by their end users. Reasons for this include the needs to (a) behave correctly in critical applications, and (b) empower the ultimate users of technology, which is a key prerequisite to introducing it into novel application domains. A number of other requirements on distributed systems can also be stated, but the above are the most relevant for our purposes.

In light of the above, we must ensure that different components of a distributed system interact with one other in a manner independent of their internal implementations. The question then arises as to how we may specify how these interactions are to take place, so that components may independently be upgraded without affecting the correctness of the entire system. Most extant research on this problem concerns itself with the low-level aspects of interaction:

typically, it worries about the formatting of data rather than its content.

Another set of problems pertains to requirements acquisition. Capturing requirements for complex systems, which is a difficult problem in centralized computing, becomes harder and more urgent for distributed computing. We need to capture both the end users' requirements and the intermediate design requirements by which the desired interactions among different components can be used to guide their implementation. Consequently, the need for high-level specification techniques is more pressing than ever. For the same reason, there is need for formalization of any proposed specification approaches.

The program of research whose initial steps are reported in the present monograph addresses the issues described above. It does not entirely solve them, for they are too complex and have many facets, but it addresses their deepest aspects directly. I propose that we think of distributed systems as composed of intelligent entities with intentions, beliefs, and know-how. These entities interact through high-level communications in order to affect each others' intentions and beliefs and, thereby, actions. I submit that, when properly formalized and understood for their computational content, the intentions and know-how of agents, and the communications that take place among them, are important scientific abstractions for complex distributed systems.

These abstractions help us meet our three desiderata quite naturally. One, the heterogeneity of system components is hidden behind concepts that are independent of implementation; interactions among the components similarly occur in a content-based and implementation-independent manner. Two, the components can easily be designed to be autonomous, being influenced by other components only to the extent desired. Such components may also be used as mediators to shield existing applications. Three, specifications phrased in terms of the proposed concepts are natural for end users and more easily correspond to their wishes and expectations.

I develop a semantics of intentions and know-how in a general model of actions and time. Using this semantics, I also provide a semantics for the different modes of communication, including, e.g., promises and prohibitions. The proposed framework involves actions, possible and actual, abstract and concrete, that agents perform. This enables us to use intentions, know-how, and communications as more than just conceptual descriptions. Their formal semantics is useful for comparing implementations and for creating design tools. It aids us in stating constraints on system behavior that more naturally capture users' requirements. The proposed framework can thus serve as a foundation on which to develop specific approaches and methodologies for specifying, designing, and implementing complex systems.

I use the term *agent* to refer to the intelligent components of distributed systems when viewed in this manner; I use the term *multiagent systems* to describe the composite systems themselves. Of course, multiagent systems are really distributed systems and have no privileged approach to computation distinct from other distributed systems. But we should not allow ourselves to be distracted by this. The power of the proposed approach resides in its making high-level concepts available for specification and design and in supplying a formal notion of correctness in terms of those concepts. Of course, almost every abstraction can be reduced to lower-level abstractions, but that does not by itself make it useless. For example, just because programming languages can be compiled all the way to microcode or hardware does not mean that we should not use them. Similarly, multiagent systems can be reduced to ordinary distributed systems, but it may not be productive to do so.

It turns out that the approach I follow is closely related, in spirit, to work in distributed artificial intelligence (DAI). Concepts such as knowledge, intentions, know-how, and communications are of key importance in DAI. The work described here can thus be seen as contributing to DAI. However, I view DAI as a means to solve the problems in distributed computing, not as an end in itself.

One always takes a risk when attempting to formalize some previously informal concepts. This risk is the acutest for mental concepts, such as intentions. One can never precisely capture every informal aspect of such concepts, which may in fact be mutually contradictory. The yardstick I use in deciding upon a particular formalization is its utility to the main program of research, namely, the high-level specification of multiagent systems. If a formalization makes impossible to naturally derive an important result, that would be reason to discard it. If a formalization requires going into the innards of an intelligent system, rather than giving a high-level specification, that too would be reason to discard it.

This is not to say that other potential approaches are necessarily useless: just that, for purposes of computing, I see them as less fit than the chosen approach. Indeed, the history of science indicates that informal concepts can be formalized as several coexisting concepts. For example, the sixteenth century concept of *impetus* has been formalized as the present-day concepts of *momentum* and *kinetic energy*. Both can be valid: the first would be preferable for computing the force required to stop a moving object in a certain time and the second for computing the energy that must be dissipated in order to stop it.

I have sought to make the present work accessible to a wide audience, including graduate students and researchers in computer science (including distributed computing and artificial intelligence), cognitive science, and philosophy. The main focus of the proposed theory is in computer science, however. No special background is required beyond a familiarity with logic and some mathematical maturity. A knowledge of temporal and modal logic would help, but is not essential.

Outline of this Monograph

The rest of this monograph is organized as follows. Chapter 1 discusses multiagent systems in some detail and shows what it means to take the intentional stance towards them. It also discusses the state of the art in computer science as it pertains to multiagent systems and points out how the present work fits in with it.

Chapter 2 motivates and develops the basic formal model, which considers the actions of agents in a framework of branching time. It admits simultaneous actions by several agents and allows the actions of different agents to be performed out of synchronization. These features help make the model correspond more closely to the multiagent systems that may occur in practice than would have been possible otherwise. The way in which all these features are brought together is novel.

In this chapter, I also motivate and describe *strategies*, which are programs denoting abstract actions. Strategies are used to define intentions and know-how in a way that makes them easy to interrelate. A notion of knowledge is also needed to properly define know-how. I describe the standard modal one, which I use here. Finally, I compare the proposed framework to the theories of action in linguistics, philosophy, and artificial intelligence.

Chapter 3 motivates a definition of intentions that is suitable for multiagent systems. It includes a discussion of the numerous dimensions of variation of intentions as studied in the pertinent artificial intelligence and philosophy literature. My goal is not to produce a philosophical treatise. However, it is crucial to obtain an understanding of the key issues, though from a strictly computer science perspective. After this discussion, I proceed to motivate and present a formalization of intentions and consider its strengths and limitations.

Chapter 4 motivates, defines, and formalizes the next core primitive in this monograph: know-how. Ability is an important special case of know-how, so it is treated first to clarify the subsequent formalization of know-how. Two formalizations are provided, one that considers the basic actions of agents directly, and another that considers abstractions over these actions. Though these formalizations have different architectural consequences, they have the same logical properties. This is as one would expect, because merely considering abstractions should not change the intrinsic meaning of a concept.

Next, Chapter 5 relates the concepts of intentions and know-how to each other. This is where the theory of this monograph really begins to fall into place. I prove the key theorem showing how an agent who (a) intends something, (b) has the necessary skills, (c) persists long enough with his intentions, and (d) is rational enough to actually use his know-how, can in fact succeed with his intention. It is "obvious" theorems like this one that are the hardest to prove formally, because, unless all the necessary ingredients are correctly formalized, spurious and counterintuitive consequences can easily result. Indeed, previous attempts to prove theorems akin to this suffer from shortcomings, which I detail.

Lastly, Chapter 6 is an exercise in using the definitions of intentions and know-how to give a semantics of communications. Like many other approaches, the proposed approach to communications is based on speech act theory. However, it differs from classical formalizations of speech acts in that it cleanly separates the semantic aspects from the syntactic and pragmatic aspects. I show that most previous attempts at the semantics of speech acts are not really semantics at all, in that they do not give the conditions of satisfaction of sentences in a formal model as required in a Tarskian model-theoretic semantics. I give a semantics of speech acts that states their conditions of satisfaction in the proposed technical framework. This facilitates the statement of various requirements and correctness constraints on communications in multi-agent systems with respect to the intentions and know-how of the participants. This semantics is used in a formal analysis of the well-known contract net protocol.

Acknowledgments

This monograph strongly reflects my personal philosophy about computational agents and their role in computer science. Thus, it is especially relevant that I acknowledge those who have influenced me and helped me formulate these views.

This monograph is based on my Ph.D. dissertation completed at the University of Texas at Austin. I am deeply indebted to my advisers, Nicholas Asher and Allen Emerson, for their constant encouragement and advice on all matters technical and presentational. They guided my work without ever attempting to impose their own will upon it. Nicholas listened patiently to my numerous harangues and pointed out the weaknesses of my various proposals. Allen helped relate my work to temporal logic and distributed computing and each instance of that exercise helped identify some superfluity or the other.

I am also indebted to the other members of my doctoral committee, Hans Kamp, Woody Bledsoe, and Robert Boyer, for their patience and trust. Bob Boyer, in particular, gave valuable comments on a previous draft that have helped me clarify and correct some claims.

I should take this occasion to thank my undergraduate professors. Shachin Maheshwari inspired me to undertake research in computer science and stressed the interplay between its practical and theoretical aspects. Niraj Sharma introduced me to distributed computing in a way that has held my interest, even in periods when I haven't actually pursued it.

Among the people I was fortunate enough to interact with in the course of my graduate career, Michael Huhns is the one I am most indebted to. He kept me thinking about multiagent systems, first in artificial intelligence and later in classical distributed computing. I learned a lot about computer science research from him. He has been a pillar of support and has given me great advice on professional and other matters.

I also benefited a lot from conversations with Benjamin Kuipers and Robert Koons, who kept me in touch with two opposite subjects that my research touches upon: reasoning about physical systems and the philosophy of mind, respectively. Rob gave me useful comments on previous versions of parts of this book. Several other people have helped me with their advice and suggestions. Kurt Konolige initially got me interested in theories of actions and intentions. Norman Martin encouraged me to pursue research in logic as applied to artificial intelligence. Manfred Krifka and Daniel Bonevac taught me much of what I know about the applications of logic in natural language.

Over the years, I have had useful discussions with a number of people, including Larry Stephens, Jürgen Müller, Wlodek Zadrozny, Raimo Tuomela, Nigel Seel, Anand Rao, Michael Georgeff, Jeff Rosenschein, Martha Pollack, Candy Sidner, and Graham Oddie. I have also gained much from interactions with fellow graduate students at the University of Texas and elsewhere, especially, Pankaj Mehra and Sakthi Subramanian. Several colleagues have helped shape my view of computer science, even though I did not always talk to them about the research reported here. These include Christine Tomlinson, Phil Cannata, Greg Lavender, Paul Attie, Greg Meredith, Wei-Min Shen, Jim Barnett, and Paul Portner.

Many of the changes from my dissertation to the present version were caused by comments from Jürgen Müller, Raimo Tuomela, Mike Huhns, Allen

Emerson, and Mona Singh. Jürgen, in particular, read a previous version extremely carefully and gave me lots of useful technical comments.

I am indebted most of all to my family for their continuous support. My son, Amitoj, was born after I completed my dissertation. He has tolerated my distractions with my research and always given me something to smile about. My wife encouraged me to pursue my research and was always there for me. She read several parts of this book, as well as papers in which some other parts were published. Her suggestions led to several improvements in the presentation. My parents gently nudged me towards completion. My father read draft versions of Chapters 1 and 3, and suggested numerous stylistic improvements, which I have tried to incorporate elsewhere also. My brother's frequent phone calls helped graduate school pass by easily. He and my sister-in-law and nephews were always exceedingly hospitable on my numerous visits to their home, mostly to work summers or attend conferences in the area.

This research was supported by various agencies. The University of Texas awarded me a Microelectronics and Computer Development (MCD) Fellowship. Kurt Konolige invited me to the Artificial Intelligence Center of SRI International for the summers of 1987 and 1988. Nicholas Asher and Carlota Smith supported me from a National Science Foundation grant (# IRI-8945845) to the Center for Cognitive Science, University of Texas. Gerhard Barth made it possible for me to visit DFKI (the German Research Center for Artificial Intelligence), Kaiserslautern, Germany during the summer of 1991. I have been supported most of all by the Microelectronics and Computer Technology Corporation. The director of the Artificial Intelligence Laboratory, Elaine Rich, supported me from June 1989 to August 1990. As director of the Carnot Heterogeneous Database Project, Philip Cannata supported me from September 1991 to May 1993. Phil encouraged me to pursue my research on multiagent systems, while giving me a great opportunity to acquire research expertise in heterogeneous databases. After Phil left, Darrell Woelk, who took over as director, has successfully managed to maintain a productive research climate in extremely tough times.

Munindar Paul Singh

Contents

Chapter 1

Multiagent Systems

Multiagent systems are distributed computing systems. Like all distributed systems, they are composed of a number of interacting computational entities. However, unlike classical distributed systems they, and their constituent entities, are intelligent. I shall adopt as my operational definition of intelligent systems one that is inspired by the works of McCarthy [1979], Newell [1982, p. 115], and Dennett [1987, pp. 13–35]. This definition sidesteps most slippery philosophical debate concerning the nature of intelligence. In essence, it states that intelligent systems are those for which it is helpful to take the *intentional stance*, to use McCarthy and Dennett's term, or those that can be said to have a distinct *knowledge level*, to use Newell's term.

In other words, a system is intelligent if you need, for intuitive or scientific purposes, to attribute cognitive concepts such as intentions and beliefs to it in order to characterize, understand, analyze, or predict its behavior. Thus one might say of an automatic teller machine that it "knows who I am," "does not want to give me more money than my account balance," "cannot give more than 100 dollars," "does not know how to approve an overdraft," and so on. Further such examples are discussed in the works cited above. The term *intentional* as used in this manner pertains not only to intentions, but also to other mental terms such as knowledge, beliefs, and desires.

Although some philosophers may dispute the validity of the above definition, and indeed it pretends to no philosophical sophistication, it proves particularly useful from the standpoint of computer science. It tells us that our intuitive conception of intelligence yields some nice abstractions for dealing with systems that behave intelligently. I shall return to this point later in this chapter, but suffice it to say here that this monograph is an exercise in providing a rigorous foundation to some of the abstractions that result from seriously taking the intentional stance towards computational systems.

The trend towards the development of increasingly intelligent systems is matched only by the trend towards the distribution of computing. The science of multiagent systems lies at the intersection of these trends. Multiagent systems are of great significance in a number of current and future applications of computer science. For example, they arise in systems for electronic data interchange, air traffic control, manufacturing automation, computer supported cooperative work, and electronic banking, as well as in robotics and heterogeneous information systems.

Besides the well-known reasons for the usefulness of distributed systems in general, continued progress in the study of multiagent systems is attractive for the following additional reasons. Advances in this study will permit intelligent systems to be developed independently of each other and to be reused as components of new systems. These components can be thought of as member *agents* in new multiagent systems. This modularization is also useful when designing systems for applications, such as medical diagnosis, in which expertise is naturally distributed over agents who specialize in different domains. A system designed as a multiagent system can also be more robust than otherwise, since the acquisition and validation of design requirements is simpler for such a system. Moreover, such a system can be simpler to design for many applications, including manufacturing planning and air-traffic control, by allowing an intelligent agent to be located at the site where the data are available and where the necessary decisions have to be taken.

Multiagent systems are thus of great practical importance in computer science. Unfortunately, no general framework is available at present that we may use to analyze, specify, design, or implement multiagent systems. In the next section, I briefly describe what the main components of the desired framework might be. These components are the high-level abstractions for multiagent systems that we must define and formalize.

Multiagent systems have usually been studied as a part of artificial intelligence (AI). This has been largely because of the experimental nature of most such systems. Also, their claims to intelligence often rest in languages and approaches, such as Lisp, rule-based expert-system shells, and blackboard architectures, which are traditionally associated with AI. It is hoped that the framework developed here will permit the expansion of multiagent systems into novel domains, partially by abstracting out the details of implementation and partially by developing a semantics that is closely related to the semantics for classical systems. Doing so would facilitate the implementation of multiagent systems on standard architectures and platforms.

1.1 Intentions, Know-How, and Communications

The term *agent* is widely used in computer science. It is variously applied to actors, to instantiated expert-system shells, to processes in general, to finite-state machines that monitor such processes, to physical robots, and to intelligent entities that react to their environment. The definition I adopt captures the most basic connotations of the term *agent*. According to this definition, agents are intelligent systems, towards which we need to take the intentional stance. In other words, agents are the basic units of intelligence that we consider. The examples from the literature listed above are all interesting realizations of agents as construed here.

The intentional stance makes available such abstractions as the intentions and know-how of agents, and the communications that take place among them. These turn out to be important scientific abstractions for multiagent systems. These abstractions no doubt have much conceptual appeal. Furthermore, there are simple pragmatic and technical reasons for considering them seriously. They

- are natural to humans, who are not only the designers and analyzers of multiagent systems, but also the end users and requirements specifiers;

- provide succinct descriptions of, and help understand and explain, the behavior of complex systems;

- make available certain regularities and patterns of action that are independent of the exact physical implementation of the agents in the system; and

- may be used by the agents themselves in reasoning about each other.

Consequently, these abstractions can be profitably applied in systems that may have unknown or evolving implementations. Their utility grows as we consider increasingly complex systems. The intentional stance gives us a way of proceeding with what we, and our agents, know or can find out about a given system. In this way, it addresses the issue of the partiality of the information we have about complex systems.

For any concept to be effectively used in science and engineering, it must have a rigorous foundation in theory. In particular, for the above abstractions to be useful in the science of multiagent systems, they must be given an objective grounding in terms of the architectures that different kinds of systems have, and the actions they perform.

I consider multiagent systems from without, i.e., from the perspective of a designer or analyzer. I do *not* directly take the point of view of the different agents who compose the system. I adopt an external perspective from which to attribute beliefs and intentions to agents, and describe their communications. Thus, issues of how they might actually be represented in the agents need not be considered here. This leaves the exact design of the agents an open issue to be settled later in the design process, provided certain minimal requirements are met. These requirements would be stated in terms of intentions, beliefs, and know-how.

The intentional stance is closely related to what Newell has called the *knowledge level*. Indeed, both Dennett and Newell agree that they agree: for instance, see [Dennett, 1987, p. 256] and [Newell, 1982, pp. 122–123]. The main differences are that Dennett defines the intentional stance as the choice of an observer, whereas Newell defines the knowledge level as a distinct level of computer architecture. In fact, even Dennett allows that the intentional stance may present objective patterns of behavior that are not visible otherwise (p. 25). Also, Dennett applies the stance to all systems, e.g., apple trees, not just computational systems (p. 22). But these distinctions are not relevant for our purposes and I shall freely use the insights of Dennett, McCarthy, and Newell.

In fact, individual agents are often described in terms of abstractions, such as knowledge, intentions, and desires. However, the abstractions are usually chosen in an *ad hoc* manner and not formalized in a uniform framework to the detail necessary. Of these abstractions, I pick knowledge, intentions, and know-how and argue that they are the most useful for the purposes of designing and understanding multiagent systems.

However, even after we formalize intentions and know-how in multiagent systems, we would not have completely established the conceptual foundations necessary for a science of multiagent systems. This is because one important ingredient, namely, communication, would still be missing. A major bottleneck in the design of multiagent systems is the design of the protocols of interaction among their member agents. Unfortunately, while individual agents are usually described in terms of their knowledge, intentions, and know-how, extant approaches to understanding the interactions among them are not able to make full use of those abstractions. Even fairly recent research, which provides primitives for communication among agents, has tended to be concerned with the workings of the TCP/IP and similar protocols. It has not been possible to ignore aspects of communication roughly at or below the so-called

Transport Layer of the classical ISO/OSI standard. And, more to the point, current theories do not provide any kind of a formal semantics for the messages exchanged in a multiagent system.

This lack of a general theory of the interactions among agents forces the system designer to think in terms of what are, from the point of view of multiagent systems, merely details of the underlying architecture. These details are important, but are simply out of place at the level at which we wish to study such systems. The concomitant mixing up of concerns often makes the behavior of the designed system depend crucially on details of the operating system and the network hardware. At the same time, the behavior of the individual agents is based on the knowledge they have at different stages. Thus there is no principled way to relate the interactions *among* the agents to the available abstract descriptions of what is *within* each of them. The designer must design some acceptable modes of interaction in an *ad hoc* fashion and relate them as effectively as possible to the agents' states. Not only is this tedious task error-prone, it also has to be redone if the system is ever reimplemented. Further, the designer is accorded no assistance when systems implemented in different ways are to be integrated. In short, the extant technology suffers from the following limitations:

1. It requires that the interactions among agents be designed from scratch each time.

2. The semantics of these interactions is embedded in different procedures, some of which involve network and operating system code. This makes the nontrivial task of validating and modifying multiagent systems even more difficult.

3. Systems designed independently cannot be easily integrated.

4. It is virtually impossible to gracefully update or redesign a system: one cannot easily replace an existing agent with a new one.

Taken together, these limitations subvert many of the main original motivations for developing distributed intelligent systems. I seek to present a theory of the interaction among agents and a formal semantics for their interactions that will form the basis for a framework for designing multiagent systems.

Consider the following example of a simple, but in some ways quite typical, multiagent system. This system comprises three agents: two air-traffic controllers and a pilot. These agents may or may not be human, but one can initially think of them as if they were. Figure 1.1 shows an example execution

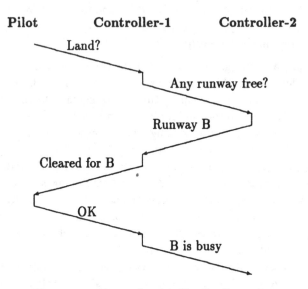

Figure 1.1: Example: Air-Traffic Control

of this system. It begins with the pilot requesting permission to land from one of the controllers. The controller does not know of any available lanes, so he asks the other controller if she knows of any vacant lanes. She informs him that Runway B is free. He offers the pilot permission to land there, if the pilot would agree to pay all applicable charges. The pilot accepts the offer and agrees to pay the charges. The first controller then prohibits the second controller from assigning Runway B to any other plane.

This brief example contains many of the interesting features of multiagent systems. The interactions among the different agents can be characterized by means of the messages they exchange. The messages fall into a handful of major logical categories: requests, queries, assertions, permissions, promises, and prohibitions. Of course, a single physical message may have the effect of two or more logical ones. Similarly, multiple physical messages may be required to achieve the effect of one logical message. However, details of the underlying communication mechanism are not our main concern here. The member agents of the system participate in different protocols for interaction: thus these protocols define the interfaces among the agents. The agents' internal structures can be modified as long as their participation in the relevant protocols is unaffected. Indeed, we would like to be able to reinstantiate the above multiagent system with different pilots and to reimplement the controllers, if we can preserve the correctness of their behavior. A clean specification of the interfaces would allow us to design the component agents independently of one another and upgrade the system incrementally.

The requirement of correct behavior imposes some constraints on how the member agents of a multiagent system should act, and the intentions and know-how they must have, at different stages in the applicable protocols. In the above example, controllers must accede to pilots' requests when possible and must respect each others' prohibitions. A pilot should intend to use a runway if he requests one. Other, more detailed, conditions can also be stated.

In order to capture correctness requirements abstractly and to allow the agents to evolve, a framework for multiagent systems must include at least the following two components: (a) a semantics for abstractions such as intentions and know-how with which the individual agents can be specified, and (b) a semantics of communications that goes beyond message transmission and considers the contents of messages in terms of the participants' intentions, know-how, and actions. A framework that includes these components is developed here.

1.2 The State of the Art

In this section, I briefly survey the state of the art in the areas of computer science that touch upon the topics of interest here. Some of these issues are discussed in greater detail in appropriate chapters. In giving this survey, I hope to identify the parts of my work that have been anticipated by others and the parts that I believe are new.

I borrow many of the underlying motivations and intuitions from the field of distributed artificial intelligence, a small cross-section of which is reported in collected volumes, such as [Huhns, 1987], [Gasser & Huhns, 1989], and [Demazeau & Müller, 1991]. A number of multiagent systems have been implemented. Examples include the GRATE system applied in the ARCHON project for controlling electrical power grids [Jennings, 1992], the Distributed Vehicle Monitoring Testbed (DVMT) for distributed sensing [Durfee *et al.*, 1987], and the MINDS system for information retrieval [Huhns *et al.*, 1987]. These implementations are usually designed to demonstrate the feasibility of some proposed architectures and sometimes to solve particular problems in specific application domains. However, despite such limitations, this kind of work is important because it builds experience and expertise for more general and deployable implementations of multiagent systems.

More immediately relevant is the increasing body of work pertaining to algorithms and mechanisms for cooperation and negotiation in multiagent systems. This work involves higher-level primitives such as the beliefs and intentions of agents and imposes various kinds of logical structures on the communications among agents. Notable work in this area includes [Bussman & Müller, 1993], [Burmeister *et al.*, 1993], [Chang, 1991], [Berthet *et al.*, 1992], and [Müller, 1993]. The present monograph can be thought as defining primitives that will capture the intuitions that emerge from the above works. This work now tends to take a moderately formal view of these mechanisms: it provides a formal language of one sort or another, but is not rigorous in terms of formal models and semantics like the present work.

Hence, whereas overall a large amount of good research has been conducted in distributed artificial intelligence, there are some limitations that it tends to suffer from. In particular, despite several implementation efforts, no principles for the systematic design of multiagent systems are available. The procedural characterizations that are usually given cannot easily be adapted to new applications. Further, typically, no formal theory of any kind is available that corresponds to these implementations. But these are precisely the issues addressed by the present work.

There has been considerable work in AI on planning. In the early days, this work was almost exclusively procedural and not quite formalized [Fikes & Nilsson, 1971; Sacerdoti, 1977]. Recent work is more rigorous and is based on formal theories of action. One of the most significant theoretical contributions to the study of actions in AI is the situation calculus, which was developed by McCarthy & Hayes [1969]. Several theories of action have been proposed in the last decade or so. However, many of these theories make assumptions that can prove quite restrictive in practice. These assumptions commonly include the following:

- only one event happens at a time, which entails that only one agent acts at a time;

- events have precisely determined effects; and

- events are necessarily associated with a state change.

Recently, Lifschitz and his coworkers have shown how the above assumptions, which are usually associated with models of the situation calculus, can be relaxed [Gelfond *et al.*, 1991]. However, this involves defining functions assigning real times to situations and real time durations to actions. Traditionally, this was not done. But, augmented in this manner, the situation calculus can be thought of as a possible metalanguage for the framework developed here.

However, since my main concern is to formalize some useful concepts, rather than to express everything in a minimal language, I shall be content with the framework described below.

Theories of action have been applied in planning. Not many of the abovementioned assumptions have yet been relaxed in this research, although events with context-dependent effects are now considered, which could not be handled by the original STRIPS approach [Pednault, 1988]. More recently, other researchers have also allowed multiple events to take place simultaneously [Allen, 1991]. Although the problem of generating plans is not addressed here, the development of a general framework of actions, time, know-how, and intentions would prove beneficial there. Indeed, classical temporal logic, which I seek to extend here, has been applied to planning [Lansky, 1989].

Besides AI, there is another body of work that I am indebted to. This is the work on logics of programs, both for sequential and concurrent systems. Two of the main strands of research in this area are on temporal logics [Emerson, 1990] and dynamic logics [Kozen & Tiurzyn, 1990]. Temporal logics have operators to deal with time, but do not consider actions explicitly. Dynamic logics provide a rich syntax for actions, but do not explicitly consider time. In the most popular variant, which is the one I use, actions are given a regular language syntax. I explicitly relate actions with time. The relationship is not complicated, but it needs to be exhibited so that we can proceed with a general logic of actions and time to use as a basis for further development.

Usually, the models considered for both temporal and dynamic logics are discrete, with only one action happening at a time. I consider nondiscrete models in my definitions. I also allow multiple actions and events to happen simultaneously and out of synchronization with each other. Even though the basic models may be nondiscrete, we can induce a discrete structure on them for the purposes of computing. The details of this are not explored here. However, having multiple actions has some ramifications on the definition of know-how, since it enables us to consider games in which the players do not take turns. Thus it enables us to consider more general cases of games than are usually considered. It is not clear that these cases can be captured in a strict interleaving framework.

Traditionally, theories of action in AI are designed for the reasoning of an intelligent agent. In other words, one expects to design an agent as a formal reasoner or theorem prover that operates by explicitly using the given theory. By contrast, theories of actions and time in classical computer science are meant to characterize models and computations from without. In other words, someone may characterize a distributed system using temporal or dynamic logic *only* to prove some results about the behavior of the system. Such results would state that the given system is correct in some sense, for instance, that it does not violate any *safety* condition and exhibits *liveness* by never entering a state of deadlock. But, no matter what the theorems exactly are, they are always proved by the designer or analyzer, and not by the system itself. In some cases, two processes that interact, for instance by sharing some storage, might be unaware of each other. Yet theorems about the system they constitute may involve joint conditions on them.

Whether the designer's or the agent's perspective is taken has major technical ramifications on the nature of a semantical framework, such as the one presented here. If an agent is to prove theorems, then his knowledge and ignorance about the relevant conditions has great significance. Given the finiteness of agents' knowledge, it is virtually essential, in this case, to adopt some kind of a defeasible or nonmonotonic formalism. Unfortunately, nonmonotonic reasoning can often be quite intractable. On the other hand, if a designer has to prove theorems, then he has to ensure that all the relevant conditions have been included in the model. Reasoning can then proceed in a monotonic framework.

An intuitively appealing way to think of this dichotomy, due to Benjamin Kuipers [Kuipers, 1986; Crawford *et al.*, 1990], is the following. Although a designer explicitly constructs a model *before* reasoning, an agent engaging in nonmonotonic reasoning effectively constructs or instantiates a model *while* reasoning. Kuipers has argued that the task of building a model can be separated from the task of reasoning in it, even when agents have to do both of these tasks. I accept this view. What I seek to describe is a formal model and language that captures many of the required properties of actions and time. I also aim to use it to give formal definitions to a number of useful concepts. The definitions lead to a clear way of computing with these concepts. However, I do not address the problem of generating good models automatically. That I leave to future work. As a result, the framework proposed here is sufficiently developed only to apply from the perspective of a designer of multiagent systems.

Interestingly, the above remarks help relate this research to Rosenschein's efforts, who too takes the designer's point of view [Rosenschein, 1985]. His goal is to convert specifications of agents into their implementations in software or hardware. Thus, in a broad sense, our respective approaches are in agreement. However, he considers only the concept of knowledge, i.e., know-that, in his theory. Therefore, I believe that my approach is more sophisticated than his. Not only have I considered time and actions explicitly, I have also incorporated concepts such as intentions, know-how, and communications.

The concepts of intentions and knowledge have been used to great advantage in user modeling and in attacking the problems of planning and understanding of speech acts and discourses. Following Grice, there is a long tradition in natural language processing (NLP) that to understand a sentence is to understand what its speaker meant by it [Grice, 1969]. It is customary to derive what is meant by an utterance from what a speaker may intend to achieve by making it. In fact, it is widely accepted that the basis for a speech act is the corresponding *communicative intention* of its speaker [Kuroda, 1989; Searle, 1969]. Communicative intentions are a special kind of the intentions studied here. Speech acts theory, which underlies much work in NLP, is based on the view that communication is a variety of action [Austin, 1962]. This observation motivates the application of planning techniques to communication [Appelt, 1986]. Theories of action apply similarly.

User modeling focuses on how a user interface may present information to, and process information from, a human being. Both these tasks depend greatly on what the interface system expects the user to know, intend, and know how to achieve. In this way, user modeling is required for effective natural language and other, e.g., graphical, interactions with human beings.

I propose a semantics for communications in Chapter 6. Although I consider communications in multiagent systems as speech acts, I do not focus on the natural language aspects of the problem. In other words, I do not provide a theory of what a given natural language utterance may be interpreted as. But I do relate speech acts to the actions, know-how, and intentions of agents. This connection, I submit, is necessary for a theory of communications to fit as an integral part of the larger theory of multiagent systems. My proposal on communication and traditional work in NLP and user modeling are complementary in one respect. The former is concerned with the *content* that different communications must have; the latter is concerned with the *form* they must take to accurately correspond to that content.

Several formal theories of knowledge and belief have been proposed in the literature. These theories are of great value to the study of multiagent systems. However, as I argue in Chapter 4, the conception of knowledge corresponding to *know-how* is by itself of great importance in the study of multiagent systems. Traditional theories of knowledge are usually about *know-that*. It is implicitly assumed that know-how poses no special challenges. A notable exception is Ryle [1949], whose views I discuss in Chapter 4. Even when this assumption is reasonable, and it is not always so, it has the effect of burying our intuitions about know-how inside the technical properties of know-that. We must tightly relate the abstractions we define for multiagent systems to the agents' possible actions. This relationship is captured more naturally when know-how is considered as an independent abstraction.

Some formal theories of intentions have also been proposed in the literature. The most well-known of these is due to Cohen & Levesque [1990]. Unfortunately, this theory is terribly complicated. Moreover, it has certain conceptual and technical shortcomings. At the conceptual level, this theory allows an agent to succeed with an intention merely through persistence. The agent simply has to be able to correctly identify the intended condition; he does not need to know how to achieve it. Clearly, this requirement is not sufficient: one can come up with several natural conditions that an agent may be able to identify, but would not be able to achieve. An example of a technical shortcoming is that the authors state certain properties as "easy to see," but it is possible to construct counterexamples to these properties in the theory itself. I have developed these arguments in greater detail elsewhere [Singh, 1992a].

Other theories of intentions include the ones of [Rao & Georgeff, 1991a] and [Singh & Asher, 1993]. The former is similar, in some respects, to the theory developed here. It is considered in detail in Chapter 3. The latter is based on Kamp's Discourse Representation Theory [Kamp, 1984] and seeks to be cognitively more accurate than the theory presented here. For example, that theory rightly invalidates the inference that an agent's intentions must be closed under logical equivalence. I discuss this inference too in Chapter 3.

Another related category of research pertains to intentions of multi-agent systems. This involves considering sets or groups of agents as having joint intentions. In effect, it attempts to define and formalize the intentions of a multiagent system itself, rather than of its component agents. The relevant literature in this area includes [Grosz & Sidner, 1988], [Cohen & Levesque, 1988a], [Singh, 1991c], [Tuomela & Miller, 1988], [Tuomela, 1991], and [Jennings, 1992]. This research is important, but from a distributed computing perspective, success in it presupposes a good understanding of the component agents themselves. Work on the social aspects of agents will eventually prove essential. However, to be useful in computer science, these social aspects must be studied and formalized to the same technical standards as classical distributed computing. The present work seeks to give a rigorous treatment of the mental and communicative aspects of agents, the need for which is more pressing given the state of the art. However, this work will facilitate the development of formalizations of social concepts as well.

Recently, some work has been done on the design of communication protocols based on a notion of knowledge [Fischer & Immerman, 1986; Halpern & Moses, 1987]. However, the knowledge considered therein is of the process of communication itself. Thus, in these approaches, the delivery of messages is significant, while their content is ignored. By contrast, my aim is to emphasize and study the semantics of the messages exchanged, not the process of exchanging them. Also, the classical work on knowledge is about protocols for lower-level data transmission, which are assumed as an available primitive here.

1.3 Major Contributions

The present work proposes a theory of intentions and know-how in a general framework of action and time. It uses these concepts to define a semantics of communications in multiagent systems. The major contributions include

- A rigorous technical framework that

    - Allows concurrent actions by multiple agents
    - Allows actions to be of varying durations
    - Allows nondiscrete models of time, which underlies actions
    - Carefully relates actions to the temporal aspects of the framework
    - Admits a notion of weak determinism in which different possible choices of agents can be simultaneously captured
    - Defines abstract actions or strategies such that they can coexist with basic or primitive actions

- A formalization of intentions and know-how, in which

    - Intentions are independent of beliefs and know-how
    - Know-How is independent of intentions
    - Constraints relating intentions, beliefs, and know-how can be stated
    - Constraints on how agents with certain intentions and know-how may act can be stated
    - Conclusions about what will transpire given the agents' intentions and know-how can be drawn

- A formalization of communications, which

    - Builds on top of speech act theory
    - Gives a semantics for communications based on their conditions of *whole-hearted* satisfaction, which in turn are determined by the content of the communication.

As discussed above, there has been much research on knowledge and belief and some on intentions. However, such concepts cannot be properly understood, except in the presence of know-how. For it is know-how that relates beliefs and intentions closely to actions, and it is actions that make ascriptions of belief and intentions nongratuitous. For example, a missionary who intends to cross a river may not be able to do so, even if he persists with his intention, and performs actions in attempts to achieve his intention. However, if he has the requisite know-how and applies it, he would succeed eventually, provided he keeps his intention to cross the river.

I propose a formalization of intentions and know-how in a general model of actions and time. This semantics captures many of the properties of intentions and know-how that are relevant from the standpoint of multiagent systems. Using this semantics, I also seek to provide a new semantics for the different modes of communication, such as promises and prohibitions. The proposed framework involves the programs that agents can, and do, execute. As a result, we can use intentions, know-how, and communications as more than just conceptual descriptions. The proposed semantics helps us compare implementations and guides the creation of design tools. It also helps assign meaning to different constraints on system behavior that are natural in a given domain.

Formal theories and formal semantics are useful not only because their properties can be precisely specified, but also because they can be used as a rigorous backdrop for various design rules. This holds even if, in one's chosen approach, these rules are applied only informally. However, the approach I prefer involves the use of a formal language and its semantics for specifying and verifying multiagent systems with mechanical tools. These tools, which include automatic theorem provers and model checkers, have been used to great advantage for classical systems [Boyer & Moore, 1979; Emerson & Clarke, 1982; Burch *et al.*, 1990]. Their development for the proposed framework would advance the state of the art in multiagent systems considerably. Formal theories can also be used to motivate and design concise and clean representations that agents may use in interacting with one another. The proposed abstractions are, in fact, often used informally. The absence of general formal theories is thus a major weakness in the science and engineering of multiagent systems.

Chapter 2

Technical Framework

In light of the goals of this research, there is need for a formal model that incorporates at least the following features:

- time,

- concurrent actions by more than one agent,

- a notion of *choice* so that intentions can be captured, and

- a notion of *control* so that know-how can be captured.

Just such a model is developed here. Only the basic model and formal language are described in this chapter. Further components of the model and extensions to the language are motivated and introduced as needed in succeeding chapters.

The formal model of this work is based on possible worlds, which are well-known from modal logic [Chellas, 1980]. The possible worlds here, in the technical sense of the term, are possible *moments*. That is, each moment plays the role of a *world* in standard modal logic. However, I shall use *moment* in the technical sense and *world* only informally. Each moment is associated with a possible state of the world, which is identified by the atomic conditions or propositions that hold at that moment (atomic propositions are explained in section 2.1.1). A condition is said to be achieved when a state in which it holds is attained. At each moment, environmental events, and agents' actions occur. The same physical state may occur at different moments. A *scenario* at a moment is any maximal set of moments containing the given moment, and all moments in its future along some particular branch.

Figure 2.1 shows a schematic picture of the formal model. Each point in the picture is a moment. There is a partial order on moments that denotes

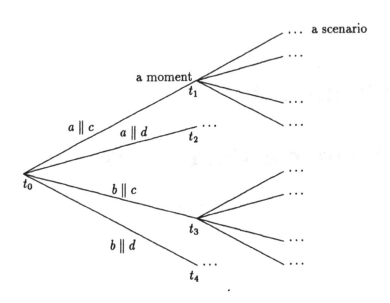

Figure 2.1: The Formal Model

temporal precedence: following usual conventions, time is shown flowing towards the right of the picture. In general, time may branch into the future. Indeed, in any interesting application, it will branch into the future. Since the past is determined at each moment, the temporal precedence relation is taken to be linear in the past. The ignorance that some agent may have about the past is captured by the general mechanism of beliefs, which I discuss in section 2.6. Figure 2.1 is labeled with the actions of two agents. Each agent influences the future by acting, but the outcome also depends on other events. For example, in Figure 2.1, the first agent can constrain the future to some extent by choosing to do action a or action b. If he does action a, then the world progresses along one of the top two branches out of t_0; if he does action b, then it progresses along one of the bottom two branches. However, the agent cannot control what exactly transpires. For example, if he does action a, then whether t_1 or t_2 becomes the case cannot be controlled by him, but rather depends on the actions of the second agent. Both *choice* and *limited control* can thus be captured in this model.

The important intuition about actions is that they are package deals. They correspond to the granularity at which an agent can make his choices. In the above example, the first agent can choose between t_1 and t_2, on the one hand, and between t_3 and t_4, on the other hand. However, he can choose neither between t_1 and t_2, nor between t_3 and t_4.

It is useful for capturing many of our intuitions about the choices and abilities of agents to identify one of the scenarios beginning at a moment as the *real* one. This is the scenario on which the world can be seen to have progressed, assuming it was in the state denoted by the given moment. The real scenario is determined by the choices of the agents and events in the environment. Thus the reality of a scenario is relativized to the moment at which it is considered. In classical modal logic, a distinguished world is sometimes identified as being the real one; however, unlike in the present approach, that world is the unique real world for the entire model. Here, the real scenarios at different moments may have no moment in common. Of course, the real scenarios for moments on the real scenario of a preceding moment must be suffixes of that scenario.

The rest of this chapter proceeds as follows. I present the core formal language, formal model, and semantics in successive subsections of the next section. Section 2.2 is about the temporal and action operators that I define. The temporal operators have standard definitions but the actions operators are quite novel. Their semantics involve subtleties, so that the same definitions can apply in a variety of models, from discrete to continuous time. Section 2.3 motivates and formalizes the several coherence constraints needed in this approach. These are required to eliminate counterintuitive models and simplify the presentation, so that expected results can still be obtained. Section 2.4 presents some simple results relating the temporal and the action operators: these show why the subtleties of some of our definitions and some of the coherence constraints were required. Section 2.5 presents *strategies* as abstract descriptions of actions necessary to understanding complex systems. Section 2.6 presents a standard modal view of belief and knowledge, which are required to complete the present theory. Section 2.7 discusses theories of actions in linguistics, philosophy, and artificial intelligence. Lastly, section 2.8 briefly gives a rationale for why the simpler approach of qualitative temporal logic is appropriate for our purposes.

2.1 The Core Formal Framework

2.1.1 The Formal Language

The proposed formal language, $\mathcal{L}$, is based on CTL*, which is a well-known propositional branching-time logic [Emerson, 1990]. $\mathcal{L}$ also includes the operators [] and $\langle\,\rangle$, and permits quantification over basic action symbols. The operators [] and $\langle\rangle$ depend on basic actions. Formally, $\mathcal{L}$ is the minimal set closed under the following rules. Here $\mathcal{L}_s$ is the set of "scenario-formulae," which is used as an auxiliary definition. The formulae in $\mathcal{L}$ are evaluated relative to moments; those in $\mathcal{L}_s$ are evaluated relative to scenarios and moments. In the following,

- Φ is a set of atomic propositional symbols,

- $\mathcal{A}$ is a set of agent symbols,

- $\mathcal{B}$ is a set of basic action symbols, and

- $\mathcal{X}$ is a set of variables.

SYN-1. $\psi \in \Phi$ implies that $\psi \in \mathcal{L}$

SYN-2. $p, q \in \mathcal{L}$ implies that $p \wedge q \in \mathcal{L}$

SYN-3. $p \in \mathcal{L}$ implies that $\neg p \in \mathcal{L}$

SYN-4. $\mathcal{L} \subseteq \mathcal{L}_s$

SYN-5. $p, q \in \mathcal{L}_s$ implies that $p \wedge q \in \mathcal{L}_s$

SYN-6. $p \in \mathcal{L}_s$ implies that $\neg p \in \mathcal{L}_s$

SYN-7. $p \in \mathcal{L}_s$ implies that $\mathsf{A}p, \mathsf{R}p \in \mathcal{L}$

SYN-8. $p \in \mathcal{L}$ implies that $\mathsf{P}p \in \mathcal{L}$

SYN-9. $p \in \mathcal{L}$ and $a \in \mathcal{X}$ implies that $(\bigvee a : p) \in \mathcal{L}$

SYN-10. $p \in (\mathcal{L}_s - \mathcal{L})$ and $a \in \mathcal{X}$ implies that $(\bigvee a : p) \in \mathcal{L}_s$

SYN-11. $p, q \in \mathcal{L}_s$ implies that $p \mathsf{U} q \in \mathcal{L}_s$

SYN-12. $p \in \mathcal{L}_s$, $x \in \mathcal{A}$, and $a \in \mathcal{B}$ implies that $x[a]p, x\langle a\rangle p, x\langle\!\langle a\rangle\!\rangle p \in \mathcal{L}_s$

The atomic propositional symbols denote the primitive propositions or conditions of our models. Conditions of interest to the given application, e.g., whether a given runway is busy or free, are mapped to different propositional symbols. Similarly, the basic actions symbols denote the elementary actions, e.g., landing or taking off, that are important in the given application. Choosing the right atomic propositions and basic actions is an important component of constructing useful formal models of a given applications. However, we shall not study this task in any detail in the present work.

2.1.2 The Formal Model

Let $M = \langle F, N \rangle$ be a model for the language $\mathcal{L}$, where $F = \langle \mathbf{T}, <, \mathbf{A} \rangle$ is a frame, and $N = \langle [\,] , \mathbf{Y}, \mathbf{B}, \mathbf{R} \rangle$ is an interpretation. Here $\mathbf{T}$ is a set of possible moments ordered by $<$. $\mathbf{A}$ assigns agents to different moments; i.e., $\mathbf{A} : \mathbf{T} \mapsto \wp(\mathcal{A})$. As described below, $[\,]$ assigns intensions to atomic propositions and to pairs of agent symbols and action symbols. $\mathbf{Y}$ assigns *strategies* (to be defined in section 2.5) to the agents at each moment. $\mathbf{B}$ assigns alternative moments to the agents at each moment. As explained in section 2.6, these are the moments that denote states of affairs that the agents imagine to be the case. $\mathbf{B}$ is used to give the semantics of belief and know-that. $\mathbf{R}$ assigns a scenario to each moment, which is interpreted as the *real* scenario at that moment.

The relation, $<$, which is a subset of $\mathbf{T} \times \mathbf{T}$, is a strict partial order. It models time as linear in the past. Time may or may not branch in the future; however, if it branches at a moment, the branches cannot join again. Indeed, if two branches join at some moment, then the linear past requirement would be violated at that moment. This makes it possible to identify periods (defined below) uniquely by their endpoints. Formally, the following properties hold of the relation $<$.

- *Transitivity:* $(\forall t, t', t'' \in \mathbf{T} : (t < t' \wedge t' < t'') \Rightarrow t < t'')$

- *Asymmetry:* $(\forall t, t' \in \mathbf{T} : t < t' \Rightarrow t' \not< t)$

- *Irreflexivity:* $(\forall t \in \mathbf{T} : t \not< t)$

It may be intuitively helpful for the reader to think of the connected components of $\mathbf{T}$ induced by $<$ as different possible worlds, in the classical sense, i.e., as entities that evolve over time. By the definition of connectedness, the actions of agents cannot begin at a moment in one such component and end in another. However, more than one such component is needed for many of the technical definitions given here, since they explicitly involve alternative states of affairs. The reader may consult [Emerson, 1990] for an introduction to temporal logic and to models of time and [Chellas, 1980] for a textbook level introduction to modal logic.

In earlier versions of this work, I also assumed that models were linear past. However, that assumption was needed only to simplify the notation for periods. If the past at each moment is linear, then branches of time never merge. Hence, periods of time can be uniquely identified by their beginning and ending moments. Since this assumption had no substantive effect on the theory, I have now decided to remove it altogether. Indeed, in determining compact representations for the proposed models, it would help to collapse moments that were in some sense the same: this process would result in models that were directed graphs rather than trees and possibly be directed graphs with cycles. This point will become clearer in section 2.3 in the discussion of weak determinism.

A scenario at a moment is any single branch of the relation $<$ that begins at the given moment, and contains *all* moments in some linear subrelation of $<$. Different scenarios correspond to different ways in which the world may develop in the future, as a result of the actions of agents and events in the environment. Only one scenario can be realized. This property is not used in the formal theory in Chapters 3 and 4, but is used in Chapter 5. It is intuitively useful throughout for understanding many of the definitions. Formally, a scenario at moment t is a set $S \subseteq \mathbf{T}$ of which the following conditions hold.

- *Rootedness:* $t \in S$

- *Linearity:* $(\forall t', t'' \in S : (t' = t'') \vee (t' < t'') \vee (t'' < t'))$

- *Relative Density:* $(\forall t', t'' \in S, t''' \in \mathbf{T} : (t' < t''' < t'') \Rightarrow t''' \in S)$

- *Relative Maximality:* $(\forall t' \in S, t'' \in \mathbf{T} : (t' < t'') \Rightarrow (\exists t''' \in S : (t' < t''') \wedge (t''' \not< t'')))$

  Intuitively, maximality means that if it is possible to extend the scenario S (here to t''), then it is extended, either to t'' (when $t''' = t''$), or along some other branch. Note that this assumption by itself does not entail that time be eternal. That is assumed separately in coherence constraint Сон-2 below.

$\mathbf{S}_t$ is the set of all scenarios at moment t. Since each scenario at a moment is rooted at that moment, the sets of scenarios at different moments are disjoint, that is, $t \neq t' \Rightarrow \mathbf{S}_t \cap \mathbf{S}_{t'} = \emptyset$. If t' is such that $t < t'$, then for every scenario, $S' \in \mathbf{S}_{t'}$, there is a scenario, S, such that $S' \subset S$ and $S \in \mathbf{S}_t$. Conversely, for every scenario $S \in \mathbf{S}_t$, for each moment $t' \in S$, there is a scenario $S' \in \mathbf{S}_{t'}$, such that $S' \subseteq S$.

$[S; t, t']$ denotes a period on scenario S from t to t', inclusive, i.e., the subset of S from t to t'. Thus, if $[S_0; t, t'] \subseteq S_1$, then $[S_0; t, t'] = [S_1; t, t']$ (because they are both the same set of moments). However, in general, $[S_0; t, t'] \neq [S_1; t, t']$. For notational simplicity, $[S; t, t']$ presupposes $t, t' \in S$ and $t \leq t'$.

The notion of basic actions needed for a general theory of intentions and know-how is different from the one that is traditionally assumed. Traditionally, only actions of unit length are considered and only one agent is

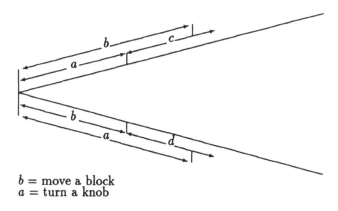

b = move a block
a = turn a knob

Figure 2.2: Actions: Nonsynchronized and of Varying Durations

assumed to act at a time (e.g., [Cohen & Levesque, 1990]). These assumptions
are both somewhat restrictive. I submit that the key intuition behind basic
actions is that they are done by the agent with a single *choice*, irrespective
of the duration for which they last. More than one agent may act simultaneously. The set of actions available to an agent can be different at different
moments. Basic actions may have different durations relative to one another in
different scenarios, including those scenarios that begin at the same moment.
For example, the actions of moving a block may take more or less time than
the action of turning a knob, depending on how another agent obstructs one
of these actions. Such a case is diagramed in Figure 2.2, which also shows that
actions may begin and end at different moments.

The intension, $[\,]$, gives the semantic content of some of the symbols
of the formal language. Intensions, to be distinguished from intentions, are
well-known from modal logic. The intension of an atomic proposition is the set
of moments at which it is true. The intension of an action symbol a is, for each
agent symbol x, the set of periods in the model in which an instance of a is
done by x. Formally, $[\,]$ is the union of two functions of types $\Phi \mapsto \wp(\mathbf{T})$ and
$\mathcal{A} \times \mathcal{B} \mapsto \wp(\wp(\mathbf{T}) \times \mathbf{T} \times \mathbf{T})$, respectively. Thus $t \in [p]$ means that p is true at
moment t; and, $[S; t, t'] \in [a]^x$ means that agent x is performing action a on

S from moment t to moment t'. As explained in constraints Сон-1 and Сон-3 of section 2.3, when $[S;t,t'] \in [\![a]\!]^x$, t' corresponds to the ending of a, but t does not correspond to the initiation of a. This is because a may already be in progress before t. All basic actions take time. That is, if $[S;t,t'] \in [\![a]\!]^x$, then $t < t'$. The superscript denoting the agent is elided when it can be understood from the context.

It is useful for some of the definitions that follow to extend the definition of intension of an action in the following way. Let $s = a_0, \ldots, a_{m-1}$ be a sequence of actions of x. Then $[\![s]\!] = \{[S;t,t'] | (\exists t_0 \leq \ldots \leq t_m : t = t_0 \wedge t' = t_m \wedge (\forall j : j \in [1\ldots m] \Rightarrow [S;t_{j-1},t_j] \in [\![a_{j-1}]\!]^x))\}$. That is, $[\![s]\!]$ is the set of periods over which sequence s is done. In other words, $[S;t,t'] \in [\![s]\!]$ means that s begins at t and ends at t'.

Finally, the component $\mathbf{R}$ of the model simply assigns a scenario to each moment. Therefore, it is of the type $\mathbf{T} \mapsto \wp(\wp(\mathbf{T}))$. In particular, $\mathbf{R}(t) \in \mathbf{S}_t$; in other words, reality is possible.

Restrictions on the intension, $[\![\,]\!]$, can be used to express the limitations of agents as well as how the actions of agents may depend on certain conditions holding at the moments at which they are begun and how they may interfere with the actions of others. For example, the proposition that Bob cannot pick up three blocks at once can be modeled by making the intension of his picking up three blocks empty. Similarly, the constraint that at most one person can enter the elevator at a time can be modeled by requiring that the intersection of the intensions of the actions of two persons entering it be empty. Each of these restrictions may be made contingent upon other conditions. Relations between beliefs and actions will be considered in subsequent chapters.

Note that, intuitively, if an agent is deemed to be performing an action at a moment, he must be alive then. Thus the births and deaths of agents can be accounted for in the formal model: all the non-wait actions performed by an agent occur between the moments of his birth and death; however, this observation is not used in any part of the formal theory here. If we wished to incorporate this in the theory, we would have to restrict different conditions, e.g., constraint Сон-5 below, to apply only to live agents.

2.1.3   Semantics

The semantics of sentences, i.e., formulae, in the formal language is given relative to a model, as defined above, and a moment in that model. $M \models_t p$ expresses "M satisfies p at t." This is the main notion of satisfaction here.

For formulae in $\mathcal{L}_s$, it is useful to define an auxiliary notion of satisfaction, $M \models_{S,t} p$, which expresses "M satisfies p at moment t on scenario S." For notational simplicity, $M \models_{S,t} p$ is taken to entail that $t \in S$. We say p is *satisfiable* iff for some M and t, $M \models_t p$; we say p is *valid* in M iff it is satisfied at all moments in M. The satisfaction conditions for the temporal operators are adapted from those in [Emerson, 1990]. It is assumed that each action symbol is quantified over at most once in any formula. Below, $p|_b^a$ is the formula resulting from the substitution of all occurrences of a in p by b. Formally, we have the following definitions:

SEM-1. $M \models_t \psi$ iff $t \in [\![\psi]\!]$, where $\psi \in \Phi$

SEM-2. $M \models_t p \wedge q$ iff $M \models_t p$ and $M \models_t q$

SEM-3. $M \models_t \neg p$ iff $M \not\models_t p$

SEM-4. $M \models_t \mathsf{A}p$ iff $(\forall S : S \in \mathbf{S}_t \Rightarrow M \models_{S,t} p)$

SEM-5. $M \models_t \mathsf{R}p$ iff $M \models_{\mathbf{R}(t),t} p$

SEM-6. $M \models_t \mathsf{P}p$ iff $(\exists t' : t' < t$ and $M \models_{t'} p)$

SEM-7. $M \models_t (\bigvee a : p)$ iff $(\exists b : b \in \mathcal{B}$ and $M \models_t p|_b^a)$, where $p \in \mathcal{L}$

SEM-8. $M \models_{S,t} (\bigvee a : p)$ iff $(\exists b : b \in \mathcal{B}$ and $M \models_{S,t} p|_b^a)$, where $p \in (\mathcal{L}_s - \mathcal{L})$

SEM-9. $M \models_{S,t} p\mathsf{U}q$ iff $(\exists t' : t \le t'$ and $M \models_{S,t'} q$ and $(\forall t'' : t \le t'' \le t' \Rightarrow M \models_{S,t''} p))$

SEM-10. $M \models_{S,t} x[a]p$ iff $(\exists t' \in S : [S;t,t'] \in [\![a]\!]^x) \Rightarrow (\exists t' \in S : [S;t,t'] \in [\![a]\!]$ and $(\exists t'' : t < t'' \le t'$ and $M \models_{S,t''} p))$

SEM-11. $M \models_{S,t} x\langle a\rangle p$ iff $(\exists t' \in S : [S;t,t'] \in [\![a]\!]^x$ and $(\exists t'' : t < t'' \le t'$ and $M \models_{S,t''} p))$

SEM-12. $M \models_{S,t} x\langle\!\langle a\rangle\!\rangle p$ iff $(\exists t' \in S : [S;t,t'] \in [\![a]\!]^x$ and $(\exists t'' : t < t'' \le t'$ and $(\forall t''' : t < t''' \le t''$ implies that $M \models_{S,t'''} p)))$

SEM-13. $M \models_{S,t} p \wedge q$ iff $M \models_{S,t} p$ and $M \models_{S,t} q$

SEM-14. $M \models_{S,t} \neg p$ iff $M \not\models_{S,t} p$

SEM-15. $M \models_{S,t} p$ iff $M \models_t p$, where $p \in \mathcal{L}$

Two useful abbreviations are **false** $\equiv (p \land \neg p)$, for any $p \in \Phi$, and **true** $\equiv \neg$**false**. The definition of $\mathcal{L}$ as given so far is by no means complete; additions to it are defined in subsequent sections of this chapter and in the succeeding chapters after further intuitive motivation.

It should be clear from the above that in this work, the term *model* is used in the standard sense of logic. Statements of fact, including statements of what a given agent intends or believes, are evaluated with respect to a model that consists of different possible moments. For example, whether the statement "it is raining" is true in the model or not depends only on the moment relative to which this statement is evaluated, *not* on the beliefs of any agent. Similarly, whether an agent intends something is to be differentiated from the question of whether he (or someone else) believes that he intends something. This point is obvious and standard, but can cause grave misconceptions if not kept in mind.

2.2   Temporal and Action Operators: Discussion

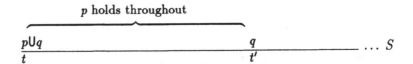

Figure 2.3: Temporal Operators: $p\mathsf{U}q$

Figure 2.4: Temporal Operators: $\mathsf{F}p$

The formula $p\mathsf{U}q$ is true at a moment t on a scenario, iff q holds at a future moment on the given scenario and p holds on all moments between t and the selected occurrence of q. The formula $\mathsf{F}p$ means that p holds sometimes in the future on the given scenario and abbreviates **true**$\mathsf{U}p$. The formula $\mathsf{G}p$ means

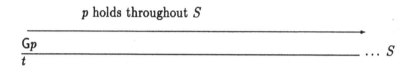

Figure 2.5: Temporal Operators: Gp

that p always holds in the future on the given scenario; it abbreviates $\neg F \neg p$. These definitions are illustrated in Figures 2.3, 2.4, and 2.5. The formula Pp denotes p held at some moment in the past. The boolean or propositional logic operators, $\wedge$ and $\neg$, are used to compose formulae in the usual manner. Implications $(p \to q)$ and disjunctions $(p \vee q)$ of formulae are defined as the usual abbreviations.

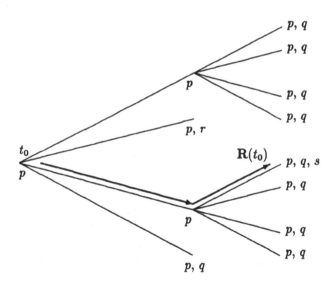

Figure 2.6: Temporal Operators: A, E, R

The branching-time operator, A, denotes "in *all* scenarios at the present moment." Here "the present moment" refers to the moment at which a given formula is evaluated. A useful abbreviation is E, which denotes "in *some* scenario at the present moment." In other words, E$p \equiv \neg A \neg p$. The reality

operator, R, captures the notion of what will really be the case. It denotes
"in the *real* scenario at the given moment." Now consider Figure 2.6. In that
figure, assume that p holds at all moments in the future of those shown. Then
at t_0, AGp holds, because p holds at all moments on all scenarios beginning at
that moment. Similarly, EFr, AFq, and EGp also hold at that moment. The
arrow marks the real scenario at t_0. Therefore, RFs also holds at t_0.

I introduce two new modalities for actions. The proposed definitions
loosely follow standard dynamic logic [Kozen & Tiurzyn, 1990], but differ in
several important respects. For an action symbol a, an agent symbol x, and
a formula p, $x[a]p$ holds on a given scenario S and a moment t on it, iff, if x
performs a on S starting at t, then p holds at some moment while a is being
performed. The formula $x\langle a\rangle p$ holds on a given scenario S and a moment t
on it, iff, x performs a on S starting at t and p holds at some moment while
a is being performed. The agent symbol is elided when it is obvious from the
context. These definitions require p to hold at any moment in the (left-open
and right-closed) period in which the given action is being performed. Thus
they are weaker than possible definitions that require p to hold at the moment
at which the given action completes.

In assigning meanings to $x[a]p$ and $x\langle a\rangle p$, it is essential to allow the
condition to hold at any moment in the period over which the action is performed. This is because we are not assuming that time is discrete or that all
actions are of equal durations and synchronized to begin and end together.
Intuitively, if we insisted that the relevant condition hold at the end of the
action, then an agent could effectively leap over a condition. In that case, even
if a condition occurs while an action is performed, we may not have $x\langle a\rangle p$.
For example, if p is "the agent is at the equator," and the agent performs the
action of hopping northwards from just south of the equator, he may end up
north of the equator without ever (officially) being at it. That would be quite
unintuitive. For this reason, the present definitions are preferred although as a
consequence of them, the operators $\langle\rangle$ and $[]$ are not formal duals of each other.
But this is made up for not only by having a more intuitive set of definitions,
but also by the natural axiomatization for know-how in section 4.2 that the
chosen definitions facilitate. Further, the present definitions enable the right
relationship between $\langle\rangle$ and U to be captured. Recall from above that pUq
considers all moments between the given moment and the first occurrence of q,
not just those at which different actions may end.

Further, $x\langle a\rangle\!| p$ holds on a scenario S and moment t if x performs
action a starting at t and p holds in some initial subperiod of the period over
which a is done. This operator is necessary to relate actions with time for
the following reason. In dense models, actions happen over periods which

contain moments between their endpoints. Even in discrete models whose actions are not all of unit length, actions can happen over nonempty periods. Consequently, if s is done at t and q holds at an internal moment of a and p holds throughout, then $p\mathsf{U}q$ holds at t. But absent the $\langle\!\langle\rangle\!\rangle$ operator, we cannot characterize $p\mathsf{U}q$ recursively in terms of actions. One useful characterization is given in section 2.4: this helps in giving the fixed point semantics of the temporal operators, which is essential to computing them efficiently.

The above dynamic modalities yield scenario-formulae, which can be combined with the branching-time operators, A, E, and R. Thus $\mathsf{A}[a]p$ denotes that on all scenarios S at the present moment, if a is performed on S, then p holds at some moment on S between the present moment and the moment at which a is completed. Similarly, $\mathsf{E}\langle a\rangle p$ denotes that a is being done on some scenario at the present moment and that on this scenario p holds at some moment between the present moment and the moment at which a is completed. In other words, $\mathsf{A}[a]p$ corresponds to the necessitation operator and $\mathsf{E}\langle a\rangle p$ to the possibility operator in dynamic logic.

One difference with the definition of the operators in dynamic logic is that here the relevant condition can hold at any moment *during* the course of the action. This is in accordance with time not being constrained to be discrete. In dynamic logic, actions are modeled as pairs of states, which usually are discrete snapshots of the world. Therefore, in that context, it does not make sense to talk of intermediate states. But in the model here, moments are defined independently of specific actions. Of course, the present definitions specialize correctly to discrete models of time in which all actions are of equal duration and synchronized. Furthermore, the operators [] and ⟨⟩ are evaluated on scenarios. The advantage of doing so is that it simplifies the connection with branching-time logic. It also allows us to express conditions like $\mathsf{A}x\langle a\rangle p$, which have no correlate in dynamic logic. In effect, $\mathsf{A}x\langle a\rangle p$ means that a is the only action (of the agent x) that can be performed at the given moment (i.e., the moment where this formula is evaluated) and p is the condition that results from doing a.

Existential quantification over basic actions is a useful feature for our purposes. Of the several basic actions that an agent may do at a given moment, we would often like to restrictively talk of the subset of actions that have some interesting property. Indeed, we need something like this to formally express the idea of *choice:* an agent may be able to do several actions, but would, in fact, choose to do one. For each action that an agent may choose to do, there is a set of scenarios over which those actions are attempted and done. Usually, this set of scenarios is not a singleton, because the actions of other agents and environmental events would contribute to determining which scenario is finally

selected. The agent constrains the scenario that would be realized by doing
some action, but the one that is, in fact, realized also depends on events beyond
his direct control. It sometimes helps to use the dual of this operator, universal
quantification over actions, as well.

2.3   Coherence Constraints

For the models introduced above to be coherent and useful as models of actions
and time for reasoning about multiagent systems, they must satisfy a number
of technical constraints. Many of these are motivated and formalized below.

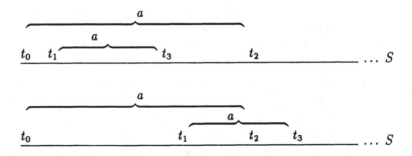

Figure 2.7: Cases Disallowed by Action Uniqueness

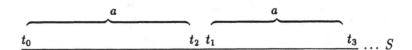

Figure 2.8: Case Allowed by Uniqueness of Termination of Actions

Coh-1. **Uniqueness of Termination of Actions:** Starting at any given
moment, each action can be performed in at most one way on any
given scenario. In other words, for any action a, scenario S, and
moments t_0, t_1, t_2, t_3 in S, we have that $[S; t_0, t_2] \in [a]$ and $[S; t_1, t_3] \in$
$[a]$ implies that, if $t_0 \leq t_1 < t_2$, then $t_2 = t_3$. This might seem
too elementary to be mentioned explicitly. However, it is needed to

exclude ill-formed models in which an action does not have a unique moment of ending. The two main classes of such ill-formed models are diagramed in Figure 2.7. If an agent performs an action and then repeats it, the repetition counts as a separate instance, because it has a distinct starting moment. Such a case is shown in Figure 2.8; this constraint allows $t_1 = t_2$ in that figure. Note that the present constraint only states that each action has a unique endpoint. It permits several different actions with possibly distinct endpoints to happen simultaneously. In discrete models with unit length actions, both endpoints are necessarily unique; here only the termination point is assumed to be unique.

COH-2. **Eternity:** At each moment, there is a future moment available in the model. Or, time never comes to an end. Formally, $(\forall t : (\exists t' : t < t'))$. In conjunction with the maximality property of scenarios, this is equivalent to the statement that there is always a scenario available along which the world may evolve. This statement is intuitively helpful to remember, even though its formalization is more complex than the above version: $(\forall t : (\exists S : S \in \mathbf{S}_t$ and $(\exists t' : t' \in S$ and $t < t')))$.

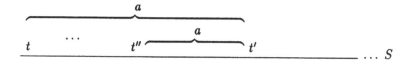

Figure 2.9: Actions in Progress

COH-3. **Actions in Progress:** It is also useful in relating moments with actions to impose the following condition on the models: $[S; t, t'] \in [a] \Rightarrow (\forall t'' : t \le t'' < t' \Rightarrow [S; t'', t'] \in [a])$. This constraint allows us to talk of an agent's actions at any moment at which they are happening, not just where they begin. Of course, in discrete models with unit length actions, there is no moment properly between t and t', so our constraint holds vacuously of such models. However, note that in accordance with condition COH-1, actions begun at a moment still have a unique ending moment. As a result of this constraint, the operators [] and $\langle \rangle$ on actions and propositions, which were defined informally in section 2.1.1, behave properly at all scenarios and moments in the model. For example, if an agent can achieve a condition by performing some action, then he can also achieve it while in the process of performing that action.

The "real" choice is exercised by the agent when he begins a particular action; the present constraint may be understood as stating that until an initiated action completes, the agent implicitly reaffirms his choice. Figure 2.9 shows how this constraint causes the intension of an action to be filled out by suffixes of the period over which it is performed. Note that the period $[S; t', t']$ is not added to $[a]$, since that would lead to a violation of our assumption that $[S; t, t'] \in [a]$ implies that $t < t'$. This would cause ambiguity between an action instance ending at t' and another beginning there. In any case, there is no additional information in $[S; t', t']$ and our definitions are simpler when it is kept out of $[a]$.

Coh-4. **Passage of Time:** For any scenario at a given moment, there is an action that is done on that scenario. That is, something must be *done* by each agent along each scenario in the model, even if it is some kind of a dummy action. In other words, even waiting is an action. This assumption ensures that time does not just pass by itself, and is needed to make the appropriate connections between time and action. And, assuming that every agent acts helps simplify some technical definitions later on. Formally, $(\forall t \in \mathbf{T}, x \in \mathbf{A}(t), S \in \mathbf{S}_t \Rightarrow ((\exists t' \in S) \Rightarrow (\exists t' \in S, a : [S; t, t'] \in [a]^x)))$.

Figure 2.10: Limit Sequences Disallowed by Reachability of Moments

Coh-5. **Reachability of Moments:** For any scenario and two moments on it, there is a finite number of actions of each agent that, if done on that scenario starting at the first moment, will lead to a moment in the future of the second moment. Formally, $(\forall S : (\forall t, t' \in S : t < t' \Rightarrow (\exists t'' : t' \leq t'' \text{ and } (\exists a_1, \ldots, a_n \text{ and } [S; t, t''] \in [a_1, \ldots, a_n])))).$ This condition is intended to exclude models in which there are moments that would require infinitely long action sequences to reach.

Such models, an example of which is diagramed in Figure 2.10, would allow a condition to be inevitable and yet unreachable though any finite sequence of actions. Since each action corresponds to a choice on the part of the agent, it is important that this not be the case for inevitability to relate properly with know-how. Infinite sequences of the kind excluded by this constraint cannot arise in discrete models, since there are only a finite number of moments between any two moments and each action consumes at least one.

Figure 2.11: Illegal Discontinuity in Reality

COH-6. **Reality does not Change:** The model component **R** assigns to each moment the real scenario at that moment. If a scenario is determined to be the real scenario at some moment, then at any moment on that scenario, the appropriate suffix of that scenario should be the real scenario. The absence of this requirement would mean that reality may change arbitrarily. This would be strange: after all, we are considering reality *per se*, not beliefs about it. The required constraint can be captured as follows: $(\forall t, t' : t' \in \mathbf{R}(t) \Rightarrow \mathbf{R}(t') \subseteq \mathbf{R}(t))$. Figure 2.11 gives an example of the discontinuity in reality that is forbidden by this constraint.

COH-7. **Atomicity of Basic Actions:** If an agent is performing an action over a part of a scenario, then he completes that action on that scenario. This makes sense since the actions in the model are basic actions, done with one choice by their agent. If an action in some domain can in fact be chopped into a prefix and suffix such that the suffix is optional, then it should be modeled as two separate basic actions, the first of which completes entirely and the second of which may not be begun at all.

Formally, let $t, t', t_1 \in \mathbf{T}$, such that $t < t' < t_1$. Let $S_0, S_1 \in \mathbf{S}_t$, such that $[S_1; t, t'] \in S_0$. Then $[S_1; t, t_1] \in [\![a]\!]^x$ implies that $(\exists t_0 \in S_0 : [S_0; t, t_0] \in [\![a]\!]^x)$.

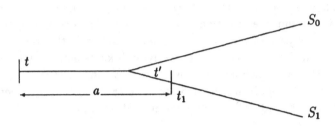

Figure 2.12: Actions Cannot be Partially Performed on any Scenario

Intuitively, $[S_1; t, t_1] \in [\![a]\!]^x$ means that x is performing a from t to t_1. Therefore, he must be performing a in any subperiod of that, including $[S_1; t, t']$, which is the same as $[S_0; t, t']$. Thus, a must be completed on S_0. By contrast, higher-level actions may not satisfy this. For example, Al may be crossing the street (on a scenario) even if he did not cross it successfully on that scenario, e.g., by being run over by a bus.

The basic formal model is now in place to reason about actions and time. However, some further assumptions are required in order to capture some important properties of the concepts to be formalized and to enable their formalization in a sufficiently general and intuitively appealing manner. One of these properties is that the intentions of an agent do not entail his know-how, and vice versa. That is, an agent who intends p may not know how to achieve it, and one who knows how to achieve p may not intend it. Another property is that intentions constrain the actions an agent may choose, roughly, to be among those that would lead to his intentions being fulfilled. Still another property is that intentions coupled with know-how can, if acted upon, lead to success. These and other such properties are studied in detail in later chapters. However, we must enforce certain additional constraints on our model to facilitate their expression in the present framework. Some of these constraints are motivated and introduced later. However, one that is particularly important and general is described next.

Our models represent physical systems, albeit nondeterministic ones. The actions available to the agents and the conditions that hold on different scenarios leading from a given state are determined by that state itself. Constraints on agent's choices, abilities, or intentions can thus be flexibly modeled.

A well-known alternative characterization of models of time is by the set of all scenarios at all states. Let $\mathbf{S} = \bigcup_{t \in \mathbf{T}} \mathbf{S}_t$. For a model to represent a physical system and be specifiable by a transition relation among different states, the corresponding set of scenarios, $\mathbf{S}$, must satisfy the following closure properties [Emerson, 1990, p. 1014]. I generalize these from discrete time.

- *Suffix closure:* If $S \in \mathbf{S}$, then all suffixes of S belong to $\mathbf{S}$.

- *Limit closure:* If for an ordered set of states $T = \{t_0 \ldots t_n \ldots\}$, scenarios containing each initial fragment $t_0 \ldots t_n$, for $n \geq 0$ are in $\mathbf{S}$, then a scenario S such that $T \subseteq S$ is also in $\mathbf{S}$.

- *Fusion closure:* If $S_0 = S_0^p \cdot t \cdot S_0^f$ and $S_1 = S_1^p \cdot t \cdot S_1^f$ in $\mathbf{S}$ include the same state t, then the scenarios $S_0^p \cdot t \cdot S_1^f$ and $S_1^p \cdot t \cdot S_0^f$ formed by concatenating the initial and later parts of S_0 and S_1 with respect to t also belong to $\mathbf{S}$ (here · indicates concatenation). Fusion closure means that the futures available at a state depend only on the state itself, not on the history by which it may be attained.

Lemma 2.1 By construction, $\mathbf{S}$ derived from the proposed model satisfies suffix and limit closures. □

However, fusion closure is not satisfied in general. I show next how to satisfy it by imposing an additional constraint on the proposed model. This constraint relies on a notion of *state*. However, the components of the proposed model are moments and periods. Therefore, I first formalize states in the proposed model. For this, I define a relation, $\sim$, which indicates the state-equivalence of moments and periods. States are the equivalence classes of moments under $\sim$.

For moments, t and t', define $t \sim t'$ iff they satisfy the same atomic propositions. For sets of moments, L and L', define $L \sim L'$ in terms of an *order-isomorphism, f*.

Aux-1. Given two sets L and L' with an order $<$, a map f from L to L' is an order-isomorphism iff

- f is onto,
- ($t \in L$ iff $f(t) \in L'$), and
- ($\forall t, t_0 \in L : t < t_0$ iff $f(t) < f(t_0)$)

Aux-2. $t \sim t'$ iff $\{\psi \in \Phi | t \in [\![\psi]\!]\} = \{\psi \in \Phi | t' \in [\![\psi]\!]\}$

Aux-3. $L \sim L'$ iff ($\exists f : f$ is an order-isomorphism and ($\forall t \in L \Rightarrow t \sim f(t)$))

Observation 2.2 $\sim$ is an equivalence relation $\square$

Thus, $t \sim t'$ means that the same physical state occurs at moments t and t'. In other words, states are the equivalence classes of $\sim$ on moments. Similarly, $L \sim L'$ means that the moments in L and L' represent the same states occurring in the same temporal order. In other words, L and L' represent the same trajectory in state space.

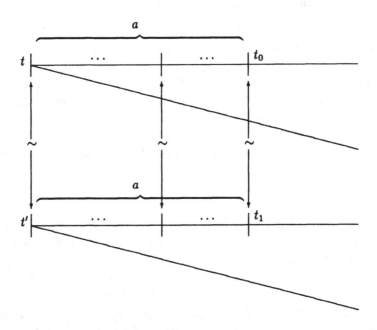

Figure 2.13: Weak Determinism

Coh-8. **Weak Determinism:** If two moments satisfy precisely the same atomic propositions, then the fragments of the model rooted at those moments must be isomorphic with respect to the temporal precedence relation and the atomic propositions in the formal language. Thus, we can define weak determinism as the following constraint.

($\forall x \in \mathcal{A}, a \in \mathcal{B}, t, t', t_0 \in \mathbf{T}, S_0 : t \sim t' \Rightarrow$ ($[S_0; t, t_0] \in [\![a]\!]^x \Rightarrow$ ($\exists S_1 \in \mathbf{S}_{t'}, t_1 : [S_1; t', t_1] \in [\![a]\!]^x$ and $[S_0; t, t_0] \sim [S_1; t', t_1]$)))

Lemma 2.3 Under weak determinism, **S** derived from the proposed model satisfies fusion closure. □

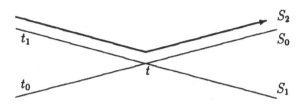

Figure 2.14: Weak Determinism as Fusion Closure in State Space

Figure 2.14 shows an example of fusion closure and how it is satisfied by weak determinism. Note that this figure shows the state space. In other words, the relation $\sim$ is replaced by identity in this figure. The figure shows that, if S_0 and S_1 are scenarios, then S_2 is a scenario at t_1. This holds by the following reasoning. Let t_0' and t_1' be the moments in S_0 and S_1, respectively, that have the state t. Then $t_0' \sim t_1'$. Therefore, by weak determinism, for all moments in S_0 after t_0', there are state-equivalent moments in **T** that follow t_1' in the same order. In Figure 2.14, these moments represent the state space trajectory of S_0 after t.

The key intuition behind the present approach is that agents and their environments are physical systems with respect to which we take the intentional stance. This means that all relevant information about how a multiagent system *might* physically evolve is captured by the state in the formal model. The actual evolution or behavior of a system is determined by the actions that the agents may perform and the events that may occur in the environment. In other words, the real scenario at a moment depends on the agents' intentions and beliefs, but the set of possible scenarios is independent of the agents' intentions and beliefs. That is, the actions that are available to the agents and the conditions that hold on different scenarios leading from a given state are determined by that state itself. The state at a moment is precisely characterized by the atomic propositions that hold at that moment.

A purely physical stance is one in which we take the agents' intentions and beliefs to be determined by the physical state of the system. Under such a stance, the actions that are physically not possible at a moment would be considered on par with the actions that are physically available, but happen not to be chosen by the agents (given the agents' intentions and beliefs). Such

a stance would lead to a model in which the only source of nondeterminism
is quantum-mechanical, i.e., physical, nondeterminism. However, as argued in
Chapter 1, a purely physical stance is not scientifically helpful for the study of
multiagent systems. Indeed, the whole point of taking the intentional stance is
to facilitate abstract, i.e., non-physical, descriptions of intelligent agents.

For the same reason, even if the underlying model were deterministic, we would prefer that the model be nondeterministic, so that the choices
that agents make and a variety of potential constraints on those choices can
be explicitly captured. Classical distributed computing models of temporal
logic also allow this kind of nondeterminism (through branching or multiple
possible computations). However, a key difference is that the notion of state
in the present work is of physical state, which explicitly excludes aspects like
intentions and beliefs. In classical temporal logic models, there is no notion of
intentions or beliefs and the state by itself characterizes the potential behaviors
of the system.

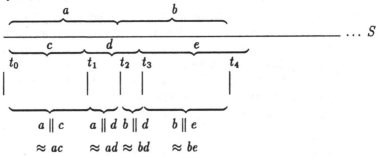

Figure 2.15: Each Agent Performs one Action at a Time

Aux-4. **Additional assumption to simplify notation.** *Each agent performs one action at a time:* It is technically convenient to limit each
agent to do exactly one basic action at a moment. This does not restrict potential models, since we can consider the set of basic actions
of an agent to contain actions that are the combinations of the actions
he would otherwise have been said to be performing simultaneously.

For example, an agent who can walk and whistle at the same time can
be thought of as having a basic action, called "walk-whistle," that has exactly
the same effects in each given state that the actions of walking and whistling
would have when done simultaneously. Figure 2.15 shows how we may convert
any model in which an agent can perform multiple actions simultaneously to

one in which he performs exactly one action at a time. The original actions can be of arbitrarily different durations. The moments at which any action is begun or completed are especially important. These are shown as moments t_i in the figure. Between any two successive such moments, the agent simultaneously performs a well-defined set of actions. We can generate a set of action symbols, one for each set of actions that the agent performs simultaneously. The agent's choices can be seen in the original model as selecting a set of actions; in the revised model, the choices pertain to the extend set of basic actions. In each model, the choices of an agent are constrained by the durations of the actions that he has already selected.

The above is not a claim about how actions should be represented in a reasoning system; it is merely an assumption designed to simplify the quantifications over actions that many of the later definitions involve. If this assumption is made, those definitions become significantly more readable. I should reiterate that nothing is lost of our ability to model different applications: we can transform any model into one in which this assumption is satisfied. This can be accomplished by changing the set of basic actions and the intensions of basic actions appropriately. As a result, while each agent does one action at a moment, different agents can act simultaneously. In the worst case, the number of basic actions in the transformed model can be exponential in the number of basic actions in the original model. However, that is not a problem since, if all combinations of actions were possible and if we wanted to reason about them, we could not have done any better anyway. For, even then, we would have to consider how an agent might select an appropriate subset of his basic actions.

Observation 2.4 Under assumption AUX-4, $(x\langle a\rangle\text{true} \wedge x\langle b\rangle\text{true}) \rightarrow a = b$ □

The formal model described above is motivated from general intuitions about actions and time. The frame component of it will remain unchanged throughout this work, although the interpretation component will need to be extended. The key intuitions behind the model are that the world is seen to be in different states at different moments. The agents can act in different ways, each combination of their choices leading to different scenarios being realized. The definitions of intentions and know-how depend on the relations between the agents' possible actions and the conditions that result from them.

2.4   Results on Time and Actions

It is helpful in intuitively understanding formal definitions to attempt to prove some technical results that should follow from them. For this reason, I state and discuss some consequences of the above model and semantic definitions next.

It appears that constraint Coh-1 is what McDermott sought to achieve by requiring that actions do not overlap. Unfortunately, that also eliminates Coh-3, which is essential, e.g., so that Fp can be concluded at all moments which precede p (Observation 2.18). Constraints Coh-4 and Coh-5 are required for Observation 2.18 and related results about G and U.

Observation 2.5 $\neg(pU\neg p)$ $\square$

Observation 2.6 $p \rightarrow Fp$ $\square$

Observation 2.7 $Gp \rightarrow Fp$ $\square$

Observation 2.8 $Fp \equiv FFp$ $\square$

Observation 2.9 $Gp \equiv GGp$ $\square$

Observation 2.10 $FGp \rightarrow GFp$ $\square$

Observation 2.11 $GFp \not\rightarrow FGp$ $\square$

Observation 2.12 $p \wedge q \rightarrow pUq$ $\square$

Observation 2.13 $Gp \not\rightarrow pUq$ $\square$

Observation 2.14 $(Gp \wedge Fq) \rightarrow pUq$ $\square$

Observation 2.15 $(pUp) \equiv p$ $\square$

Observation 2.16 $(x\langle a\rangle p) \rightarrow Fp$ $\square$

Observation 2.17 $(x\langle a\rangle Fp) \rightarrow Fp$ $\square$

Observation 2.18 $\mathsf{F}p \rightarrow p \vee (\vee a : x\langle a \rangle \mathsf{F}p)$ □

Observation 2.19 $\mathsf{G}p \rightarrow (\vee a : x\neg[a]\neg\mathsf{G}p)$ □

Observation 2.20 $(p \wedge x\neg[a]\neg\mathsf{G}p) \rightarrow \mathsf{G}p$ □

Observation 2.21 $(p \wedge q) \rightarrow p\mathsf{U}q$ □

Observation 2.22 $(p \wedge x\neg[a]\neg(p\mathsf{U}q)) \rightarrow p\mathsf{U}q$ □

Observation 2.23 $(p \wedge x\langle\!\langle a \rangle\!\rangle(p\mathsf{U}q)) \rightarrow p\mathsf{U}q$ □

Observation 2.24 $p\mathsf{U}q \rightarrow ((p \wedge q) \vee (p \wedge (\vee a : x\neg[a]\neg(p\mathsf{U}q))) \vee (p \wedge (\vee a : x\langle\!\langle a \rangle\!\rangle(p\mathsf{U}q))))$ □

The following shows that one action operator suffices in discrete models with unit length actions.

Observation 2.25 In models with unit length actions, $x\langle a \rangle p \equiv x\neg[a]\neg p$ and $x\langle a \rangle p \equiv x\langle\!\langle a \rangle\!\rangle p$ □

In the presence of constraint Сон-1, we can simplify the semantic condition for $x[a]p$ as follows. I will freely use this version in the sequel.

Observation 2.26 $M \models_{S,t} x[a]p$ iff $(\forall t' \in S : [S; t, t'] \in [a]^x$ implies that $(\exists t'' : t < t'' \leq t'$ and $M \models_{S,t''} p))$ □

The following observation highlights that $x\neg[a]\neg p$ means that a is performed and p holds throughout a.

Observation 2.27 $M \models_{S,t} \neg[a]\neg p$ iff $(\exists t' \in S : [S; t, t'] \in [a]^x$ and $(\forall t'' : t < t'' \leq t'$ implies that $M \models_{S,t''} p))$ □

2.5   Strategies

It is useful to think of intelligent systems as having a *reactive* component. This is the component that takes care of the actions that agents do at the greatest level of detail. Typically, these are actions that cannot be planned in advance, because of uncertainty about the state of the world and the rapidly changing nature of the relevant parameters. These actions are selected by an agent on the fly on the basis of the state of the environment he finds himself facing. For example, a detailed plan of how a robot should walk down a hall would in general not be feasible. For, even if the locations of all the objects in the hall were known precisely initially, the exact path taken would depend on the paths taken by other agents and objects in the hall while the robot was in it.

To the extent that it has been developed in the preceding sections, the proposed formal model can accommodate the reactive component of intelligent systems most naturally. This is because it can model actions fairly generally and nothing more is required. It will, however, help to be able to define useful abstractions over the behaviors of agents. These abstractions make it simple for us to understand, specify, and implement intelligent agents.

These abstract descriptions of behavior, I call *strategies.* The idea of using strategies such as these for describing intelligent agents can be traced back to [Miller *et al.*, 1960, p. 17], who credit [Kochen & Galanter, 1958] (p. 47). To my knowledge, the first computer science usage of this term in a related sense is in [McCarthy & Hayes, 1969]. Strategies here are taken simply to characterize an agent's behavior, possibly in quite coarse terms. This is in greater agreement with the definition of [Miller *et al.*, 1960] than of [McCarthy & Hayes, 1969]. Also, there is no commitment here to strategies being implemented as symbolic structures or as programs. They could just be the compact descriptions of a particular architecture, i.e., realized in the hardware. How strategies are realized is clearly of great importance to the implementor. However, from a logical point of view, we can fruitfully study them independent of the form in which they ultimately may be realized.

The formal definition of strategies here is derived from regular programs in dynamic logic, which are a standard notation for describing programs and computations in theoretical computer science [Fischer & Ladner, 1979; Kozen & Tiurzyn, 1990]. I define the set of strategies, $\mathcal{L}_y$, recursively as below. This set includes the empty strategy and the abstract strategies of achieving different conditions. It is closed under sequencing, conditionalization, and iteration. An important feature of this language is that it is deterministic. That is, all choices concerning what substrategy to execute next have guard conditions. A particular option is selected only if its guard is satisfied or, sometimes, only if its guard is known to be satisfied.

STRAT-1. **skip** $\in \mathcal{L}_y$

STRAT-2. $q \in \mathcal{L}$ implies that **do**$(q) \in \mathcal{L}_y$

STRAT-3. $Y_1, Y_2 \in \mathcal{L}_y$ implies that $Y_1 ; Y_2 \in \mathcal{L}_y$

STRAT-4. $q \in \mathcal{L}$ and $Y_1, Y_2 \in \mathcal{L}_y$ implies that **if** q **then** Y_1 **else** $Y_2 \in \mathcal{L}_y$

STRAT-5. $q \in \mathcal{L}$ and $Y_1 \in \mathcal{L}_y$ implies that **while** q **do** $Y_1 \in \mathcal{L}_y$

Thus the main difference between strategies and deterministic regular programs is that the former are composed of abstract strategies for achieving different conditions, while the latter are composed from a finite alphabet of basic action symbols. Intuitively, the strategy **do**(q) denotes an abstract action, namely, the action of achieving q. It could be realized by any sequence of basic actions that yields q.

Thus, in architectural terms, strategies can serve as macro-operators over the reactively realized behaviors of agents. For instance, we might implement the following agent. This agent would have a simple sensory system through which it would be assigned one of a limited repertoire of household tasks. These tasks could include making dinner, getting a newspaper, or checking the mail. It is natural to think of different strategies being associated with these tasks. While the strategies for the different tasks would have to be distinct, they could share significant components. For example, the strategies of getting a newspaper and checking the mail, respectively, share the components of getting to the front door, opening and closing it, going down and up the porch steps, and so on. These subtasks are not trivial. However, they do call for reactive solutions. This is because the movements of other agents, the changes in the location of the furniture, the intensity of the breeze, and the wetness of the porch are unpredictable factors that determine the exact actions that the agent must perform to succeed with the relevant subtasks. On the other hand, if we have designed the agent to be able to perform these subtasks successfully, then we can simply invoke them as higher-order primitives from the other strategies.

Strategies do not add any special capability to the agents. They simply help us, designers and analyzers, better organize the skills and capabilities that agents have anyway. Hierarchical or partial plans of agents, thus, turn out to be good examples of strategies. Considering strategies explicitly as a part of the formal language allows us to model agents who have plans, but who are also capable of acting reactively and must usually do so. Such agents are important in current research into intelligent systems [Mitchell, 1990; Spector & Hendler, 1991]. Furthermore, we can use strategies to describe computational entities that do not explicitly have plans, but simply execute programs. Thus we can consider agents who may not explicitly symbolically represent and manipulate their action descriptions. This is in concordance with the spirit of the intentional stance, which I have adopted here: this stance can apply to all interesting systems, not just those that are, for independent reasons, known to be intelligent. In this way, strategies help put the different schools of thought about intelligent systems in a unifying perspective.

The component Y of the model was defined in section 2.1.2 as a function that assigns a strategy to each agent at each moment. Now we can formalize its type as $\mathcal{A} \times T \mapsto \mathcal{L}_y$. Intuitively, the strategy assigned to an agent is the one that the agent is currently following or attempting to follow. Of course, there is no guarantee that the agent will succeed with it. I return to these points in section 3.1.

It is common in the AI literature to consider *goals* as primitives that determine what an agent seeks to achieve [Georgeff, 1987]. Goals are just seen to be descriptions of states that may be passed as inputs to a planning program to determine a sequence of actions for an agent. In some cases, goals are considered as possible descriptions of states that an agent may decide to achieve; then, adopted goals correspond to intentions. The notion of goals can be easily accommodated in the present approach. Indeed, one can associate a goal for a condition q as the simple strategy $\mathbf{do}(q)$. The definition of strategies given here allows more complex specifications of goals; however, goals as given traditionally can be captured here. Just as in the traditional approaches, it is possible to consider goals independently of whether they have actually been adopted by an agent. However, details of how one might plan an agent's actions are not focused on here.

Strategies are also powerful enough to capture many classes of behavior that may seem to be, and may be presented as being, non-teleological. I submit that many varieties of such behavior must be expressible in standard programming languages, such as Pascal. Since strategies are deterministic regular programs, albeit with abstraction (as in $\mathbf{do}(q)$), they can directly capture just about any kind of terminating behavior that can be expressed in Pascal and other imperative programming languages. Indeed, deterministic regular programs have been found interesting in theoretical computer science precisely because of their similarity with standard programming languages. Once a strategy can be specified, it can be used to assign intentions to agents. In this way, we can take the intentional stance even towards systems that are initially given as not engaging in goal-directed behavior.

Y	$\downarrow_t Y$
skip	**skip**
do(q)	if $M \models_t \neg q$ then **do**(q) else **skip**
$Y_1;Y_2$	if $\downarrow_t Y_1 \neq$ **skip** then $\downarrow_t Y_1$ else $\downarrow_t Y_2$
if q **then** Y_1 **else** Y_2	if $M \models_t q$ then $\downarrow_t Y_1$ else $\downarrow_t Y_2$
while q **do** Y_1	if $M \models_t \neg q$ then **skip** else $\downarrow_t Y_1$

Table 2.1: Definition of $\downarrow$ of Strategies

Y	$\uparrow_t Y$
skip	**skip**
do(q)	**skip**
$Y_1;Y_2$	if $\downarrow_t Y_1 \neq$ **skip** then $(\uparrow_t Y_1);Y_2$ else $\uparrow_t Y_2$
if q **then** Y_1 **else** Y_2	if $M \models_t q$ then $\uparrow_t Y_1$ else $\uparrow_t Y_2$
while q **do** Y_1	if $M \models_t \neg q$ then **skip** else if $\downarrow_t Y_1 \neq$ **skip** then $(\uparrow_t Y_1);Y$ else **skip**

Table 2.2: Definition of $\uparrow$ of Strategies

It is useful to define two metalanguage functions, $\downarrow$ and $\uparrow$, on strategies. These functions depend on the moment at which they are evaluated; the relevant moment is notated as a subscript. Let Y be a strategy. $\downarrow_t Y$ denotes the part of Y up for execution at moment t, and $\uparrow_t Y$ the part of Y that would remain after $\downarrow_t Y$ has been done. It is convenient to assume that strategies are normalized with respect to the following constraints, although it is not technically essential to do so.

- **skip**$;Y = Y$, for all Y, and

- $Y;$**skip** $= Y$, for all Y.

Both the $\downarrow_t$ and $\uparrow_t$ of a strategy depend on the moment t. For example, the $\downarrow$ of a conditional strategy depends on whether the relevant condition is true or false at t. It should be easy to see from the above that for any strategy, Y, $\downarrow_t Y = $ **skip** or is of the form $\mathbf{do}(q)$, for some q. And if $Y \neq $ **skip**, then $\downarrow_t Y$ is necessarily of the latter form. Tables 2.1 and 2.2 give the definitions of $\downarrow$ and $\uparrow$. A consequence of those definitions is Lemma 2.28 below.

Lemma 2.28 $\downarrow_t Y = $ **skip** entails that $\uparrow_t Y = $ **skip**

Proof. By inspection of the conditions in Tables 2.1 and 2.2, for each form of a strategy. $\square$

This lemma simplifies the statement of certain conditions later on, especially, the condition of persistence discussed in Chapters 3 and 5. It is not needed for most of the other definitions, however.

In succeeding chapters, I will use the set $\mathcal{L}_y$ and the metalanguage functions defined on it to give the semantics of the operators for intentions and know-how.

2.6   Belief and Knowledge

Two main kinds of formal definitions of knowledge (or belief) are known in the literature. The *sentential* approach states that an agent knows every proposition that is stored in his knowledge base [Konolige, 1986]. The *possible-worlds* approach states that an agent knows every proposition that is true in all the worlds (or moments, in the present terminology) that he "considers" possible [Hintikka, 1962]. Since typically these worlds are not characterized separately, but only through the agent's knowledge, the agent may be said to know every proposition that is true in all the worlds that are compatible with what he knows. Each approach has its trade-offs. The sentential approach does not consider models of the world and, thus, does not assign semantic content to knowledge. The possible-worlds approach gives a perspicuous semantics, but at the cost of validating inferences such as: an agent knows all logical consequences of his knowledge. This is in direct conflict with the fact that agents are not perfect reasoners and, in general, do not know what the consequences of their knowledge might be. Alternative approaches exist [Asher, 1986; Fagin & Halpern, 1988; Singh & Asher, 1993] that seek to avoid both these problems, but they are technically more complex than either of the approaches mentioned above.

The definition given below is a possible-worlds definition and thus imperfect in the ways mentioned above. However, it relates quite naturally to our model of actions and time; it is, therefore, a reasonable first approximation. The interpretation function, $\mathbf{B}$, defined in section 2.1.2 assigns a set of moments to each agent at each moment. At a given moment, the set of moments assigned to an agent by $\mathbf{B}$ denotes the states of affairs that the agent considers as possible (at the given moment). Thus, what the agent really believes are the propositions that hold in each of the moments he considers possible. This motivates the following semantic definition for $x\mathbf{B}p$:

SEM-16. $M \models_t x\mathbf{B}p$ iff $(\forall t' : (t,t') \in \mathbf{B}(x)$ implies $M \models_{t'} p)$

An important special case occurs when for all moments, t, $(t,t) \in \mathbf{B}(x)$. In that case, $x\mathbf{B}p \to p$. That is, all of x's beliefs are true. Following standard practice, true beliefs are identified with knowledge. In that case, it is mnemonically helpful to use the formula $x\mathsf{K}_t p$ instead of $x\mathbf{B}p$, where K_t stands for *know-that*.

It is customary to assume that each of the relations $\mathbf{B}(x)$ has the following properties [Moore, 1984].

1. *Reflexivity:* $(\forall t : (t,t) \in \mathbf{B}(x))$

2. *Transitivity:* $(\forall t, t', t'' : (t,t'), (t',t'') \in \mathbf{B}(x) \Rightarrow (t,t'') \in \mathbf{B}(x))$

In that case, the $\mathbf{B}$ operator defined above can be replaced by K_t. The following axioms hold of it.

Ax-BEL-1. $x\mathsf{K}_t p \to p$

Ax-BEL-2. $x\mathsf{K}_t p \to x\mathsf{K}_t x\mathsf{K}_t p$

Ax-Bel-3. $x\mathsf{K}_t\mathsf{true}$

Ax-Bel-4. $x\mathsf{K}_t(p\rightarrow q)\rightarrow (x\mathsf{K}_t p\rightarrow x\mathsf{K}_t q)$

Theorem 2.29 Axioms Ax-Bel-1 through Ax-Bel-4 constitute a sound and complete axiomatization for the operator K_t.

This theorem is due to Kripke. A proof is available in [Chellas, 1980, pp. 177–178]. □

The primary relationship between knowledge and actions is that, given a particular strategy, the actions an agent chooses are determined by his knowledge. This connection is studied in detail in Chapters 4 and 5. One constraint between actions and knowledge that is often applicable is the following.

Coh-9. **Knowledge of Choices:** This states that an agent knows what actions he can perform. In other words, if an agent can perform an action at a given moment, then he can perform it at all belief-alternative moments. Formally,

$(\forall t : (\exists S, t_0 : [S; t, t_0] \in [a]^x) \Rightarrow (\forall t' : (t, t') \in \mathbf{B}(x) \Rightarrow (\exists S', t_1 : [S'; t', t_1] \in [a]^x)))$

Lemma 2.30 If a model satisfies constraint Coh-9, then it validates the following formula: $\mathsf{E}x\langle a\rangle\mathsf{true}\rightarrow \mathsf{K}_t\mathsf{E}x\langle a\rangle\mathsf{true}$ □

2.7   More on Actions and Other Events

The formal framework described above includes actions and other events and relates them to time. Only actions, which are events due to an agent, are included in the formal language because actions is all we need for our purposes. But it is easy to augment the formal language to refer to non-action events as well, if that is needed.

Although the formal framework allows several actions and events to happen concurrently and asynchronously, it presents only a bare-bones view of them. Actions and events have been intensively studied in linguistics [Vendler, 1967; Link, 1987; Krifka, 1989], philosophy [Davidson, 1980; Goldman, 1970; Thomason & Gupta, 1981; Asher, 1992], and AI [McDermott, 1982; Allen, 1984; Shoham, 1988; Bacchus et al., 1989]. The most sophisticated of these studies have been the ones in linguistics and philosophy. The former is especially useful, since most of our intuitions about events are derived from how they are referred to in natural language. I shall, therefore, concentrate on linguistic and philosophical theories and consider AI approaches only at the end.

2.7.1 Events in Natural Language

The classification of events proposed in [Vendler, 1967, chapter 4] is based on data from natural languages. It captures many of our commonsense intuitions about events and is fundamental to much of the other work on events. At the top level, events are distinguished from states. The major categories of events are *telic* and *atelic*. Telic events are those that have a well-defined endpoint; atelic events are those that do not. Examples of telic event types are "build a house" or "eat an apple," which have a set moment of ending. Examples of atelic event types are "push a cart" or "walk in the park." There are subtle relationships between the event category denoted by a natural language sentence and certain properties of the different parts of speech in that sentence [Krifka, 1989]. These shall not concern us here.

The important observation from our point of view is that these theories are, for the most part, not about the nature of events *per se*, but rather about descriptions of those events. The description of an event typically refers to the entities involved in it, its result state, its structure (whether it is telic, whether it iterates, and so on), and the manner in which it happens. These can be taken care of in the proposed framework, provided we extend the formal language to make it sufficiently expressive: the model itself need not be augmented.

The introduction of strategies in section 2.5 serves to extend the formal language to describe actions based on their resulting states. The strategy $do(q)$ denotes the action of achieving a state in which q holds. This is common to many natural language descriptions of actions, for instance, "He shut the door" and other telic sentences. Although the model does not admit instantaneous basic actions and events, strategies can be instantaneously satisfied: this happens when the relevant condition holds already. As a result, instantaneous events can be said to have occurred wherever the given condition holds. This might seem problematic, since events such as "Al woke up" cannot be said to have happened in every state in which Al is awake. However, the status of zero-duration events is suspect, given our knowledge of Physics. Therefore, we can avoid modeling events as instantaneous, even though natural languages allow some of them to be treated as if they were.

When events are described in terms of states, they usually involve entering or exiting a certain state. This change of state can be modeled by strategies of the form $\mathbf{do}(\neg q);\mathbf{do}(q)$. Such strategies require that an appropriate condition, q, come to hold after its negation has held. Thus they are satisfied only if we can find two moments, the earlier of which satisfies $\neg q$ and the later of which satisfies q. Such strategies cannot be begun and satisfied at a moment at which q holds; in fact, they always take time. Such strategies may be used to model events such as reaching a mountain peak, which happen when one is not initially on the peak. However, this proposal permits someone on the peak to reach it by leaving it and then returning to it. This might seem counterintuitive since, in natural language, reaching a place *again* is different from reaching it the first time. This distinction too can be captured by explicitly using the past operator, P, to state whether the given condition was achieved for the first time or not. Ultimately, however, the present qualitative formal language is too weak to directly represent all natural language phenomena, e.g., the anaphoric nature of temporal reference [Partee, 1973]. An indirect approach, which suffices for most purposes of specifying multiagent systems, is discussed in section 2.8.

However, atelic events cannot naturally be expressed as involving changes of state. Such events are, therefore, not easily captured in the proposed approach. Fortunately, though, such events do not arise in the specifications of artificial systems. For example, one never requires that an agent take a walk, but rather that an agent take a walk for a certain duration or walk until he arrives at some destination or achieves some other condition.

Link's and Krifka's theories allow composite events to be formed by joining atomic events [Link, 1987; Krifka, 1989]. Their approach is abstract in that no constraints are stated on how and when two events may be composed. Their main aim is to be able to derive certain properties of natural language sentences and, thereby, to explain certain linguistic phenomena. The obvious connection to the proposed framework is that only events that are on the same scenario may be composed. Single events distinguish scenarios on which they occur from those on which they do not. Similarly, compositions of events can distinguish scenarios too. The properties of events studied by these researchers include telicity and others that depend on event descriptions. These are not of interest here.

2.7.2   Trying to Act

Basic actions were defined as the choices that an agent can make. Agents thus automatically succeed with the basic actions they try. But, as described above, it is often useful to be able to identify actions by their effects. However, usually, the effects of actions are far from certain. This observation is captured in the model by allowing each action begun at a moment to be performed on several different scenarios, possibly leading to different states on each. As a result, when actions are described by their effects, there is a profound distinction between trying to perform an action and actually performing it.

Indeed, this is one reason why the study of know-how and intentions is interesting: know-how and intentions are means of talking about abstract actions that are defined by their effects. When we are interested in such abstract actions, the present framework allows us to distinguish between successful performances of them and unsuccessful attempts to perform them. I shall formalize a constraint later that states that, if agents can, they act in ways to best achieve their strategies; such actions constitute attempts at achieving the given strategies and at satisfying the associated intentions. Those attempts can be guaranteed to be successful only in the presence of know-how.

It is possible in natural language to distinguish between an action and an attempt to perform it, for instance, by using an explicit indicator like the verb "try." Quite often, the same verb is used for both purposes. For example, we can use the verb "push" in the sense of "trying to push" to felicitously say "He pushed the box, but it did not move." The same verb can also be used in its normal sense, as in "He pushed the box to the left wall." This usage specifies the resulting state and it is impossible for the following sentences, which refer to the same box, to both be true at once: "John is pushing the box to the left wall" and "Al is pushing the box to the right wall." However, attempts of the described actions can occur simultaneously, because an attempt to perform an abstract action may occur, even though that action does not.

Telic events, when they occur simultaneously, necessarily have the effects that define them individually. Their joint ramifications could, of course, vary significantly from their individual ramifications. For example, John's and Al's pushing different boxes to different sides of a ship cabin may individually cause the ship to tilt, but jointly may not. The ramifications of atelic events vary similarly. Although atelic events are not defined in terms of any specific terminal effects as such, they can be associated with some effects on some salient objects. For example, one takes a walk only for so long as one actually walks. And, one pushes a block only so long as one keeps it moving. It is worth considering the example that Allen gives of the actions of pushing a block one unit to the left, and one unit to the right [1984, p. 125]. He says that performing both actions simultaneously does not cause the block to move. But, it seems that he is using the verb "push" in the sense of "tried to push." The action of pushing a block one unit to the left could not possibly have occurred if the block did not move: it could at most have been unsuccessfully attempted. The point of this is to show that, in formalizing commonsense domains, one must carefully distinguish actions from attempts to perform them.

The philosopher Goldman proposed the theory of *generation* [1970]. An action *generates* another action if it is the means of performing the second action. In other words, *a* generates *b* iff the given agent performs *b* by doing *a*. Goldman defines generation as applying between instances of actions that are spatiotemporally identical, but are in some other way distinct. Most of the time, the only distinction possible between these actions is their descriptions. For our purposes, the more relevant component of Goldman's theory is the relation of conditional generation between action types, which presupposes the truth of some salient conditions under which an instance of the first action will generate an instance of the second action. In the present framework, when abstract actions are identified with strategies, the basic actions associated with those strategies can be seen as generating the abstract actions with which they are associated. This is also related to the notion of trying, since an agent may perform a sequence of basic actions, but not succeed in generating the corresponding abstract action: in that case, in the presence of appropriate intentions, the agent may be said to have tried to perform that abstract action.

2.7.3   Actions and Events in Artificial intelligence

Actions and time have drawn much attention in AI. However, most extant approaches are shallow. They do not formalize the properties that coherent models of actions should support and focus instead on the language aspects, e.g., whether predicates like *holds* should be used or not. In other words, they are metalinguistic and not model-theoretic [Turner, 1984, p. 88]. Further, though these theories are advanced in some respects, e.g., in allowing continuous time, they validate too few natural inferences to facilitate formalization of concepts that build on actions, e.g., intentions and ability. Thus most work on those concepts assumes that time is discrete and actions are performed one at a time (e.g., [Rao & Georgeff, 1991a]).

Much of the AI work on actions and events has been concerned with either specifying the time intervals over which they occur, or with their normal preconditions and effects. The internal structure of actions and events, as discussed in the preceding subsections, has drawn much less attention, although some AI researchers have borrowed heavily from the linguistic and philosophical literatures. Most of such contributions have been in the subarea of natural language processing. Events are studied in other parts of computer science, notably in frameworks for semantics of distributed computation. The internal structure of events has not been intensively studied there either. Thus most of mainstream computer science and AI work on events has been closer in focus to the present approach than linguistic or philosophical work. McDermott's approach bears the greatest similarities to the present framework [1982].

Logics and models of time fall into two major categories: branching-time and linear-time, respectively. The former category variously considers basic temporal structures as branching into the past or the future or both; the latter category requires them to be scenarios. There has been much debate in theoretical computer science about the relative merits of the above two approaches with respect to the specification and verification of classical distributed systems. For our purposes, branching-time approaches yield a natural framework for describing the behavior of multiagent systems. This is because multiagent systems are composed of intelligent agents who have limited control on the future of the world and exercise their choices independently of each other. Our models must incorporate the different choices available to agents explicitly, if we are to represent and reason about those choices and their optimality in our framework. Indeed, any formal framework that is sufficiently powerful for this purpose must involve at least some notion of branching time, implicit or explicit.

Allen presents an interval-based linear-time theory of actions in [1984]. Turner [1984, p. 88] and Shoham [1988, ch. 2] show that Allen's theory is not clear, especially with regard to intervals. Allen objects to branching-time approaches on grounds that branching times are required only for hypothetical reasoning, due to incomplete knowledge about the future [1984, p. 131]. Shoham agrees with this view; he too restricts his models to be linear (p. 36). Allen, who discusses this subject in greater detail, argues that hypothetical reasoning about the future is essentially the same as hypothetical reasoning about anything else, including the past or the present. This remark embodies a fundamental confusion between models and representations. What the branching futures at a moment capture is not the incompleteness of some agent's knowledge, but rather the fact that there are several different ways in which agents may act and the world may evolve. We need to capture different branches of time into the future in order to explicitly consider the choices that agents can make. Since there are no choices to be made about the past, we can allow it to be linear. (Sometimes, efficiency may be gained by treating even the past as branching: I allow this.) The incompleteness of the agents' knowledge, be it about the past, present, or future, is captured by the alternativeness relations that are assigned to each of them. A similar point is made by McDermott [1982, p. 108].

McDermott's temporal models are in some ways similar to the ones developed here. McDermott, however, requires his models to be dense; no such requirement is imposed here, though density is permitted. Scenarios as defined above are related to the *fullpaths* of Emerson [1990, p. 1014] and the *chronicles* of McDermott [1982, p. 106]. The key differences are that fullpaths are defined over discrete models and are necessarily discrete; and, chronicles are necessarily dense. By contrast, scenarios are maximally dense relative to the temporal precedence relation. That is, they derive their structure from $<$. McDermott does not impose any of the coherence constraints described here; it is not clear if he makes use of any of them implicitly.

2.8   Rationale for Qualitative Temporal Logic

The qualitative temporal logic approach adopted here captures the essential aspects of the concepts being formalized, beginning with basic actions and going on to intentions and know-how. One can always move to a quantitative framework or to one in which times are explicit in the formalization. For the former, one may assign dates or clock values to each moment, such that dates are totally ordered and are shared by moments along different scenarios. The present framework can easily accommodate dates. For the latter, one may base the language not on propositions, but on predicates with an explicit temporal argument. Alternatively, one may modify operators, such as U and P, to have quantitative arguments and interpretations. Doing so would allow us to reason about real time within the logic.

Extensions of notation would, of course, be needed to formalize certain kinds of applications. For example, the prohibitive "do not assign runway B" would apply only for a salient interval, say till 2:10 pm, not forever. It can be formalized as if it were the following prohibitive: "do not assign runway B when the time is prior to 2:10 pm." Once the time becomes 2:10 pm, this prohibitive can no longer be violated. Thus we can capture this aspect of temporal specifications simply by enriching the sublanguage from which the atomic propositions of our formal language are drawn. The syntax and semantics of the formal language remain unchanged.

Interestingly enough, the qualitative temporal logic CTL*, on which the present formal language is based, is as expressive as the monadic second-order theory of two successors with set quantification restricted to infinite paths (i.e., scenarios), over infinite models. A similar result holds for the linear fragment of CTL* with respect to the first order language of linear order [Emerson, 1990, pp. 1021–1026]. Thus, in a qualitative framework, expressiveness is not a concern.

I see the steps of augmenting the framework with explicit dates or moving to a language in which moments are explicit as adding notational complexity. However, neither of these steps significantly aids our understanding of the concepts of intentions, know-how, and communications, which are what I primarily focus on here. They are needed solely to make the language more expressive for the lower-level details of a specification.

Another, methodological, reason for proceeding with a qualitative temporal (and dynamic) logic framework is to draw as many similarities as possible with classical distributed computing. Ideally, only the conceptually significant distinctions would be apparent. An important goal of the present approach is to develop a semantics for multiagent systems that is closely related to the semantics for classical systems, thereby making the implementations of such systems on standard platforms with close to standard techniques more obvious.

As remarked above, the underlying language from which the atomic propositions are drawn would need to be extended for most practical languages. Such extensions may be specialized to different applications. Considering only an abstract language makes the framework simpler to understand. However, it leaves two shortcomings. One, we are unable to reason about quantitative durations, since they are packaged inside the atomic propositions. Two, we are unable, without metarules, to refer to times relativized to some salient moment that would be determined during execution. Such relativized times are required in specifications such as "the controller responds within 1 minute of receiving a request for permission to land." On the other hand, languages that are expressive enough to admit such specifications have high computational complexity for problems such as validity checking.

Chapter 3

Intentions

I argued in Chapter 1 that intentions are an important scientific abstraction for characterizing agents in multiagent systems. This view is justified by the power with which we, humans, can use concepts such as intentions to understand, predict, and explain the behavior of other humans. The relevant point here is that humans are intelligent beings whose internal physical states we do not have precise knowledge of. I submit that a formalized, though necessarily somewhat restrictive, notion of intentions would prove equally useful in the study of artificial multiagent systems.

In this chapter, I first review the logical and intuitive properties that intentions may, or may not, be taken to have. These properties involve several aspects of our pretheoretic understanding of intentions and constrain how we may formalize them. I then present a formalization of intentions in the framework developed in Chapter 2. Next, I formalize several important properties of intentions, some by imposing additional constraints on models. I then briefly discuss the related concept of desires. I conclude with some general remarks on intentions.

3.1 Dimensions of Variation

Like all commonsense concepts, intentions have several senses or connotations. For the case of humans, especially, many of the intuitions associated with intentions are not always clear, or are mutually contradictory. Intentions are also related to other commonsense concepts, such as desires and hopes. It is common in the philosophical literature, however, to distinguish intentions from these other concepts on the following grounds. An agent's intentions are often taken to be necessarily mutually consistent or, at least, believed to be mutually consistent. And, they are almost always taken to be consistent with the given agent's beliefs. Intentions are also closely related to actions and are taken to be causes of the agent's actions. Indeed, there are several dimensions of variation in the study of intentions. I enumerate and discuss the major ones below with the aim of delineating the issues that are of particular relevance to multiagent systems. I have benefited the most from the work of the philosophers Bratman and Brand for much of this discussion [Bratman, 1987; Brand, 1984].

I-DIM-1. *Propositions versus actions:* Intentions can variously be taken to be towards (a) propositions that an agent is deemed to intend to *achieve,* i.e., achieve a state in which they are true, or (b) actions that an agent is deemed to intend to *perform.* Different natural language examples fit these views to different degrees. This dichotomy is largely irrelevant in the approach taken here. Intentions *per se* are taken to apply to propositions, which makes for a natural discussion of their logical properties. However, since I explicitly consider strategies in this framework, it is possible to obtain the effects of applying intentions to actions. An agent having a certain strategy can be said to intend the abstract action which that strategy denotes. Since the language of strategies allows fairly complex procedures to be described, the present approach can accommodate intentions towards action.

The notion of intending to perform a basic action can also be captured. For example, the condition $Ax\langle a\rangle$true denotes that action a is about to be completed on all available scenarios: it holds when the agent has chosen and begun action a, but not yet completed it. That is why it *will* be completed on all possible scenarios. However, it is not clear what this notion of intending basic actions might be used for. This is because in the proposed approach, intentions are supposed to be *abstractions* of agents' states and behaviors. Still, it is good to know that such requirements can be captured here, should they ever be needed for some applications.

I-DIM-2. *Future-directed versus present-directed:* It should be clear that intentions cannot be about past times. In the philosophical literature, they are taken to be either towards future states of the world or future actions, or towards present actions. The terms used here are due to Bratman [1987, p. 4]. Searle uses the term *intention-in-action* to denote the latter sense [1983, p. 106]. Brand uses the terms *prospective* and *immediate* to distinguish them. However, there is general agreement in the recent literature that the former, i.e., prospective, sense is the primary sense of intentions. For the purposes of multi-agent systems too, intending to achieve a particular future state of the world is the more useful notion. This is because it is the one that relates intentions to the strategies that agents execute and can be used as a predictor of their behavior.

Indeed, the notion of present-directed intentions is used primarily by philosophers to address some of their concerns about whether a given behavior of an agent is indeed an action. For instance, a popular example is a person's moving his arm: this behavior counts as an action only if he intends it *while* doing it and this intention causes the arm to move. It would not be an action if he intended it before it happened, but it happened because a neurosurgeon sent an electrical pulse on an appropriately connected electrode. Such conundrums are of limited value in computer science, at least at present. A possible use of present-directed intentions is to determine whether a certain putative action was intended. But the relevant aspects of this case are readily subsumed by future-directed intentions: an agent can be said to have intended an action if it was done as part of a prior future-directed intention of his [Brand, 1984, p. 28].

In our formal model, agents are assigned different actions on different periods: if it helps we can think of each of those actions as being intended during the periods in which they are performed. But in the sequel, I shall use the term *intention* exclusively to refer to future-directed intentions.

I-DIM-3. *Intending versus doing intentionally:* Another dimension of variation relevant to intentions is perhaps more useful in computer science. This concerns the difference between intending something and doing it intentionally. The former involves the true intentions or preferences of an agent; the latter applies to actions or states that the agent purposefully performs or brings about, but not with any prior intention to do so [Bratman, 1987, p. 119]. For example, an agent who intends to load paper into a photocopier may have to pick some ream of paper to do so. However, while he picks a specific ream deliberately and knowingly, he may not have intended in advance to pick that particular one. In the proposed approach, the conditions that an agent brings about intentionally are the ones that occur as, possibly contingent, consequences of his following his strategy. Only the conditions that are intended may be used to explain an agent's actions. However, the conditions he brings about intentionally, but does not intend, may be used in understanding or estimating his priorities. I discuss a related point in item I-DIM-6 below.

I-DIM-4. *Satisfiability:* It is usually believed that an agent's intentions are satisfiable in some future state of the world. More weakly, it is assumed that an agent believes that his intentions are satisfiable. For example, Bratman requires that an agent's plan be consistent with his beliefs, assuming that the beliefs are themselves not inconsistent [1987, p. 31]. An agent's plans should be executable if his beliefs are correct. Roughly, the motivation for this is that intentions are taken to apply to agents who are rational in some sense. Rationality is not formally characterized here; however, a constraint is stated in section 3.3 below that captures the requirement of the satisfiability of intentions.

I-DIM-5. *Mutual consistency:* It is commonly suggested that a rational agent's intentions should not preclude each other [Bratman, 1987, p. 31] [Brand, 1984, pp. 125–126]. Brand argues that inconsistency among an agent's intentions would make his mental state too incoherent for him to act.

Mutual consistency follows as a natural consequence of the present approach. If the intentions of an agent are satisfiable, then the strategies assigned by Y must be doable, at least on some scenarios. In that case, the intentions of the agent are also mutually consistent. This is because the model considers only those moments and actions that are consistent in the given domain. The above argument applies only if the intentions of one agent are considered. The intentions of different agents may not be mutually consistent. For example, when two agents are playing a zero-sum game, each intends that he win (and the other be forever from prevented from winning that instance of the game). This is allowed by the present approach.

I-DIM-6. *Closure under logical consequence:* In general, if one is talking about human beings, intentions are not closed under logical consequence. This is because the given agent may not have realized the appropriate connection or may have realized it, but does not prefer it, nevertheless. For example, you may intend to be operated on, but even though (let us stipulate) that entails spending a day in a hospital, you may not intend spending a day in a hospital. It is possible to develop formal theories of intentions that preserve this feature, and I have done so in joint work with Nicholas Asher [Singh & Asher, 1993].

However, for the purposes of designing and analyzing multiagent systems, it may be acceptable to let one's theory validate this inference. The reason is similar to those that motivate modal approaches to knowledge, as applied in distributed systems [Chandy & Misra, 1986; Halpern & Moses, 1987]. If one is considering a system from without, one has to consider its possible actions. By definition, a logical consequence of a proposition holds at all moments where that proposition holds. Therefore, it cannot be distinguished from the given proposition on the basis of the results of possible actions for achieving it. Thus there is no principled ground for preventing the given inference.

Newell cites this inference as an example of the profound limitation of the knowledge level. As a result of this inference, the knowledge level cannot aspire to be more than an approximation, and a "radically incomplete" one at that [Newell, 1982, pp. 104–105 and 111]. That is, it may fail to describe "entire ranges of behavior." Robert Boyer has independently argued that the only safe way to use this approach is to check, for each putative claim, whether it improperly relies on the closure inference [Boyer, 1992]. This contrasts with mathematical reasoning in general, where all conclusions of a theory are valid. Here we need an additional filter that looks at the proofs of theorems, rather than the theorems themselves. This restricts the applicability of the proposed approach.

One reason for allowing closure under logical consequence is that sometimes we can take a normative stance towards an (artificial) agent's actions. With such a stance, we can require that an agent have figured out his priorities and decided rationally on a course of action: such an agent is then responsible for whatever actions he performs. Also, a framework that prevents closure under logical consequence can easily become technically intractable. But when one wishes to clarify one's intuitions about complicated concepts such as intentions and to develop tools based on them for designing actual systems, closure under logical consequence remains a shortcoming.

I should note parenthetically that it is possible, in principle, to formally distinguish a proposition from its logical consequences. However, it is not clear if that can be done intuitively acceptably on the basis of possible actions as described here. In any case, logically equivalent propositions cannot be distinguished from each other in any possible worlds framework. Since the intuitive arguments against closure under logical consequence also apply against closure under logical equivalence, I explicitly discuss only the former case.

I-DIM-7. *Closure under believed effects:* It is sometimes argued that, for human beings, intentions are not closed even under beliefs. An agent may intend p, believe that p necessarily entails q and not intend q. Bratman gives the example of a strategic bomber who intends to bomb a munitions plant, believes that this will cause the adjacent school to blow up, but nevertheless does not intend to blow up the school [1987, p. 139]. Rao & Georgeff, who agree that this inference is not desirable, have termed it the *side-effect* problem [Rao & Georgeff, 1991a].

I-DIM-8. *Closure under means:* Item I-DIM-7 contrasts with the following claim. An agent who intends p, and believes that q is a necessary *means* to p, should intend q. Bratman calls this phenomenon *means-ends coherence* (p. 35). Brand too considers it an essential property of intentions [1984, p. 126]. In this case, it is rational for the agent to intend q; indeed he might intend q even if it was only of several possible means to p. In the case of item I-DIM-7, however, not only does intending the expected side-effects of an intention seem an incorrect description of people's intentions, it is also irrational, since it would only distract an agent from his real intention [1987, p. 142].

I-DIM-9. *Commitment:* A property of intentions that has recently gained acceptance is that usually they involve some measure of commitment on part of the agent [Harman, 1986, p. 94] [Bratman, 1987, ch. 2]. That is, an agent who has an intention is committed to achieving it and will persist with it through changing circumstances. I agree with the usefulness of persistence for the purposes of allowing agents to infer one another's strategies with greater ease and to feasibly coordinate their actions. However, the extent of an agent's persistence with a specific intention is intimately connected with some notion of rationality and involves the costs and benefits of different actions as well as the cost of computation. For example, it is clear that agents should not persist with their intentions forever. If they did, they would end up acting irrationally on intentions that were no longer useful or compatible with their true goals. I do not believe that there is any purely qualitative solution to the problem of when, and for how long, an agent must persist with an intention. However, certain qualitative constraints on intentions and beliefs can be meaningfully stated: an example constraint is described in item I-DIM-11. I have addressed this problem in some related research [1991b; 1991e]; however, I shall not focus on it in this work.

I-DIM-10. *Causation of action:* Another important intuition concerning intentions is that they are causes of actions by agents. This feature is supposed to conceptually differentiate intentions from desires and beliefs. It is not clear how we might use this explicitly in a theory of multiagent systems (recall the discussion in item I-DIM-3 above). However, it can be used to motivate an important constraint on models that intuitively captures a useful property of the architecture of intelligent agents. This is discussed in section 3.3 below.

I-DIM-11. *Intentions must be consistent with beliefs:* Since intentions are somehow related to an agent's rationality, it makes sense to assume that an agent's intentions are consistent with his beliefs about the future. If an agent believes that something is impossible, there is no purpose in his intending it. Similarly, if an agent who has a certain intention later comes to believe that it is, or has become, impossible to achieve, he would do well to drop that intention and concentrate his resources elsewhere. In other words, it should be inconsistent for an agent to intend p and simultaneously believe that p will not occur.

I-DIM-12. *Intentions do not entail beliefs:* While an agent cannot have beliefs that contradict his intentions, it is usually too much to require that an agent believe that he will in fact succeed with whatever intentions he has, or that he will be able to act appropriately for them. In other words, it should be consistent for an agent to intend p and yet not believe that p will occur. This view has been supported by several philosophers, e.g., Bratman [1987, pp. 38]. I return to this point in section 3.3.

I-DIM-13. *Intentions versus beliefs:* Intentions are usually taken to be distinct from beliefs, although they are always taken to be related to them. Allen, however, defines a prior or future-directed intention towards an action as being identical to a belief on part of the agent that he will execute a plan that includes the given action [1984, pp. 145–146]. This definition has some shortcomings. An agent may believe that he will perform a certain action but not be committed to actually performing that action, in the sense of retrying it under appropriate circumstances. Also, it is not clear how an agent's beliefs about the future may actually cause him to act one way or another. One, the agent may have several such beliefs about future happenings and may even intend to prevent some of them. Two, he may intend to do an action, but may not believe that he will necessarily be able to perform it.

It seems that the key ingredient of adopting a plan or strategy is missing from Allen's definition. It may be possible to define an agent's beliefs about his future actions in such a way as to differentiate them from his other beliefs and to capture many of the important properties of intentions. However, it is not clear what one might gain by that exercise. If one takes the trouble to differentiate the relevant kinds of beliefs from others, one might as well treat them as a distinct concept, and use the term "intentions" to describe them.

Intentions can be assigned several other philosophically motivated properties as well. However, my aim here is to take a minimalist stance, i.e., to study the simplest concept that will suffice for our needs. I submit that for the purposes of multiagent systems, the semantics of intentions should relate them to the strategies of agents and to the actions those agents may possibly perform. Intentions here are assigned on the basis of strategies and are computed in models that consider the possible actions of agents and the possible states of the world. As a result, several of their interesting properties can be derived from model-theoretic constraints on strategies. For example, we can state a constraint on models that ensures that the agents' intentions are satisfiable. Roughly, this constraint says that the strategies assigned to agents at different moments are doable (by them) on at least some scenarios at those moments.

Many intuitive properties of intentions, including their role as causes of action, are properly seen as matters of agent architecture. In the case of causing action, the relevant features of the architecture are the procedures of action selection that an agent employs. Taking strategies as primitive entities not only throws some light on how these properties may be realized in an agent's architecture, but also on how they may be captured in our formal model. Since each intention must be founded on some strategy, we can model the desired property by having agents' strategies restrict their actions appropriately.

For example, we can constrain the selection of actions so that an agent may begin an action only if it, at least potentially, leads to the satisfaction of the current part of the assigned strategy. Thus an agent with an as-yet-unsatisfied strategy must act in a manner that may lead to its satisfaction. There is no guarantee that he would succeed. However, this assumes that his strategy is not impossible to satisfy. The suggested constraint would allow the agent to try different actions on different scenarios, but that is only reasonable: in general, there may be more than one way to satisfy an intention or to carry out a strategy. In Chapter 5, where a constraint on the selection of actions is formally stated, it is somewhat stronger than the one here. There, an agent is required to select actions with which he can force the success of his strategy, assuming, of course, that such actions are available. The technical basis for this is developed in Chapter 4.

Some of the other properties of intentions, e.g., the tendency of agents to persist with them, are not a part of their *semantics*. Rather, these are consequences of constraints on how intentions are updated or agents' strategies revised. These constraints can be motivated on grounds of rationality. They can stated as additional requirements on agents. We can use the semantics developed here to assign meaning to these constraints, to formally infer their properties, and to define a notion of consistency among them.

Further desiderata for a theory of intentions are the following. For a theory of intentions to be of general applicability in computational systems, it should not be committed to a plan-based architecture of intelligent agents. It has recently been argued by several researchers that intelligence is not solely a matter of explicitly representing and interpreting symbolic structures, or at least not necessarily so [Agre & Chapman, 1987]. It would be useful to accommodate the kinds of systems these researchers consider, which are systems that involve a significant reactive component. A good theory of intentions should, however, be compatible with a plan-based architecture. This is because the main intuition behind adopting the intentional stance is that we must proceed without explicit knowledge of the details of the given system's design.

3.2 Intentions Formalized

Perhaps the most basic conception of intentions is to associate them with the preferences of an agent. It is helpful to think of an agent as somehow having "selected" some scenarios as those that he prefers (prefers to realize, as it were). In other words, of all the possible future courses of events, some courses of events are preferred by the agent. These are the ones that correspond to the agent's intentions.

For example, consider Figure 3.1. Assume that $\neg p$ and $\neg q$ hold everywhere other than as shown. Let the agent x (whose actions are written first in the figure) at moment t_0 prefer the scenarios S_1 and S_2. Then, by the informal definition given above, we have that x intends q (because it occurs eventually on both the preferred scenarios) and does not intend p (because it never occurs on S_1). At t_0, x can do either action a or action b, since both can potentially lead to one of the preferred scenarios being realized. Note, however, that if the other agent does action d, then no matter which action x chooses, he will not succeed with his intentions, because none of his preferred scenarios will be

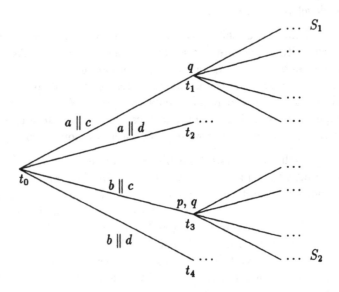

Figure 3.1: Intentions

realized. It is this observation that largely motivates the concept of know-how, which I discuss in Chapter 4.

A standard modal approach would do no more than assume the assignment of preferred scenarios to agents. However, in the approach taken here, I show how the selection of scenarios can itself be founded on the strategies that the agents have. Technically, this has the advantage of grounding claims about agents' intentions in the strategies they follow. It also has the intuitively appealing property that we can apply it to agents who may not be said to have a goal or preference. This is because, as discussed in section 2.5, even an agent who is given as not trying to achieve any goals is following some strategy and, therefore, can be said to have certain appropriate intentions.

Thus we arrive at the following general definition of intentions: *an agent intends all the necessary consequences of his performing his strategy.* Note that only the consequences of the *successful* performance of the strategy are included. There is no guarantee that a given strategy will in fact be successfully performed.

Despite its simplicity, this definition is quite powerful. It considers as intentions only the *necessary* consequences of the performing of the agent's strategy. This is important, because we do not wish to claim that an agent intends even the merely contingent consequences of his performing his strategy. For example, an agent with a strategy for loading paper in a photocopier will have to pick some ream of paper or the other. But he cannot be said to have had the intention of picking the specific one he in fact picks on a particular occasion. This is because he could just as well have picked another one and still satisfied his strategy. This point is related to the discussion in item I-DIM-3 in section 3.1.

3.2.1 Formal Language and Semantics

The formal language of this chapter, $\mathcal{L}^i$, is $\mathcal{L}$ augmented with four operators, $\langle\rangle_i$, $\langle\!\langle\rangle\!\rangle$, $*$, and I (which stands for Intends).

SYN-13. All the rules for $\mathcal{L}$, with $\mathcal{L}^i$ substituted for $\mathcal{L}$

SYN-14. All the rules for $\mathcal{L}_s$, with $\mathcal{L}^i_s$ substituted for $\mathcal{L}_s$

SYN-15. All the rules for $\mathcal{L}_y$, with $\mathcal{L}^i_y$ substituted for $\mathcal{L}_y$

SYN-16. $p \in \mathcal{L}^i_s$, $x \in \mathcal{A}$, and $Y \in \mathcal{L}^i_y$ implies that $x\langle Y\rangle_i p$ and $\langle\!\langle Y\rangle\!\rangle p \in \mathcal{L}^i_s$

SYN-17. $p \in \mathcal{L}^i_s$, $x \in \mathcal{A}$, and $Y \in \mathcal{L}^i_y$ implies that $x * Y \in \mathcal{L}^i$

SYN-18. $p \in \mathcal{L}^i_s$ and $x \in \mathcal{A}$ implies that $(x|p) \in \mathcal{L}^i$

It is convenient to define $x[Y]_i p$ as an abbreviation for $x\neg\langle Y\rangle_i\neg p$.

Before giving the formal semantics of the newly introduced operators, it is useful to extend the definition of $[\,]$ to apply to strategies. Recall that for a basic action, a, $[\![a]\!]^x$ denotes the set of periods over which a is performed by agent x. Essentially the same intuition is meant to be captured here for the case of strategies. That is, $[\![Y]\!]^x$ will denote the set of periods over which Y is successfully performed by agent x. Thus we have the following definitions. The agent is the same throughout and so is not mentioned.

AUX-5. $[\![\text{skip}]\!] = \{[S; t, t]|t \in \mathbf{T}\}$

The empty strategy is performed on all the trivial periods, i.e., those which consist of just one moment each.

AUX-6. $[S; t, t'] \in [\![do(q)]\!]$ iff $M \models_{t'} q$ and $(\forall t'' : t \leq t'' < t' \Rightarrow M \not\models_{t''} q)$

The strategy $do(q)$ is performed over all those periods that begin at any moment where q is achievable and that end at the first occurrence of q after their beginning. This is essentially the property of *action uniqueness*, which was defined as constraint COH-1 in section 2.3, extended to the case of strategies. This extension is only natural, since strategies are abstract actions. A related intuition is that a strategy calls upon an agent to perform some basic actions. There is no reason for the agent to perform a basic action after the relevant strategy has been performed. This is why it makes sense to allow $t = t'$ here, whereas for basic actions, we always have $t < t'$.

AUX-7. $[S; t, t'] \in [\![Y_1; Y_2]\!]$ iff $(\exists t'' : t \leq t'' \leq t'$ and $[S; t, t''] \in [\![Y_1]\!]$ and $[S; t'', t'] \in [\![Y_2]\!])$

In other words, $Y_1; Y_2$ is performed over those periods over which first Y_1 is performed and then, starting at the moment where it ends, Y_2 is performed. Observe that $[\![do(q); do(q)]\!] = [\![do(q)]\!]$. Intuitively, the second $do(q)$, which is performed in a state in which q holds, does not take any time at all. The first $do(q)$ may or may not take any time depending on the state where it is performed.

AUX-8. $[S; t, t'] \in [\![\text{if } q \text{ then } Y_1 \text{ else } Y_2]\!]$ iff $(M \models_t q$ and $[S; t, t'] \in [\![Y_1]\!])$ or $(M \not\models_t q$ and $[S; t, t'] \in [\![Y_2]\!])$

That is, a conditional strategy is performed by performing the substrategy corresponding to the appropriate branch.

AUX-9. $[S; t, t'] \in [\![\text{while } q \text{ do } Y_1]\!]$ iff $(t = t'$ and $M \not\models_t q)$ or $(\exists t_0, \ldots, t_n :$ $t = t_0$ and $t' = t_n$ and $(\forall l : 0 \leq l \leq n - 1 \Rightarrow ([S; t_l, t_{l+1}] \in [\![Y_1]\!]$ and $M \models_{t_l} q))$ and $M \not\models_{t_n} q)$

That is, an iterative strategy is performed by performing a finite number of iterations of its substrategy. The substrategy is repeated zero or more times until the *first* moment at which the relevant condition does not hold. A consequence of this definition is that $[\![\text{while true do } Y_1]\!]$ is an empty set. And, if $M \models_t q$, then $[\![\text{while } q \text{ do skip}]\!]$ is also empty.

Note that the above definitions differ from the corresponding definition for basic actions in at least the following respect: whereas actions always take time, strategies may be trivially performed at a given moment. With these definitions in hand, I can now give the semantics of the operators introduced in this chapter.

SEM-17. $M \models_{S,t} x\langle Y\rangle_i p$ iff $(\exists t' : [S; t, t'] \in [Y]^x$ and $M \models_{S,t'} p)$

SEM-18. $M \models_t x * Y$ iff $\mathbf{Y}(x, t) = Y$

SEM-19. $M \models_t x\langle\!\langle Y\rangle\!\rangle p$ iff $M \models_t \mathsf{A}(x\langle Y\rangle_i \mathsf{true} \rightarrow \mathsf{F}p)$

SEM-20. $M \models_t x|p$ iff $(\exists Y : M \models_t x * Y$ and $M \models_t x\langle\!\langle Y\rangle\!\rangle p)$

Thus the core semantic definition is that of $x\langle Y\rangle_i p$. Under the above set of definitions, an agent's intentions are determined not only on the basis of the strategy he is currently following, but also on the basis of the actions he can perform on different scenarios. I now state and prove some useful results about auxiliary definition $[\,]$ as applied to strategies, following which I shall consider an axiomatization for intentions.

Lemma 3.1 states that a strategy of the form $\mathsf{do}(q)$ can be begun from any moment before its termination at which it is executing. This corresponds to the similar property of basic actions, which was assumed as coherence constraint COH-3 in Chapter 2.

Lemma 3.1 $[S; t, t'] \in [\mathsf{do}(q)]$ iff $(\forall t_0 : t \le t_0 \le t' \Rightarrow [S; t_0, t'] \in [\mathsf{do}(q)])$

Proof. The right to left direction of the lemma follows by instantiating t_0 as t. For the left to right direction, consider the following. We have that $[S; t, t'] \in [\mathsf{do}(q)]$ iff $M \models_{t'} q$ and $(\forall t'' : t \le t'' < t' \Rightarrow M \not\models_{t''} q)$. But, since, $t \le t_0 \Rightarrow (t_0 \le t'' \Rightarrow t \le t'')$, the preceding expression implies that $M \models_{t'} q$ and $(\forall t'' : t_0 \le t'' < t' \Rightarrow M \not\models_{t''} q)$. This holds iff $[S; t_0, t'] \in [\mathsf{do}(q)]$. $\square$

Lemma 3.2 states that, before its termination, an iterative strategy can be begun from any of the intermediate moments at which its substrategy has been executed an integral number of times.

Lemma 3.2 $[S; t, t'] \in [\mathsf{while}\ q\ \mathsf{do}\ Y_1]$ iff $(t = t'$ and $M \not\models_t q)$ or $(\exists t_0, \ldots, t_n : t = t_0$ and $t' = t_n$ and $(\forall l : 0 \le l \le n-1 \Rightarrow ([S; t_l, t_{l+1}] \in [Y_1]$ and $M \models_{t_l} q$ and $[S; t_l, t'] \in [\mathsf{while}\ q\ \mathsf{do}\ Y_1]))$ and $M \not\models_{t_n} q)$

Proof. For brevity, let $Y = \mathsf{while}\ q\ \mathsf{do}\ Y_1$. The right hand side of the above expression is stronger than definition AUX-9 (of when $[S; t, t'] \in [Y]$). Hence, the right to left direction follows trivially. Now assume $[S; t, t'] \in [Y]$. Let t_k be any of the intermediate moments, t_0 through t_n. We have $[S; t_n, t_n] \in [Y]$, since $M \not\models_{t_n} q$ holds by the definition. Also, $[S; t_0, t_n] \in [Y]$, by assumption. Consider $0 < k < n$. Then, by definition AUX-9 applied for $[S; t_0, t_n]$, $(\exists t_k, \ldots, t_n : t_k = t_k$ and $t_n = t_n$ and $(\forall l : k \le l \le n-1 \Rightarrow ([S; t_l, t_{l+1}] \in [Y_1]$ and $M \models_{t_l} q))$ and $M \not\models_{t_n} q)$. Thus, $[S; t_k, t_n] \in [Y]$. This proves the left to right direction of the lemma. $\square$

Lemma 3.3 $M \models_t \langle Y_1; Y_2 \rangle_i p \equiv (\langle Y_1 \rangle_i \langle Y_2 \rangle_i p)$

Proof. By semantic definition SEM-17, $M \models_t \langle Y_1; Y_2 \rangle_i p$ iff ($\exists t'$: $[S; t, t'] \in [Y_1; Y_2]$ and $M \models_{S,t'} p$), which by definition AUX-7 holds iff ($\exists t'$: ($\exists t'' : [S; t, t''] \in [Y_1]$ and $[S; t'', t'] \in [Y_2]$) and $M \models_{S,t'} p$). But this reduces to ($\exists t'' : [S; t, t''] \in [Y_1]$ and $M \models_{S,t''} \langle Y_2 \rangle_i p$). Hence, the desired result. $\square$

Lemma 3.4 $[S; t, t'] \in [Y]^x$ iff ($\exists t_1 : [S; t, t_1] \in [\downarrow_t Y]^x$ and $[S; t_1, t'] \in [\uparrow_t Y]^x$)

Proof. The proof proceeds by induction on the structure of strategies. Recall the definitions of $\downarrow$ and $\uparrow$ given in Tables 2.1 and 2.2. The claim holds trivially for strategies of the forms **skip** and **do**(q), since in each case $\uparrow_t Y =$ **skip**. These are the two base cases.

Let $Y = Y_1; Y_2$. By definition AUX-7, $[S; t, t'] \in [Y_1; Y_2]$ iff ($\exists t'' : t \leq t'' \leq t'$ and $[S; t, t''] \in [Y_1]$ and $[S; t'', t'] \in [Y_2]$). Assume, by the inductive hypothesis, that the given claim holds for Y_1 and Y_2. First, consider the case of $\downarrow_t Y_1 \neq$ **skip**. Then, $[S; t, t''] \in [Y_1]$ iff ($\exists t_1 : [S; t, t_1] \in [\downarrow_t Y_1]^x$ and $[S; t_1, t''] \in [\uparrow_t Y_1]^x$). Also by definition AUX-7, $[S; t_1, t''] \in [\uparrow_t Y_1]^x$ and $[S; t'', t'] \in [Y_2]$ iff $[S; t_1, t'] \in [(\uparrow_t Y_1); Y_2]$. Thus, $\downarrow_t Y_1 \neq$ **skip** implies that $[S; t, t'] \in [Y]$, which is equivalent to ($\exists t_1 : [S; t, t_1] \in [\downarrow_t Y]$ and $[S; t_1, t'] \in [\uparrow_t Y]$) . If $\downarrow_t Y_1 =$ **skip**, then the claim trivially follows from the inductive hypothesis for Y_2. Thus the given claim holds for strategies of the form $Y_1; Y_2$.

Let $Y =$ **if** q **then** Y_1 **else** Y_2. Let $M \models_t q$. Then, $\downarrow_t Y = \downarrow_t Y_1$ and $\uparrow_t Y = \uparrow_t Y_1$. Since Y_1 is structurally smaller than Y, the desired result holds by the inductive hypothesis. A similar argument applies if $M \not\models_t q$.

Let $Y =$ **while** q **do** Y_1. The case where $M \not\models_t q$ is trivial, since in that case, $t = t'$ and $\downarrow_t Y = \uparrow_t Y =$ **skip**. The case where $M \models_t q$ and $\downarrow_t Y_1 =$ **skip** is also trivial, since then $[Y] = \emptyset$. Now let $M \models_t q$ and $\downarrow_t Y_1 \neq$ **skip**. Then, $\downarrow_t Y = \downarrow_t Y_1$ and $\uparrow_t Y = \uparrow_t Y_1$. Let t_1 be the same as t_1 in the definition of $[ ]$ for **while**. Then, $[S; t, t_1] \in [Y_1]$. Since Y_1 is structurally smaller than Y, by the inductive hypothesis, we have that ($\exists t'' : [S; t, t''] \in [\downarrow_t Y_1]$ and $[S; t'', t_1] \in [\uparrow_t Y_1]$). By Lemma 3.2 and the choice of t_1, we also have that $[S; t_1, t'] \in [Y]$. Using Lemma 3.3, we obtain that $[S; t'', t'] \in [(\uparrow_t Y_1); Y]$. Thus, ($\exists t'' : [S; t, t''] \in [\downarrow_t Y]^x$ and $[S; t'', t'] \in [\uparrow_t Y]^x$), which by appropriate relabeling is the present lemma. $\square$

Lemma 3.5 At all moments, t, $M \models_t x \langle Y \rangle_i p \equiv (x \langle \downarrow_t Y \rangle_i x \langle \uparrow_t Y \rangle_i p)$

Proof. The semantic definition of $x \langle Y \rangle_i p$ involves the definition of $[ ]^x$. The proof is a trivial consequence of Lemma 3.4. $\square$

3.2.2 Axioms for Intentions

I now present a sound and complete axiomatization of $\langle Y \rangle_i p$. The agent is not relevant in the following discussion and, therefore, is not mentioned.

Axiom Ax-INT-6 below is a way of relativizing this axiomatization to that of the underlying logic, which includes the boolean operators, i.e., $\wedge$ and $\neg$, the belief or knowledge operator B (or K_t), the temporal operators, i.e., [], $\langle \rangle$, U, and A, and existential quantification over actions. There are two reasons for relativizing this axiomatization to that of the underlying logic. The first is that we would like to focus attention on the novel contributions here. The other, more subtle, reason is that sometimes no axiomatization may be known for the underlying logic. For example, the logic CTL*, which is decidable, has no known axiomatization [Emerson, 1992]. Axiom Ax-INT-6 can thus be thought of as implicitly invoking an oracle for the underlying logic. This idea is used Chapter 4 also.

Ax-INT-1. $\langle \mathbf{skip} \rangle_i p \equiv p$

Ax-INT-2. $\langle Y_1; Y_2 \rangle_i p \equiv \langle Y_1 \rangle_i \langle Y_2 \rangle_i p$

Ax-INT-3. $\langle \mathbf{if} \ q \ \mathbf{then} \ Y_1 \ \mathbf{else} \ Y_2 \rangle_i p \equiv (q \rightarrow \langle Y_1 \rangle_i p) \wedge (\neg q \rightarrow \langle Y_2 \rangle_i p)$

Ax-INT-4. $\langle \mathbf{while} \ q \ \mathbf{do} \ Y_1 \rangle_i p \equiv (q \rightarrow \langle Y_1 \rangle_i \langle \mathbf{while} \ q \ \mathbf{do} \ Y_1 \rangle_i p) \wedge (\neg q \rightarrow p)$

Ax-INT-5. $\langle \mathbf{do}(q) \rangle_i p \equiv (q \wedge p) \vee (\neg q \wedge (\bigvee a : \langle a \rangle \langle \mathbf{do}(q) \rangle_i p))$

Ax-INT-6. All substitution instances of the validities of the underlying logic

Theorem 3.6 Axioms Ax-INT-1 through Ax-INT-6 constitute a sound and complete axiomatization of $\langle Y \rangle_i p$ for any model M as described in section 2.1.2.

Proof.

Soundness and Completeness: The proofs of soundness and completeness are developed hand-in-hand. Only formulae of the form $\langle Y \rangle_i p$ are considered here. Construct a model whose indices are maximally consistent sets of sentences of $\mathcal{L}^i$ and $\mathcal{L}^i_i$. The other components of the model, especially, $<$, **B**, **R**, and [] are constrained by the formulae that are true at the different moments and at different scenario and moment pairs. Completeness means that $M \models_{S,t} \langle Y \rangle_i p$ entails $\langle Y \rangle_i p \in (S,t)$ and soundness means that $\langle Y \rangle_i p \in (S,t)$ entails $M \models_{S,t} \langle Y \rangle_i p$.

The proof is by induction on the structure of strategies. It follows as a consequence of the lemmas proved earlier in this chapter. It uses the definition of $[\,]^x$ extensively, which is the key primitive in the semantic definition of $\langle Y \rangle_i p$. It also uses the fact that $M \models_{S,t} q$ iff $M \models_t q$, which is a consequence of semantic definition SEM-15 of section 2.1.3, which applies since $q \in \mathcal{L}^i$.

For axiom AX-INT-1, $M \models_{S,t} \langle \mathbf{skip} \rangle_i p$ iff $(\exists t' : [S; t, t'] \in [\mathbf{skip}]$ and $M \models_{S,t'} p)$. But, $[S; t, t'] \in [\mathbf{skip}]$ iff $t = t'$. Therefore, $M \models_{S,t} \langle \mathbf{skip} \rangle_i p$ iff $M \models_{S,t} p$. This accounts for axiom AX-INT-1.

By the definition of $[\,]$, $(\exists t' : [S; t, t'] \in [Y_1; Y_2]$ and $M \models_{S,t'} p)$ iff $(\exists t' : (\exists t'' : [S; t, t''] \in [Y_1]$ and $[S; t'', t'] \in [Y_2])$ and $M \models_{S,t'} p)$. Therefore, $M \models_{S,t} \langle Y_1; Y_2 \rangle_i p$ iff $(\exists t'' : [S; t, t''] \in [Y_1]$ and $(\exists t' : [S; t'', t'] \in [Y_2])$ and $M \models_{S,t'} p)$. By induction on the structure of strategies, this is identical to $(\exists t'' : [S; t, t''] \in [Y_1]$ and $M \models_{S,t'} \langle Y_2 \rangle_i p)$. By the same induction, this holds iff $M \models_{S,t} \langle Y_1 \rangle_i \langle Y_2 \rangle_i p$. This takes care of axiom AX-INT-2.

Similarly, $[S; t, t'] \in [\mathbf{if}\ q\ \mathbf{then}\ Y_1\ \mathbf{else}\ Y_2]$ iff $(M \models_t q$ and $[S; t, t'] \in [Y_1])$ or $(M \not\models_t q$ and $[S; t, t'] \in [Y_2])$. Therefore, $M \models_{S,t} \langle \mathbf{if}\ q\ \mathbf{then}\ Y_1\ \mathbf{else}\ Y_2 \rangle_i p$ iff $(\exists t' : (M \models_t q$ and $[S; t, t'] \in [Y_1])$ or $(M \not\models_t q$ and $[S; t, t'] \in [Y_2])$ and $M \models_{S,t'} p)$. Which is identical to $(M \models_t q$ and $(\exists t' : [S; t, t'] \in [Y_1]))$ or $(M \not\models_t q$ and $(\exists t' : [S; t, t'] \in [Y_2]))$. Thus by induction, the previous expression reduces to $M \models_{S,t} q \wedge \langle Y_1 \rangle_i p$ or $M \models_{S,t} \neg q \wedge \langle Y_2 \rangle_i p$. But this condition is equivalent to $M \models_{S,t} (q \rightarrow \langle Y_1 \rangle_i p) \wedge (\neg q \rightarrow \langle Y_2 \rangle_i p)$. This takes care of axiom AX-INT-3.

By Lemma 3.5, $M \models_{S,t} \langle \mathbf{while}\ q\ \mathbf{do}\ Y_1 \rangle_i p$ iff $M \models_{S,t} \langle \downarrow_t (\mathbf{while}\ q\ \mathbf{do}\ Y_1) \rangle_i \langle \uparrow_t (\mathbf{while}\ q\ \mathbf{do}\ Y_1) \rangle_i p$. If $M \models_t q$ and $\downarrow_t Y_1 \neq \mathbf{skip}$, then this reduces to $M \models_{S,t} \langle \downarrow_t Y_1 \rangle_i \langle (\uparrow_t Y_1); (\mathbf{while}\ q\ \mathbf{do}\ Y_1) \rangle_i p$. By Lemma 3.3, we obtain $M \models_{S,t} \langle \downarrow_t Y_1 \rangle_i \langle \uparrow_t Y_1 \rangle_i \langle \mathbf{while}\ q\ \mathbf{do}\ Y_1 \rangle_i p$. By Lemma 3.5, this reduces to $M \models_{S,t} \langle Y_1 \rangle_i \langle \mathbf{while}\ q\ \mathbf{do}\ Y_1 \rangle_i p$. If $M \models_t q$ and $\downarrow_t Y_1 = \mathbf{skip}$, then $M \not\models_{S,t}$ $\langle \mathbf{while}\ q\ \mathbf{do}\ Y_1 \rangle_i p$, so this case is also taken care of. Lastly, if $M \not\models_t q$, then $\downarrow_t Y = \mathbf{skip} =\uparrow_t Y$. Hence, $M \models_{S,t} \langle \mathbf{while}\ q\ \mathbf{do}\ Y_1 \rangle_i p$ iff $M \models_{S,t} p$. Thus, in all cases, $M \models_{S,t} \langle \mathbf{while}\ q\ \mathbf{do}\ Y_1 \rangle_i p$ iff $M \models_{S,t} (q \rightarrow \langle Y_1 \rangle_i \langle \mathbf{while}\ q\ \mathbf{do}\ Y_1 \rangle_i p) \wedge (\neg q \rightarrow p)$, as desired.

Finally, $M \models_{S,t} \langle \mathbf{do}(q) \rangle_i p$ iff $(\exists t' : [S; t, t'] \in [\mathbf{do}(q)]$ and $M \models_{S,t'} p)$. If $M \models_t q$, then by definition AUX-6, $t = t'$ and $M \models_{S,t} p$. If $M \not\models_t q$, then by definition AUX-6, $t < t'$. By coherence constraint COH-4, $(\exists a, t_0 : t < t_0 \leq t'$ and $[S; t, t_0] \in [a]^x$ and $(\forall t_1 : [S; t, t_1] \in [a]^x \Rightarrow t_1 \leq t_0)$ (here x is the given agent, usually elided).

We choose the maximal t_0, so that by coherence constraint COH-5, only a finite number of applications of this axiom will suffice. Using coherence constraint COH-5, for each agent, we can associate with any period the number of actions that are taken by that agent over that period. This number can serve as a metric for mathematical induction, since it decreases over the subperiods of a period and equals zero for the trivial period.

By Lemma 3.1, $[S; t_0, t'] \in \llbracket \mathbf{do}(q) \rrbracket$), which entails that $M \models_{S, t_0}$ $\langle \mathbf{do}(q) \rangle_i p$. Hence, $M \models_{S, t} (\bigvee a : \langle a \rangle \langle \mathbf{do}(q) \rangle_i p)$. Therefore, $M \models_{S, t} \langle \mathbf{do}(q) \rangle_i p$ iff $M \models_{S, t} q \wedge p$ or $M \models_{S, t} \neg q \wedge (\bigvee a : \langle a \rangle \langle \mathbf{do}(q) \rangle_i p)$. $\square$

3.3 Properties of Intentions

Several interesting properties of intentions may be obtained from the definition given above, especially when certain intuitively nice constraints are imposed on the models. Different constraints may be chosen depending on the purpose one has and the precise concept one requires. Certain particularly important constraints are discussed in Chapter 5, where conditions leading to the success of an agent with his intentions are formalized.

I-Cons-1. **Satisfiability:**

$x|p \rightarrow \mathsf{EF}p$

This says that if p is intended by some agent, then it occurs eventually on some scenario. That is, the given intention is satisfiable on some future. This does not hold in general, since the strategies assigned to the agents may be unexecutable. If a strategy assigned to an agent is unexecutable, then $x|$ false holds. The simplest such strategy is $\mathbf{do}(\mathsf{false})$. The desired constraint may be expressed as below. It essentially corresponds to the requirement that one of the executions of one of the actions of the agent be on a scenario on which p occurs.

$x * Y \Rightarrow \mathsf{E}x \langle Y \rangle_i \mathsf{true}$

I-Cons-2. **Temporal Consistency:**

$(x|p \wedge x|q) \rightarrow x|(\mathsf{F}p \wedge \mathsf{F}q)$

This says that if an agent intends p and intends q, then he (implicitly) intends achieving them in some temporal order: p before q, q before p, or both simultaneously. This holds in general because the function Y assigns exactly one strategy to each agent at each moment. Thus if both p and q, which are scenario-formulae, occur on all scenarios on which that strategy is performed, then they occur in some temporal order on each of those scenarios. The formula $(\mathsf{F}p \wedge \mathsf{F}q)$ is true at a moment on a scenario precisely when p and q are true at (possibly distinct) future moments on the given scenario.

I-Cons-3. **Persistence does not entail success:**

$EG((x|p) \land \neg p)$ is satisfiable

This is quite obvious intuitively: just because an agent persists with an intention does not mean that he will succeed. Technically, two main ingredients are missing. The agent must know-how to achieve the intended condition and must act on his intentions. I include this here to point out that in the theory of Cohen & Levesque, persistence is sufficient for success [1990, p. 233]. This is a major weakness in any theory of intentions [Singh, 1992a]. Secondly, the need to state the conditions under which an agent can succeed with his intentions is one of the motivations for the concept of know-how, which is formalized in Chapter 4.

I-Cons-4. **Limiting choices:**

I discussed above the causal role that intentions are sometimes taken to have in getting an agent to act. A related idea is that intentions limit an agent's choices [Bratman, 1987, pp. 44–45]. Thus the following constraint, which I do not accept, may seem intuitively quite plausible. At any moment, the only actions that an agent may perform are those which can lead to the satisfaction of the current part of his strategy. There need be no guarantee, however, that any of those actions would ensure success.

$(\mathbf{Y}(x,t) = Y$ and $\downarrow_t Y = \mathbf{do}(q)) \Rightarrow (\forall S \in \mathbf{S}_t, t' \in S, a \in \mathcal{B} :$
$[S; t, t'] \in [a]^x \Rightarrow (\exists S'', t'' \in S'' : [S; t, t''] \in [a]^x$ and $M \models_{S'',t} Fq))$

This violates the weak determinism constraint, Coh-8, of section 2.3. Although it does not validate the statement that intentions entail ability, it validates something almost as unintuitive. Under some additional but fairly weak assumptions, it validates the claim that an agent who intends p is not able to achieve something incompatible with p. For example, assume that $AG(p \rightarrow AGp)$ holds in every moment in the model. Then the above constraint ensures that as long as $x * \mathbf{do}(p)$ holds, x is unable to achieve $AG\neg p$ at t. While it may be worth considering whether an agent with a certain intention will in fact achieve something else, it is surely too strong to require that he loses all ability to do so the moment he adopts that intention. In contrast to constraint I-Cons-1, this applies to all actions of the agent. The acceptable sense of what an agent will achieve in fact is captured by the notion of real scenarios in Chapter 5.

I-Cons-5. **Persist while succeeding:**

If $\downarrow_t Y \neq$ **skip**, then $M \models_t x * Y \rightarrow (A[\downarrow_t Y]_i(x* \uparrow_t Y)) \wedge A([\downarrow_t Y]_i$**true**$\rightarrow ((x * Y \vee x* \uparrow_t Y) U x* \uparrow_t Y))$

This constraint is a possible restriction on the architectures of agents. It requires that agents desist from revising their strategies as long as they are able to proceed properly. If $\downarrow_t Y =$ **skip**, then the strategy is over and this constraint does not apply. Many robots and planners are designed to satisfy this constraint: plans are revised only on failure. The present approach allows the agents to benefit from opportunities that might arise unexpectedly, albeit in a limited way. This is because agents' strategies are composed of abstract actions. As a result, if a condition comes to hold fortuitously, or if a simple course of action becomes feasible because of the actions of other agents, then the given agent can take advantage of these opportunities, without having to revise his strategy.

$(Y(x,t) = Y$ and $\downarrow_t Y \neq$ **skip** and $[S; t, t'] \in [\downarrow_t Y]^x) \Rightarrow Y(x, t') = \uparrow_t Y$ and $(\forall t'' : t \leq t'' < t' : Y(x, t'') = Y)$

I-Cons-6. **Absence of closure under beliefs:**

$x|p \wedge x\mathsf{BAG}(p \rightarrow q) \wedge \neg x|q$ is satisfiable

This holds only in general, since intentions are determined independently of the agents' beliefs. As remarked in item I-Dim-7 of section 3.1, closure under beliefs is sometimes called the *side-effect* problem [Rao & Georgeff, 1991a]. By the present result, the proposed theory avoids this problem.

I-Cons-7. **Consistency with beliefs about future possibility:**

$x|p \wedge x\mathsf{B}\neg\mathsf{EF}p$ is not satisfiable

This holds only in the presence of the following constraint, which can be readily imposed on the models.

$M \models_t x|p$ implies that $(\exists t' : (t, t') \in B(x)$ and $M \models_{t'} \mathsf{EF}p)$

I-Cons-8. **Non-entailment of beliefs about future possibility:**

$x|p \wedge \neg x\mathsf{BEF}p$ is satisfiable

This holds in general. Indeed, it holds on each moment at which the following constraint applies.

$M \models_t x|p$ implies that $(\exists t' : (t, t') \in B(x)$ and $M \models_{t'} \neg\mathsf{EF}p)$

Constraints I-Cons-7 and I-Cons-8 are not accurate formalizations of the properties of intentions discussed in items I-Dim-11 and I-Dim-12 of section 3.1. This is because the beliefs involved in those properties are not beliefs about all possible futures, as treated in constraints I-Cons-7 and I-Cons-8, but rather are beliefs about the real future. Therefore, a better formalization of these properties is in terms of the scenarios assigned by **R**, a component of the formal model introduced in section 2.1.2.

I-Cons-9. **Consistency with beliefs about reality:**

$\neg(x|p \land xB\neg RFp)$

This property holds in the presence of the following constraint. This constraint may be understood as requiring that an agent with an intention considers at least one alternative in which that intention is realized. One might think of this as the hopeful alternative, which makes it worthwhile for the agent to undertake his intention.

$M \models_t x|p$ implies that $(\exists t' : (t, t') \in \mathbf{B}(x)$ and $M \models_{t'} RFp)$

I-Cons-10. **Non-entailment of beliefs about reality:**

$x|p \land x\neg BRFp$ is satisfiable

This property holds at all those moments at which the following constraint is true. This constraint may be understood as meaning that the agent with an intention considers at least one alternative moment from which that intention is not realized. One might think of this as the cautious alternative, which the agent may believe may be realized unless he exercises his know-how and acts to achieve his intention. Know-how is discussed in Chapter 4 and related to intentions in Chapter 5.

$M \models_t x|p$ implies that $(\exists t' : (t, t') \in \mathbf{B}(x)$ and $M \models_{t'} \neg RFp)$

I-Cons-11. **Entailment of belief in possible success:**

$x|p \rightarrow xBEFp$

This is the opposite of the property mentioned in item I-Cons-8 above. However, the justification for it is perhaps apparent from the discussion above. Even though an agent may not believe that his intention will succeed, he should surely believe that it may succeed. The incompleteness òf one's beliefs about the future should not preclude that. For, an agent would have to be quite irrational if he did not even believe it possible that his intention would succeed but still continued to hold it. This property, which is also validated in the approach of [Singh & Asher, 1993], holds when the following constraint applies.

$$M \models_t x|p \text{ implies that } (\forall t' : (t, t') \in \mathbf{B}(x) \text{ and } M \models_{t'} \mathsf{EF}p)$$

Postulates I-CONS-9 and I-CONS-10 are jointly termed the *asymmetry thesis* by Bratman [1987, pp. 38]. He argues that they are among the more basic constraints on the intentions and beliefs of rational agents.

3.4 Desires

The concept of desires, which is quite closely related to that of intentions, has been studied extensively in the literature. Earlier works, e.g., [Davidson, 1980], attempted to reduce intentions to desires or to desires combined with beliefs. Such attempts are not considered viable any more [Brand, 1984; Bratman, 1987]. However, desires themselves are still often considered, especially in the computer science literature on the subject [Georgeff, 1987].

Desires are different from intentions in that they have a weaker connection with an agent's rationality. For example, the desires of an agent may be mutually inconsistent and may be inconsistent with that agent's beliefs. Also, an agent who desires something may not desire the necessary means for achieving it. These properties contrast with the relevant properties of intentions, as discussed in items I-DIM-4, I-DIM-5, and I-DIM-8 in section 3.1. The lack of these properties make desires *per se* difficult to relate with an agent's actions. Even the strongest desires of agents, which if unique would trivially be mutually consistent, lack the other two properties and are, therefore, of limited value in the specification of artificial multiagent systems.

We could require that an agent have certain desires in certain conditions, but then we could not use them to constrain his behavior significantly: if the agent's desires are mutually contradictory, or inconsistent with his beliefs, we can hardly state any rationality constraints according to which he might successfully act. The concept of desires could of course be used in general economics-style theories of rationality to relate an agent's desires with his intentions. No such theory is available at present. Thus, given the state of the art, the concept of desires is not of sufficient utility in the study of multiagent systems to merit treatment besides intentions. Therefore, I concentrate my attention on the more restrictive concept of intentions. Ultimately, formalizations such as the present one might shed some light on the form that a theory of desires ought to take for application in multiagent systems.

Sometimes, *goals* are identified with desires. When that is the case, they suffer from all the problems described above. When it is not the case, they are readily subsumed by strategies. This point is developed in greater detail in section 2.5.

3.5   Other Formal Theories of Intentions

In this section, I briefly review the computer science literature on intentions. The concept of goals, which is related to intentions, has been studied since the early days of AI [Georgeff, 1987]. However, much of this work has been architectural in nature. Here I consider only the formal theories of intentions. One of the earliest works on intentions is that of Allen who attempts to reduce intentions to beliefs about future actions [1984, pp. 145–146]. As discussed in item I-DIM-13 in section 3.1 above, this view turns out to be problematic. Allen's main focus in that paper is not on intentions, however, and his paper is better known for its other contributions.

Cohen & Levesque formalize intentions in a framework of discrete linear-time logic with precisely one event between any two successive instants [Cohen & Levesque, 1990]. Each linear fragment of time is isomorphic to the integers and is considered as a possible world. Primitive alternativeness relations are defined for beliefs and goals. A *persistent goal* of an agent is a proposition such that (a) the agent believes it to be false, (b) the agent has it as a goal, and (c) the agent will not give up that goal until he either comes to believe (i) that it is true, or (ii) that it will never become true. Intentions are then defined as special kinds of persistent goals: an agent intends p iff he has a persistent goal for the following condition: (a) he performs an event sequence, e, after which p holds, and (b) before performing e he believes there is an event sequence, e', that he will do immediately and at the end of which p will hold, and (c) he does not have a goal for the negation of the following: e happens followed by p (p. 248).

The nesting of the definitions makes Cohen & Levesque's theory the most complicated of the works on intentions. Their theory also suffers from several conceptual and technical shortcomings. Their definition confuses the semantics of intentions with constraints on intention revision. Thus the concept of intentions is tied to a particular policy of intention revision. A technical shortcoming is that certain properties are stated as "easy to see," but it is possible to construct counterexamples to these properties in the theory itself. I have developed these arguments in greater detail elsewhere [Singh, 1992a]. Cohen & Levesque's success theorem [1990, p. 233] is discussed in Chapter 5.

Seel has proposed a formalization of intentions systems theory [Seel, 1989]. Seel's theory includes a modal logic of beliefs and wants in a framework of discrete linear time. His aim is to capture the essential aspects of certain behavioral experiments. Seel's work shares some intuitions with the present approach. But there are some significant differences.

Seel assumes a set of *world axioms*. Agents are assumed to have perfect memory: they know all *strict-past* formulae, i.e., formulae not involving future time operators. The agents' knowledge at any time is given by the world axioms and the strict-past formulae that are true at that time (pp. 22–23). The agents' behavior is also determined by a set of axioms. These, along with world axioms, yield the agents' wants (pp. 25–26). A consequence of these definitions is that knowledge implies wants (p. 28), which means that wants are closed under knowledge (this inference was discussed in item I-Cons-6 above). Another, more troublesome, consequence is that a formula that is wanted in a given state must hold in that state (p. 28). Thus agents are guaranteed to succeed with their wants. This is at odds with our pretheoretic intuitions about wants or intentions. Seel's framework cannot accommodate changing wants, since that would require the axioms describing an agent's behavior to change, and they cannot. But Seel obtains useful results on how agents may acquire knowledge about their environment.

Rao & Georgeff have also recently proposed a theory of intentions [Rao & Georgeff, 1991b; Rao & Georgeff, 1991a]. While their main theory is based on branching-time logic, they seem to be neutral as to the distinction between branching-time and linear-time frameworks: they include formalizations and results for each kind. The best features of Rao & Georgeff's theory are the following: (a) it does not validate closure of intentions under beliefs and (b) it satisfies the asymmetry thesis. These issues were discussed items I-Cons-6, I-Cons-9, and I-Cons-10 in section 3.3 above.

Rao & Georgeff identify goals with desires and give a semantics to goals based on a primitive alternativeness relation. This is problematic. The given semantics ensures that the goals of each agent are mutually consistent. But, as discussed in section 3.4, the main property of desires is that they need not be mutually inconsistent, and indeed often are not. Desires need not even be believed to be consistent by the given agent. And, agents are not constrained by rationality to make their desires consistent. This is one of the major differences between desires and intentions. Thus goals, as formally defined, cannot be identified with desires. Therefore, the formalization of goals as a separate concept from intentions is not well-justified. Rao & Georgeff argue that this allows them to keep an agent's goals (i.e., ends) separate from his intentions (i.e., means) [Rao & Georgeff, 1991a, p. 6]. But this argument is not entirely satisfactory. A rational agent may need to perform means-ends reasoning to an arbitrary level of nesting. A theory should not require a separate concept for each such level of reasoning. Some related aspects of Rao & Georgeff's approach are discussed in Chapter 5.

Werner has also proposed a theory of intentions [Werner, 1991]. According to his definition, an agent, A, intends to X, if (a) A has a general plan to X, and (b) A's actions are guided by that plan (p. 119). A *general plan* is defined as a class of game-theoretic strategies (thus the term *strategy* is used differently than in the present approach). A strategy is a function from the agent's information state to an action. The agent may pick actions according to any of the applicable strategies in the given class. This makes it possible to partially specify actions. Note that this effect is attained more simply in the present approach by allowing abstract specifications, such as do(q). Also, the present approach makes the relevant conditions explicit in the conditional and iterative forms.

Although Werner's models involve time, his formal language does not. He gives no postulates relating intentions and beliefs, or intentions and time. A counterintuitive component of his definitions is that they do not distinguish between past, present, and future. Thus a strategy may be for a condition in the past. This makes it possible for agents to intend past conditions, which is problematic if intentions are meant to lead to action. More significant, perhaps, is the following problem. By the given definitions, agents cannot revise their strategies within the model. Entire histories are compared with strategies to test for compatibility. Thus if an agent is in the same information state at two points in a history, he must behave the same way at both, relative to whatever strategy he may have. Consequently, the important notions of persistence of intentions or how they are updated, which Werner also considers as important (p. 119), cannot be studied within his own framework.

Werner requires that if an agent intends something, then he must believe that he can achieve it. He also states that an intention presupposes the corresponding ability (pp. 110, 119). These requirements are unnecessarily strong. Agents often intend to achieve conditions of which they cannot guarantee the success. Indeed, they may not even believe that they will succeed with their intentions. This point was discussed in items I-Cons-8 and I-Cons-10 in section 3.3. Some other aspects of Werner's approach are discussed in Chapter 5.

The above approaches are all modal in nature and are based on possible worlds models. In joint work with Nicholas Asher, I have also developed a different logic of intentions [Singh & Asher, 1993]. That logic is based on Kamp's Discourse Representation Theory [Kamp, 1984] and seeks to be cognitively more accurate than any of the modal approaches. For example, it rightly invalidates the inference that an agent's intentions must be closed under logical equivalence. However, as discussed in item I-DIM-6 of section 3.1 above, doing so takes us away from the intentional stance and into the design stance. This makes it harder to apply that theory in the specification of multiagent systems. I return to this point in Chapter 7.

3.6 Philosophical Remarks

In the definitions given above, an agent's intentions are determined on the basis of his strategies and on how he may act on them in a formal model consisting of possible states of the world. Thus an agent's (possible) actions are significant to the process of assigning intentions to him. In this sense, the proposed approach is *pragmatist*, as that term is defined by Stalnaker [1984, pp. 15–19]. Pragmatism is the philosophy behind the logics that are based on "possible worlds" models. Such models arise in a number of formal theories besides the one proposed here, e.g., in the logic of knowledge of [Halpern & Moses, 1987] and in dynamic logic as surveyed in [Kozen & Tiurzyn, 1990].

The main technical consequence of considering possible states of the world is that agents' intentions are closed under logical equivalence. However, agents can have intentions they do not act on and, of course, those that they act on but fail with. While the agents' intentions are not associated with their actual actions, they are associated with their possible actions. Thus if an agent intends p, he automatically intends q, where q is logically equivalent to p. As discussed in item I-DIM-6 in section 3.1, while this is not always desirable, it is quite all right for many of our purposes.

Another point that is sometimes raised is about whether agents can really have intentions. An alternative view, seemingly quite plausible when one is talking of artificial entities, is that they do not have any intentions of their own, but merely reflect their designer's "intent." Leaving issues of philosophy aside, there are technical and pragmatic reasons for not taking such a view seriously in one's theorizing:

- Intelligent systems are conceivable that have no unique designer or, at least, whose intentions can be attributed to no unique designer. Examples of such systems include markets, which have evolved into complex entities and of which we can speak in intentional terms.

- The designer's intent would involve *types* of states (e.g., "in conditions of heavy local load, the agent should intend to obtain another agent's assistance"). However, the intentions of the agents, as we need that concept, involve *tokens* or specific conditions (e.g., "the agent intends now to request its nearest neighbor's help").

- The designer usually is not around to supervise the functioning of the given system. If a system can be considered autonomous, it can, and must, be ascribed intentions of its own. The states of the environment an agent faces can include those that were not anticipated by the designer. Additionally, if the designer's intent really mattered, no system would ever perform incorrectly. Therefore, we must evaluate agents by their possible actions and validate claims about their intentions accordingly.

3.7 Conclusions

Strategies allow us to succinctly describe the relevant aspects of the agents' design. These strategies yield the intentions of the agents in a simple and direct way. This is quite important. Usually, modal approaches to intentions simply postulate a primitive alternativeness relation that captures the relevant dispositions of the given agents. However, it is not clarified how such a relation may be implemented in the agent's design. When strategies are used as proposed here, this connection is at once rigorous and obvious. It also allows us to state natural model-theoretic constraints that capture important properties of the architectures of our agents.

The definition of intentions proposed here differs from most other approaches in at least one other respect: the proposed definition is separated in the logic from beliefs and knowledge. Clearly, an agent may adopt or update his intentions based on his knowledge. I do not prevent this. However, the concept of intentions is formalized so that the fact of whether or not an agent intends a particular proposition is largely independent of what he believes or knows (modulo the constraints introduced in section 3.3). A consequence of this separation is that certain counterintuitive inferences (pertaining to the entailment of beliefs or ability) that the other approaches validate are quite naturally prevented here.

The proposed approach also highlights the additional assumptions or constraints needed to ensure the success of an agent's intentions. To be assured success, an agent must have the relevant skills or basic actions as well as possess the knowledge needed to select his actions and to identify the conditions he intends to achieve. These are necessary, but not sufficient, conditions. The above prerequisites may be bound and studied together as one concept: know-how. This is the subject of the next chapter.

Chapter 4

Know-How

Given my goal of developing a framework for multiagent systems, it is only natural that I should attempt to formalize the concept of know-how. There are several reasons for this. In light of the formal framework developed in Chapter 2 and used to formalize intentions in Chapter 3, one might ask under what conditions an agent with limited control would be guaranteed to succeed. Such conditions are technically studied in Chapter 5, but suffice it to note here that know-how is an important component of those conditions. An agent cannot be guaranteed to succeed with his intentions if he lacks the know-how to achieve them.

Know-How can also be used in specifying complex systems succinctly for the purposes of designing them or analyzing their behavior. We can require that a given agent under certain conditions have certain know-how. For example, a robot that is designed for helping a handicapped person should, when called upstairs, know how to climb the stairs. This requirement might, for a particular design, reduce to the requirement that the robot's batteries be fully charged, that its load be light, and that it have sufficiently extendible legs. These requirements can be further analyzed in designing the robot, e.g., we might decide that the robot must recharge itself every hour and that it carry only small packages on its stair-climbing missions. But, once the know-how of the robot is established, it can also be used in different circumstances as well, e.g., when the robot has to go upstairs on its own initiative to deliver an unexpected express mail package.

Requirements of the kind described above arise naturally when one gives a formal semantics to the communications between the agents in a multiagent system. This proposal is elaborated in Chapter 6; an example of its use was given in section 1.1. Such a semantics for communications provides a mechanism by which constraints on the interactions among agents, e.g., that directives to come upstairs are satisfied, are reduced to constraints on the design of individual agents, e.g., that the robot assistant has the know-how and the intention to come upstairs.

I base the proposed theory of know-how on the framework of actions and time that was developed in Chapter 2. In section 4.1, I discuss know-how and present some intuitions about how we should proceed. In section 4.2, I define and axiomatize ability for the case of purely reactive agents; in section 4.3, I define and axiomatize it relative to strategies. In section 4.4, I state and prove some theorems about the logical properties of ability and its interactions with the modalities of time and action. In section 4.5, I define and axiomatize know-how for the case of purely reactive agents; in section 4.6, I define and axiomatize know-how relative to strategies. These definitions involve extensions to dynamic logic [Kozen & Tiurzyn, 1990].

4.1   Intuitive Considerations on Know-How

I shall take it as a starting point that intelligence is intimately tied to action. It is an agent's ability or potential to take effective action, and the skills he exhibits in doing things that make us attribute intelligence to him. For this reason, a useful conception of knowledge for our purposes is *know-how*, i.e., the knowledge of how to act, or the knowledge of skills. Thus a theory of know-how is needed that gives a definition with an appropriate formal semantics and logic. This would allow us to capture our intuitions about know-how straightforwardly and to use that concept directly whenever we need to.

Traditionally, however, preeminence is given to know-that, or the knowledge of facts. And know-how is reduced to know-that. While, no doubt, there are profound connections between know-how and know-that, know-how cannot be trivially reduced to know-that. Such a reduction buries intuitions about know-how and its logical properties within those of know-that. Also, this reduction, which was designed for classical planning agents, is inappropriate in general. Indeed, it is inappropriate even for planning agents who perform many of their actions reactively. This is an important class of agents in current theory and practice [Mitchell, 1990; Spector & Hendler, 1991]. I present a formal theory of know-how that applies to a wide-range of agents, and especially those who plan *and* react.

Newell defines knowledge as "[w]hatever can be ascribed to an agent, such that its behavior can be computed according to the principle of rationality" [Newell, 1982, p. 105]. He sees this definition as corresponding to the common scientific practice in AI (p. 125). I agree. However, I submit that unless know-how is also considered, ascriptions of beliefs or knowledge, and intentions must necessarily seem contrived. For example, we cannot conclude from an agent's not opening his umbrella that either he does not believe that it is raining or intends to get wet. It could just as well be that he does not know how to open his umbrella. The point of this example is simply that one cannot assume, as is traditionally done, that know-that is theoretically more fundamental than know-how, and that the latter should be reduced to it. An independent study of know-how would be beneficial in obtaining a better understanding important aspects of intelligence and rationality.

The philosopher Ryle was one of the early proponents of the distinction between know-how and know-that [Ryle, 1949]. His primary motivation, however, was to debunk "the dogma of the Ghost in the Machine," which is Descartes' doctrine of the separation and independence of minds from bodies (p. 15). Ryle's argument runs roughly as follows: intelligence is associated more with know-how than know-that; know-how involves bodies; therefore, intelligence (a quality of minds) is not independent of bodies. He rejects the view that a performance of an action is preceded or accompanied by explicit consideration of different rules (p. 29). He also rejects the claim that every component of an intelligent action must be planned (p. 31). Thus the now popular view that intelligent agents must have reactive components is in agreement with, and indeed was anticipated by, Ryle [Mitchell, 1990; Spector & Hendler, 1991].

I shall show that the intuitions motivated above are naturally captured in the proposed framework, and it is good to have some philosophical support for them. However, Ryle provides no insights into how know-how may be formalized and what technical properties it must have.

4.1.1 Traditional Theories of Action

Moore's work is among the most well-known theories of knowledge and action [1984]. Moore's focus is not on know-how and, when he discusses it, it is as the know-how to execute a given action description. But he also considers the know-how of achieving a certain condition relative to an action description (p. 347). An agent knows how to achieve p by doing an action (description), P, iff the agent knows that P achieves p, and that he can execute P. He can execute P iff he can identify each of the actions in P, i.e., if he knows what their rigid designators are. Thus, according to this definition, the agent knows how to achieve p only if he knows that for some plan P, that it will yield p, and that he will be able to execute it.

Moore's work has been extended by Morgenstern to allow an agent's plan to include actions such as asking others for information [Morgenstern, 1987]. However, Morgenstern does not define know-how either, just *know-how-to-perform*, which corresponds to *can execute* in Moore's theory. Roughly, an agent knows-how-to-perform a plan iff he knows all the required rigid designators occurring in that plan. Morgenstern's main aim, like Moore's, is to give the know-that requirements for the execution of plans; she does not address know-how *per se*.

The approaches described above incorporate useful intuitions about the relationship between know-how and know-that. They provide an analysis of the knowledge requirements of plans. Unfortunately, however, they also embody some restrictive assumptions about actions. I hope to relax some of the assumptions of these approaches, while retaining their useful components.

Many of these assumptions were considered in Chapter 2. In particular, I have generalized the underlying model of actions by allowing concurrent and asynchronous ones. I have also explicitly considered time and related it to actions. Furthermore, I admit a reactive layer of the architecture. Strategies, which were defined in section 2.5, correspond to plans in traditional theories. They do not directly involve basic actions, but instead are macros over them.

4.1.2 The Proposed Definition

I now motivate a definition of know-how that, I submit, captures the important aspects of our pretheoretic intuitions about it. As argued in section 4.1, even if the traditional theories could not be improved upon, it would be useful to have an independent treatment of know-how. But, relaxing some of the traditional assumptions provides us with a nice opportunity to consider the definition anyway.

The notion of know-how has to do with the ability to perform actions in a changing world. The agent is *competing* with the world, as it were. However, unlike in board games, the simplistic notion of turn-taking does not apply here. Of course, the world includes other agents. Thus, while the environment need not be opposed to the agent, it may be so. The environment and the agent must act concurrently: although the agent may wait for some time, the environment will not wait for him. As explained in Chapter 2, the outcome of an agent's actions depends on other events that take place in the world. These events may include the actions of other agents. For example, if I slide a mug over a table, it will simply move to its new location, unless someone sticks a hand in the way, in which case its contents may spill. By performing his actions, an agent exercises limited control over what transpires in the world. An agent must have some control over the world to ever know how to do anything; however, in general he cannot have perfect control over it. This is because events can always occur that potentially influence the outcome of any of the agent's actions.

The proposed definition of know-how is as follows. An agent, x, knows how to achieve p, if he is able to bring about the conditions for p through his actions. The world may change rapidly and unpredictably, but x is able to *force* it into an appropriate state. He has only limited knowledge of his rapidly changing environment and too little time to decide on an optimal course of actions. He can succeed only if he has the required physical resources and is able to choose them correctly.

This definition can be formalized both in terms of basic actions and strategies. Therefore, it contrasts both with situated theories of know-that [Rosenschein, 1985], and informal, and exclusively reactive, theories of action [Agre & Chapman, 1987]. Strategies were defined in section 2.5 as abstract descriptions of an agent's behavior. In section 4.3, I give a strategic definition of ability and in section 4.6, a strategic definition of know-how.

I first formalize the concept of ability, which depends solely on the actions that an agent can do and the effects of those actions, and ignores the agent's knowledge. This concept is simpler than know-how; it is a useful first step to formalize it and examine its properties. It is also useful in its own right.

4.2 Reactive Ability

As will soon become clear, it is useful to define ability relative to a *tree* of actions. A tree of actions consists of an action, called its *radix*, and a set of subtrees. The idea is that the agent does the radix action initially and, then, picks out one of the available subtrees to pursue further. In other words, a tree of actions for an agent is a projection to the agent's actions of a fragment of **T**. Such a fragment is diagramed in Figure 2.1. Thus a tree includes *some* of the possible actions of the given agent. For technical simplicity, I shall assume that when a tree is defined at a given moment, it is derived from a fragment of the model rooted at that moment. Thus it would automatically be executable along some scenarios at that moment.

An agent is able to achieve p relative to a tree of actions, iff on *all* scenarios where he performs the radix of the tree, either p occurs or the agent can choose one of the subtrees of the tree to pursue, and thereby achieve p. The definition does not require p to occur on all scenarios where the radix is done, only on the scenarios corresponding to the selected subtree. The agent gets to choose one subtree after the radix has been done. This is to allow the choice to depend on how the agent's environment has evolved. However, modulo this choice, the agent must achieve p by forcing it to occur. For example, a sailor's tree might call on him to head straight for the equator and then, depending on the wind, to adjust his sails accordingly. He would be able to arrive at his destination if, on his arrival at the equator, there is a setting for his sails with which he can succeed.

It is important to note that the tree need not be explicitly symbolically represented by the agent. The tree simply encodes the selection function the agent uses in picking out his actions at each stage. When a tree is finite in depth, it puts a bound on the number of actions that an agent may have to perform to achieve something. Since, intuitively, for an agent to be able to achieve some proposition, we expect him to be able to achieve the required proposition in finite time, this restriction is imposed here.

Since trees encode the choices that an agent may make while perform actions, there is no loss of generality in requiring that the different nonempty subtrees of a tree have different radices, i.e., begin with different actions. Given a tree in which this is not the case, we can easily transform it into one in which this restriction is satisfied. Let $\tau' = \langle a; \tau_1', \ldots, \tau_m' \rangle$ and $\tau'' = \langle a; \tau_1'', \ldots, \tau_n'' \rangle$. Then define a new tree, $\tau = \langle a; \tau_1, \ldots, \tau_k \rangle$, where $\{\tau_1, \ldots, \tau_k\} = \{\tau_1', \ldots, \tau_m'\} \cup \{\tau_1'', \ldots, \tau_n''\}$. Thus one can replace τ' and τ'' by τ in the original tree. τ encodes precisely the same choices as τ' and τ'' do together. This procedure can be generalized to any set of subtrees with a given radix. Intuitively, this results in a better tree than before. This is because the choices of the agent are required to be made one action at a time. The agent is not called upon to look ahead and predict the state in which his current action might lead him.

Let Υ be the set of trees. $\emptyset$ is the empty tree. Then Υ is defined as follows.

TREE-1. $\emptyset \in \Upsilon$

TREE-2. $a \in \mathcal{B}$ implies that $a \in \Upsilon$

TREE-3. $\tau_1, \ldots, \tau_m \in \Upsilon$, $\tau_1, \ldots, \tau_m$ have different radices, and $a \in \mathcal{B}$ implies that $\langle a; \tau_1, \ldots, \tau_m \rangle \in \Upsilon$

In the sequel, I shall always assume that τ is of one of the forms above.

The formal language of this chapter, $\mathcal{L}^h$, is an extension of $\mathcal{L}$. At this point, we require $\mathcal{L}^h$ to have the following operators. The operator $\{\ \}$ denotes ability relative to trees and the operator $(\!|\,\,|\!)$ ability relative to strategies (see section 4.3). The operators K_{rab} and K_{sab} are, respectively, the reactive and strategic versions of ability. $\mathcal{L}_s^h$ is used later in this chapter.

SYN-19. All the rules for $\mathcal{L}$, with $\mathcal{L}^h$ substituted for $\mathcal{L}$

SYN-20. All the rules for $\mathcal{L}_s$, with $\mathcal{L}_s^h$ substituted for $\mathcal{L}_s$

SYN-21. All the rules for $\mathcal{L}_y$, with $\mathcal{L}_y^h$ substituted for $\mathcal{L}_y$

SYN-22. $p \in \mathcal{L}_s^h$ and $x \in \mathcal{A}$ implies that $(xK_{rab}p), (xK_{sab}p) \in \mathcal{L}^h$

SYN-23. $p \in \mathcal{L}_s^h, Y \in \mathcal{L}_y^h$, and $x \in \mathcal{A}$ implies that $(x(\!|Y|\!)p) \in \mathcal{L}^h$

SYN-24. $\tau \in \Upsilon$, $x \in \mathcal{A}$, and $p \in \mathcal{L}^h$ implies that $x(\tau)p \in \mathcal{L}^h$

Other extensions will be described as needed.

Now $\mathcal{L}^h$ is powerful enough to express the definition of ability via the auxiliary operator, $(\ )$. Intuitively, $x(\tau)p$ is true iff the agent, x, can use τ as a selection function and, thereby, force p to become true. For the empty tree, p must already be true. For a nonempty tree, assuming p is not already true, the agent first does the radix of the tree. Depending on the other events that take place then, this action progresses along some scenario. If that is the only action of the tree, p may occur at any moment while it is being done. Otherwise, one of the subtrees is chosen in the state where the initial action ends. From there, the process iterates.

SEM-21. $M \models_t x(\emptyset)p$ iff $M \models_t p$

SEM-22. $M \models_t x(a)p$ iff $M \models_t (Ex(a)\text{true} \wedge Ax[a]p)$

SEM-23. $M \models_t x(\langle a; \tau_1, \ldots, \tau_m \rangle)p$ iff $(\exists S, t' : [S; t, t'] \in [\![a]\!]^x)$ and $(\forall S, t' : [S; t, t'] \in [\![a]\!]^x \Rightarrow (\exists \tau \in \{\tau_1, \ldots, \tau_m\} : M \models_{t'} x(\tau)p))$

Figure 4.1 shows how the above definition applies in our formal model. Assume that $\neg p$ and $\neg q$ hold everywhere other than as shown. Let us consider the agent whose actions are written first in the figure and see whether he has the ability to achieve p. Since $\neg p$ holds at t_0, the agent will have to do some actions to achieve p. Clearly, action b would not do him much good, since p never occurs on any scenario on which b is performed. If the agent does action a and the other agent does action d, then the state of the world is t_2, where p holds. Therefore, the agent is trivially able to achieve p at t_2. Thus at that moment, the agent would be done. However, action a could just as well lead

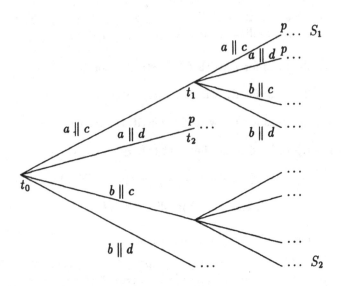

Figure 4.1: Ability

to moment t_1 (if the other agent does action b), where p does not hold. But fortunately, at t_1, if the agent does action a again, p is guaranteed. In other words, at t_1, the agent is able to achieve p. Thus the agent is able to achieve p even at t_0, since action a always leads to a state where he is able to achieve p. Thus the appropriate tree for this agent is $\langle a; a, \emptyset \rangle$.

Now reactive ability may be defined as follows:

SEM-24. $M \models_t x\mathsf{K}_{rab}p$ iff $(\exists \tau : M \models_t x\langle \tau \rangle p)$

$x\mathsf{K}_{rab}p$ means that agent x can force p to occur by performing actions in whose resultant states he can perform further actions, and so on, until p occurs. $\mathsf{K}_{rab}p$ is vacuously true if p holds in the given state. For example, if p stands for "open(door)," then $\mathsf{K}_{rab}p$ holds if the door is already open. $\mathsf{K}_{rab}p$ also holds if p is inevitable, i.e., if p will eventually occur no matter what happens. For example, let p be "returns(Halley's comet)." Assuming it is inevitable that Halley's comet will return, $\mathsf{K}_{rab}p$ holds. I shall return to this point in section 4.4.

The above is a definition of raw ability. It attributes ability to an agent, even if he may not be able to make the right choices, just as long as he has the right set of basic actions available. The choices that an agent makes depend on his beliefs. Indeed, incorporating beliefs into the picture, as I attempt in section 4.5, yields a general theory of know-how itself.

Now I present an axiomatization for the definition of K_{rab} given above and a proof of its soundness and completeness. As for the case of intentions, discussed in section 3.2.2, axiom AX-AB-REACT-3 below is a way of relativizing this axiomatization to that of the underlying logic. Note that $E\langle a \rangle$true means that a is a basic action of the agent at the given moment and is performed by him on at least one scenario.

AX-AB-REACT-1. $p \rightarrow xK_{rab}p$

AX-AB-REACT-2. $(\bigvee a : E\langle a \rangle\text{true} \wedge A[a](xK_{rab}p)) \rightarrow xK_{rab}p$

AX-AB-REACT-3. All substitution instances of the validities of the underlying logic

Theorem 4.1 Axioms AX-AB-REACT-1 through AX-AB-REACT-3 yield a sound and complete axiomatization for K_{rab}.

Proof.

Construct a branching-time model, M. The moments of M are notated as t and are maximally consistent sets of formulae that contain all the substitution instances of the validities of the underlying logic. The other components of the model, especially, $<$, $\mathbf{B}$, $\mathbf{R}$, and $[\,]$ are constrained by the formulae that are true at the different moments. Furthermore, these sets are closed under the above two axioms for K_{rab}. We can ignore the agent symbol in the following discussion.

Soundness: For axiom AX-AB-REACT-1 above, soundness is trivial from the definition of $(\emptyset)p$. For axiom AX-AB-REACT-2, let $(\bigvee a : E\langle a \rangle\text{true} \wedge A[a]K_{rab}p)$ hold at t. Then $(\exists S, t' : [S; t, t'] \in [a])$ and $(\forall S : (\forall t' \in S : [S; t, t'] \in [a] \Rightarrow (\exists t'' : t < t'' \leq t' \text{ and } M \models_{t''} K_{rab}p)))$. At each t'' in the preceding expression, $(\exists \tau' : M \models_{t''} (\tau')p)$. Soundness may be shown by exhibiting a tree, τ, such that at moment t, $(\tau)p$ holds. Clearly, action a must be the radix of τ. To construct it, note that if $t'' = t'$, τ' must be a subtree of τ. And, if $t'' < t'$, then action a is being performed at moment t''. Thus the radix of τ' is a. But, in the definition of $(\tau)p$, we need to look at the subtrees of τ only at the moments where its radix, i.e., a, has ended. With this motivation, define $T_1 = \{\tau' | \tau' \text{ is the tree used to make } K_{ab}p \text{ true at } t'\}$. Define $T_2 = \bigcup\{\tau'' | \tau'' \text{ is the tree used to make } K_{ab}p \text{ true at } t'', \text{ where } t'' < t'\}$. Now define τ as $\langle a; \tau_1, \ldots, \tau_m \rangle$, where $\{\tau_1, \ldots, \tau_m\} = T_1 \cup T_2$. Thus $M \models_t (\tau)p$, or $M \models_t K_{rab}p$. Hence, axiom AX-AB-REACT-2 is sound.

Completeness: The proof is by induction on the structure of formulae. Only the case of formulae of the form $K_{rab}p$ is described below. Completeness means that $M \models_t K_{rab}p$ entails $K_{rab}p \in t$. $M \models_t K_{rab}p$ iff $(\exists \tau : M \models_t \langle\!\langle \tau \rangle\!\rangle p)$. This proof is by induction inside the induction on the structure of formulae. This induction is on the structure of trees with which a formula of the form $K_{rab}p$ is satisfied. One base case is the empty tree $\emptyset$. And $M \models_t \langle\!\langle \emptyset \rangle\!\rangle p$ iff $M \models_t p$. By Ax-Ab-React-3, $p \in t$. By axiom Ax-Ab-React-1 above, $K_{rab}p \in t$, as desired. The other base case is for single-action trees: $M \models_t \langle\!\langle a \rangle\!\rangle p$ iff $(\exists S, t' : [S; t, t'] \in [\![a]\!])$ and $(\forall S : (\forall t' \in S : [S; t, t'] \in [\![a]\!] \Rightarrow (\exists t'' : t < t'' \leq t'$ and $M \models_{t''} p)))$. But, by axiom Ax-Ab-React-3, we have $(\bigvee a : \mathsf{E}\langle a \rangle \mathsf{true} \wedge \mathsf{A}[a]p)$. Thus by axiom Ax-Ab-React-2, we have $K_{rab}p$.

For the inductive case, $M \models_t \langle\!\langle \langle a; \tau_1, \ldots, \tau_m \rangle \rangle\!\rangle p$ iff $(\exists S, t' : [S; t, t'] \in [\![a]\!])$ and $(\forall S : (\forall t' \in S : [S; t, t'] \in [\![a]\!] \Rightarrow (\exists i : 1 \leq i \leq m$ and $M \models_{t'} \langle\!\langle \tau_i \rangle\!\rangle K_{rab}p)))$. But since τ_i is a subtree of τ, we can use the inductive hypothesis on trees to show that this is equivalent to $(\exists t' : [S; t, t'] \in [\![a]\!])$ and $(\forall S : (\forall t' \in S : [S; t, t'] \in [\![a]\!] \Rightarrow M \models_{t'} K_{rab}p))$. But it is easy to see that $(\exists t' : [S; t, t'] \in [\![a]\!])$ iff $\mathsf{E}\langle a \rangle \mathsf{true}$. And, using the definition of $[\,]$, we see that the second conjunct holds only if $\mathsf{A}[a]K_{rab}p$. Thus $M \models_t \langle\!\langle \tau \rangle\!\rangle p$ only if $M \models_t (\bigvee b : \mathsf{E}\langle b \rangle \mathsf{true} \wedge \mathsf{A}[b]K_{rab}p)$. But, by axiom Ax-Ab-React-3, $(\bigvee b : \mathsf{E}\langle b \rangle \mathsf{true} \wedge \mathsf{A}[b]K_{rab}p) \in t$. Thus by axiom Ax-Ab-React-2, $K_{rab}p \in t$. Hence we have completeness. $\square$

4.3 Strategic Ability

The definition of ability given above involves trees of basic actions of a given agent. Strategies were introduced in section 2.5 as abstractions over agents' basic actions. I now define the ability of an agent relative to a strategy. Defining ability and know-how relative to a strategy not only shows us how abstractions over basic actions relate to the concepts considered, but also help make the connection to intentions clearer.

The operator $\langle\!\langle \, \rangle\!\rangle$ is defined as follows. $x\langle\!\langle Y \rangle\!\rangle p$ means that the agent, x, is able to perform all the substrategies of Y that he may need to perform, and furthermore that he can perform them in such a way as to force the world to make p true. Basically, this allows us to have the ability of an agent to achieve the conditions in different substrategies combined to yield the ability to achieve some composite condition. This is especially important from the point of view of designers and analyzers of agents, since they can take advantage of the abstraction provided by strategies to consider the ability of an agent in terms of his ability to achieve simpler conditions. Not just intuitively, but even formally, the ability to achieve simpler conditions as used here is purely reactive, as defined in section 4.2 (see Theorem 4.3 below for the technical justification).

In order to define $x\langle\!\langle Y\rangle\!\rangle p$ formally, I need the auxiliary concept of the *ability-intension* of a tree. The ability-intension of a tree τ, for an agent x, and a strategy Y, is notated as $[\tau]_Y^x$. This is the set of periods on which the given agent is able to achieve the given strategy, by following the given tree. Precisely those periods are included on which the success of the given strategy is assured or forced, and not fortuitous. The ability-intension of trees needs to be defined only for the $\downarrow$ of strategies, which are always of the forms, **skip** or **do**(q). As usual, the agent symbol is omitted when obvious from the context. Formally, we have

1. The empty strategy, **skip**, is achieved by the empty tree.

    $[S; t, t'] \in [\![\emptyset]\!]_{\text{skip}}$ iff $t = t'$.

2. τ follows **do**(q) iff the agent can achieve q in doing τ.

    $[S; t, t'] \in [\![\tau]\!]_{\text{do}(q)}$ iff

    (a) $\tau = \emptyset$ and $t = t'$ and $M \models_t q$;

    (b) $\tau = a$ and $M \models_{t'} q$ and $(\exists t_1 : t < t' \le t_1$ and $[S; t, t_1] \in [\![a]\!]$ and $(\forall t_2 : t \le t_2 < t'$ implies $M \not\models_{t_2} q))$; or

    (c) $\tau = \langle a; \tau_1, \ldots, \tau_m\rangle$ and $M \models_{t'} q$ and $M \models_t (\tau)q$ and $(\exists t_1 : [S; t, t_1] \in [\![a]\!]$ and $(\exists t_2, i : 1 \le i \le m$ and $[S; t_1, t_2] \in [\![\tau_i]\!]_{\text{do}(q)}$ and $t_1 \le t' \le t_2))$ and $(\forall t_3 : t \le t_3 < t'$ implies $M \not\models_{t_3} q)$

An important feature of this definition is that a period, $[S; t, t']$, is included in the ability-intension of **do**(q), only if no other period is available that begins at or before t and ends sooner than t'. This captures the intuition that, in order to achieve q, an agent has to act only till its first occurrence. Another consequence of this definition is that, for some strategies, the tree $\langle a; \emptyset\rangle$ may have a different ability-intension than the tree a. The former requires the relevant condition to hold when a ends, whereas the latter allows it to hold any time during the execution of a. This is not a problem, since, whenever the tree $\langle a; \emptyset\rangle$ is available to an agent, so is the tree a.

The ability-intension of a tree for a strategy of the form **do**(q) helps relate the notion of strategic ability as defined in this section to the notion of reactive ability as defined in section 4.2. In particular, a period is in the ability-intension of a tree relative to **do**(q) iff the tree can be used as a selection function by the agent to force q. Thus, we have the following result.

Lemma 4.2 Let $\tau = \langle a; \tau_1, \ldots, \tau_m \rangle$. Then, $M \models_t \langle\!\langle \tau \rangle\!\rangle q$ iff $(\exists S, t' : [S; t, t'] \in [\![\tau]\!]_{\mathbf{do}(q)})$

Proof.

The cases of the empty tree and single-action trees are trivial. The inductive case in the right to left direction is also trivial. In the left to right direction, let t_0 be the moment at which a is done. Then, by the definition of $\langle\!\langle\;\rangle\!\rangle$, $(\exists i : 1 \leq i \leq m$ and $M \models_t \langle\!\langle \langle \tau_i \rangle \rangle\!\rangle q)$. By the inductive hypothesis, $(\exists S, t' : [S; t_0, t'] \in [\![\tau_i]\!]_{\mathbf{do}(q)})$. Therefore, $(\exists S, t' : [S; t, t'] \in [\![\langle a; \tau_1, \ldots, \tau_m \rangle]\!]_{\mathbf{do}(q)})$ □

Using the definition of ability-intension, the satisfaction conditions for $\langle\!\langle\;\rangle\!\rangle$ can be given as below.

SEM-25. $M \models_t x\langle\!\langle \mathbf{skip} \rangle\!\rangle p$ iff $M \models_t p$

SEM-26. $M \models_t x\langle\!\langle Y \rangle\!\rangle p$ iff $(\exists \tau : (\exists S, t' : [S; t, t'] \in [\![\tau]\!]^x_{1,Y})$ and $(\forall S, t' : [S; t, t'] \in [\![\tau]\!]^x_{1,Y} \Rightarrow M \models_{t'} x\langle\!\langle \uparrow_t Y \rangle\!\rangle p))$

This definition says that an agent is able to achieve p relative to strategy Y iff there is a tree of actions for him such that he can achieve the current part of his strategy by following that tree, and that on all scenarios where he does so, he either achieves p or can continue with the rest of his strategy (and is able to achieve p relative to that). This definition allows the tree for the current part of Y to overlap with the tree for the rest of it. This is desirable, since we expect the strategy $\mathbf{do}(q);\mathbf{do}(q)$ to behave the same as $\mathbf{do}(q)$, which it would not if a different action were required for each substrategy.

Now $\mathsf{K}_{sab}p$ may be defined as given below.

SEM-27. $M \models_t x\mathsf{K}_{sab}p$ iff $(\exists Y : M \models_t x\langle\!\langle Y \rangle\!\rangle p)$

The execution of a strategy by an agent is equivalent to its being unraveled into a sequence of substrategies, each of the form $\mathbf{do}(q)$. The agent follows each substrategy by performing actions prescribed by some tree. Thus the substrategies serve as abstractions of trees of basic actions. In this way, the definition of ability exhibits a two-layered architecture of agents: the bottom layer determining how substrategies of limited forms are achieved, and the top layer how they are composed to form complex strategies.

Since strategies are structured, the axiomatization of ability relative to a strategy must involve their structure. This comes into the axiomatization of $\langle\!\langle Y \rangle\!\rangle p$. These axioms resemble those for standard dynamic logic modalities, but there are important differences. Just as for reactive ability, the axiomatization below is relativized to the underlying logic.

Ax-Ab-Strat-1. $(\!|skip|\!)p \equiv p$

Ax-Ab-Strat-2. $(\!|Y_1;Y_2|\!)p \equiv (\!|Y_1|\!)(\!|Y_2|\!)p$

Ax-Ab-Strat-3. $(\!|\text{if } q \text{ then } Y_1 \text{ else } Y_2|\!)p \equiv (q \rightarrow (\!|Y_1|\!)p) \wedge (\neg q \rightarrow (\!|Y_2|\!)p)$

Ax-Ab-Strat-4. $(\!|\text{while } q \text{ do } Y_1|\!)p \equiv (q \rightarrow (\!|Y_1|\!)(\!|\text{while } q \text{ do } Y_1|\!)p) \wedge (\neg q \rightarrow p)$

Ax-Ab-Strat-5. $(\!|\text{do}(q)|\!)p \equiv (q \wedge p) \vee (\neg q \wedge (\bigvee a : E\langle a \rangle \text{true} \wedge A[a](\!|\text{do}(q)|\!)p))$

Ax-Ab-Strat-6. All substitution instances of the validities of the underlying logic

Theorem 4.3 Axioms Ax-Ab-Strat-1 through Ax-Ab-Strat-6 yield a sound and complete axiomatization of $(\!|Y|\!)p$.

Proof.

Soundness and Completeness: The proofs of soundness and completeness are developed hand-in-hand. Only formulae of the form $(\!|Y|\!)p$ are considered here. As in section 4.2, construct a model whose indices are maximally consistent sets of sentences of the language. Completeness means that $M \models_t (\!|Y|\!)p$ entails $(\!|Y|\!)p \in t$, the corresponding moment in the model, and soundness means that $(\!|Y|\!)p \in t$ entails $M \models_t (\!|Y|\!)p$. The proof is by induction on the structure of strategies.

$M \models_t (\!|skip|\!)p$ iff $M \models_t p$. But by axiom Ax-Ab-Strat-1, $(\!|skip|\!)p \in t$ iff $p \in t$. Thus we simultaneously have soundness for axiom Ax-Ab-Strat-1, and completeness for this case of strategies.

Similarly, $M \models_t (\!|\text{if } q \text{ then } Y_1 \text{ else } Y_2|\!)p$ iff there exists a tree that follows $\downarrow_t(\text{if } q \text{ then } Y_1 \text{ else } Y_2)$ and some further properties hold of it. But the truth of q entails that $\downarrow_t(\text{if } q \text{ then } Y_1 \text{ else } Y_2) = \downarrow_t Y_1$ and $\uparrow_t(\text{if } q \text{ then } Y_1 \text{ else } Y_2) = \uparrow_t Y_1$. The corresponding condition holds for $\neg q$. Thus $M \models_t (\!|\text{if } q \text{ then } Y_1 \text{ else } Y_2|\!)p$ iff $M \models_t (q \rightarrow (\!|Y_1|\!)p)$ and $M \models_t (\neg q \rightarrow (\!|Y_2|\!)p)$. But by axiom Ax-Ab-Strat-3, $(\!|\text{if } q \text{ then } Y_1 \text{ else } Y_2|\!)p \in t$ iff $(q \rightarrow (\!|Y_1|\!)p) \in t$ and $(\neg q \rightarrow (\!|Y_2|\!)p) \in t$. By induction, since Y_1 and Y_2 are structurally smaller than the above conditional strategy, and since we have axiom Ax-Ab-Strat-6 (which applies for $\rightarrow$), we have that $(\!|\text{if } q \text{ then } Y_1 \text{ else } Y_2|\!)p \in t$.

The case of $(\!|\text{do}(q)|\!)p$ is quite simple. This is because axiom Ax-Ab-Strat-5 closely resembles the axioms for reactive ability given in section 4.2. Using the definition of $\downarrow_t$ and $\uparrow_t$ we have that $M \models_t (\!|\text{do}(q)|\!)p$ iff $(\exists \tau : (\exists S, t' : [S; t, t'] \in [\![\tau]\!]_{\text{do}(q)})$ and $(\forall S : (\forall t' \in S : [S; t, t'] \in [\![\tau]\!]_{\text{do}(q)} \Rightarrow M \models_{t'} p)))$. If

$\tau = \emptyset$, then the right hand expression reduces to $M \models_t (q \wedge p)$. By axiom Ax-AB-STRAT-6, $q \wedge p \in t$, which by axiom AX-AB-STRAT-5 entails that $\langle\!\lfloor do(q)\rfloor\!\rangle p \in t$, as desired. If $\tau \neq \emptyset$, we can proceed as follows.

$(\exists S, t' : [S; t, t'] \in [\![\tau]\!]_{do(q)})$ entails that $(\exists S, t'' : [S; t, t''] \in [\![a]\!])$, which means that $M \models_t E\langle a\rangle \text{true}$. It also entails that $M \not\models_t q$. Also, by Lemma 4.2, $(\exists S, t' : [S; t, t'] \in [\![\tau]\!]_{do(q)})$ iff $M \models_t \langle\!\langle\tau\rangle\!\rangle q$. By definition, $M \models_t \langle\!\langle\tau\rangle\!\rangle q$ iff $(\forall S, t'' : [S; t, t''] \in [\![a]\!] \Rightarrow (\exists i : 1 \leq i \leq m$ and $M \models_{t''} \langle\!\langle\tau_i\rangle\!\rangle q))$. Moreover, $(\forall S, t' : [S; t, t'] \in [\![\tau]\!]_{do(q)} \Rightarrow M \models_{t'} p)$ entails that $(\forall S, t'' : [S; t, t''] \in [\![a]\!] \Rightarrow (\exists i : 1 \leq i \leq m$ and $(\forall S, t' : [S; t'', t'] \in [\![\tau_i]\!]_{do(q)} \Rightarrow M \models_{t'} p)))$. Thus the condition for $M \models_t A[a](\langle\!\lfloor do(q)\rfloor\!\rangle p)$ is met. By axiom AX-AB-STRAT-6 (which applies for quantification over actions), we have $(\vee a : E\langle a\rangle \text{true} \wedge A[a](\langle\!\lfloor do(q)\rfloor\!\rangle p))$. But by the given axiom, this entails $\langle\!\lfloor do(q)\rfloor\!\rangle p$, as desired. This proves completeness for strategies of the form $do(q)$. It also proves soundness of axiom AX-AB-STRAT-5 in the left to right direction.

For soundness of axiom AX-AB-STRAT-5 in the right to left direction, we just need to note that for the first disjunct of axiom AX-AB-STRAT-5, we can use an empty tree to make $\langle\!\lfloor do(q)\rfloor\!\rangle p$ hold; for the second disjunct, using the action a for which the quantified expression holds and the trees corresponding to the occurrences of $\langle\!\lfloor do(q)\rfloor\!\rangle p$ at the moments it has been done, we can construct a tree that would cause the satisfaction of $\langle\!\lfloor do(q)\rfloor\!\rangle p$ at the given moment. This parallels the construction given in the proof of Theorem 4.1 in section 4.2 for reactive ability, and is not repeated here.

Surprisingly, the trickiest case in this proof turns out to be that of sequencing. When $\downarrow_t Y_1 = \textbf{skip}$, the desired condition for axiom AX-AB-STRAT-2 follows trivially. But, when $\downarrow_t Y_1 \neq \textbf{skip}$, the satisfaction condition for $\langle\!\langle Y_1; Y_2\rangle\!\rangle p$ recursively depends on that for $\langle\!\langle\uparrow_t Y_1; Y_2\rangle\!\rangle p$. However, this strategy does not directly feature in axiom AX-AB-STRAT-2. Also, it is not necessarily the case that $\uparrow_t Y_1; Y_2$ is a structurally smaller strategy than $Y_1; Y_2$, e.g., if Y_1 is an iterative strategy, $\uparrow_t Y_1$ may be structurally more complex than Y_1. However, we can use the fact that here, as in standard dynamic logic, iterative strategies are finitary or, in other words, lead only to a finite number of repetitions when executed at any time. Thus we can assume that for any strategy, $Y \neq \textbf{skip}$ and moment t, the fragment of $<$ in the model restricted to the execution of Y has a finite *depth*. Here *depth* of a strategy at a moment is defined as the maximum number of recursive invocations of $\downarrow$ along any scenario at that moment. If Y is followed at t, then the $\uparrow_t Y$ is followed at those moments where $\downarrow_t Y$ has just been followed. The depth of $\uparrow_t Y$ equals (depth of Y) $- 1$. The depth of **skip** is 0. Thus the depth is a metric to do the necessary induction on. The remainder of the proof is quite simple.

The case of iterative strategies is now quite simple. Axiom AX-AB-

STRAT-4 directly captures the conditions for $\downarrow_t$ and $\uparrow_t$ of an iterative strategy. Using the above result for sequencing, and the fact that iterative strategies are finitary, we can perform induction on the depth of the strategy. This yields the desired result.

Thus for all cases in the definition of a strategy, $M \models_t \langle\!\langle Y\rangle\!\rangle p$ iff $\langle\!\langle Y\rangle\!\rangle p \in t$. This proves soundness and completeness. $\square$

4.4 Results on Ability

The axioms for strategies of the form $\langle\!\langle \mathbf{do}(q)\rangle\!\rangle p$, which is the nontrivial base case for strategies, are similar to the axioms for reactive ability given in section 4.2. Indeed, the following theorem states that the two concepts are logically identical, even though they have differing significance in terms of implementations.

Theorem 4.4 $\mathsf{K}_{rab}p \equiv \mathsf{K}_{sab}p$

Proof.

For the left to right direction, $\mathsf{K}_{rab}p$ yields $\langle\!\langle \mathbf{do}(p)\rangle\!\rangle p$, which yields $\mathsf{K}_{sab}p$. For the other direction, associate with $\langle\!\langle Y\rangle\!\rangle p$ a fragment of the model at the root of which $\langle\!\langle Y\rangle\!\rangle p$ holds and at the leaves of which is the first occurrence of p after the root. From this, construct a tree as required in the definition of $\mathsf{K}_{rab}p$. The tree for **skip** is the empty tree. The definition given above unravels a strategy into a finite sequence of strategies of the form $\mathbf{do}(q)$. Consider the last such strategies that apply in different parts of the model fragment. For each of them, an appropriate tree may be obtained by working from the bottom up in the given model fragment. Since coherence constraint COH-5 of section 2.3 holds, for each of the leaves of the fragment, there is a last action that ends there. Consider the nodes at which those actions are begun. At those nodes, we have a set of trees, each consisting of precisely one action that begins there and whose consequences are entirely within the fragment. If the original fragment is well-formed with respect to ability, there must be at least one action that satisfies this requirement. Repeated applications of this yield a tree for each strategy of the form $\mathbf{do}(q)$, and with respect to which, the agent has the required ability. Because of constraint COH-5, only a finite number of applications of this step are required. At each of the nodes where these trees are defined, we have a condition of the form $\langle\!\langle \mathbf{do}(q)\rangle\!\rangle p$. Continuing further in this way, we obtain a tree for the entire strategy. $\square$

It is convenient to refer to reactive and strategic ability jointly as K_{ab}. We are now able to state and prove some results characterizing the formal properties of ability.

Theorem 4.5 $K_{ab}p \rightarrow EFp$; and, therefore, $\neg K_{ab}$false

   Proof.

   Consider the two axioms for reactive ability. Note that $p \rightarrow EFp$: this takes care of the base case. Also, $(\bigvee a : E\langle a \rangle\text{true} \wedge A[a]EFp)$ entails EFp: this takes care of the inductive case.

   It is a trivial consequence of the definitions of E and F that $\neg EF$false is valid. $\square$

Theorem 4.6 $K_{ab}p \wedge AG(p \rightarrow q) \rightarrow K_{ab}q$

   Proof. Consider the two axioms for reactive ability. From axiom Ax-AB-REACT-1, $K_{rab}p$ holds if p holds. Since $AG(p \rightarrow q)$ is a premise, we also have q, which by axiom Ax-AB-REACT-1 entails $K_{ab}q$. From axiom Ax-AB-REACT-2, $K_{rab}p$ holds if $(\bigvee a : E\langle a \rangle\text{true} \wedge A[a]K_{rab}p)$. But for all actions, a, $AG(p \rightarrow q) \rightarrow A[a]AG(p \rightarrow q)$. Therefore, we have $(\bigvee a : E\langle a \rangle\text{true} \wedge A[a](K_{rab}p \wedge AG(p \rightarrow q)))$. By the inductive hypothesis, we can conclude $(\bigvee a : E\langle a \rangle\text{true} \wedge A[a]K_{rab}q)$ which, by axiom Ax-AB-REACT-2, entails $K_{rab}q$, as desired. $\square$

Theorem 4.7 $AFp \rightarrow K_{ab}p$

   Proof. Here, we need coherence condition COH-5 of section 2.3, which states that each moment on each scenario may be reached by a finite number of actions. Consider the subtree of the model at the leaves of which we have the first occurrences of p, which make AFp true. At those moments, we have $K_{rab}p$, due to axiom Ax-AB-REACT-1. Assign a depth to each of these moments that equals the number of actions required to reach that moment. Begin with the deepest moments. Let their depth be n. Let the nth action on some scenario be a, and let it begin at t. At the moment where that action is begun, we have $E\langle a \rangle$true, since the action is done on that scenario. Since this is the last action begun in the given subtree of the model, we also have $A[a]K_{rab}p$. Hence, axiom Ax-AB-REACT-2 applies, and we have $K_{rab}p$ at t. The we simply use induction to repeat this step n times to obtain $K_{rab}p$ at the root of the subtree, which is where AFp holds. $\square$

Theorem 4.8 $K_{ab}K_{ab}p \rightarrow K_{ab}p$

   Proof. Using the definition of reactive ability, construct a single tree out of the trees for $K_{rab}K_{rab}p$. For the base case, simply use axiom Ax-AB-REACT-1. $K_{rab}K_{rab}p$ holds if $K_{rab}p$ does, which trivially implies $K_{rab}p$. For the inductive case, $K_{rab}K_{rab}p$ holds if $(\bigvee a : E\langle a\rangle true \wedge A[a]K_{rab}K_{rab}p)$. By the inductive hypothesis, we obtain $(\bigvee a : E\langle a\rangle true \wedge A[a]K_{rab}p)$ which, by axiom-Ax-AB-REACT-2 implies $K_{rab}p$, as desired. $\square$

This seems intuitively quite obvious: if an agent can ensure that he will be able to ensure p, then he can already ensure p. But see the discussion following Theorem 4.10.

In section 4.2, I gave an example involving Halley's comet. If p is "returns(Halley's comet)," then assuming its return is inevitable, $K_{ab}p$ holds. But this may seem strange relative to our pretheoretic intuitions about ability: we would not ordinarily state that an agent such as ourselves is able to make Halley's comet return. Intuitively, it seems that an agent can be said to be able to achieve something only if it is not inevitable anyway.

For this reason, it is useful to consider an alternative notion, namely, of *proper ability*. Let K_{ab}^p denote this concept. Then $K_{ab}^p p$ holds only if p is not inevitable and does not hold currently. An obvious formalization of this is given next.

SEM-28. $M \models_t x K_{ab}^p p$ iff $M \models_t (x K_{ab} p)$ and $(\exists S : (\forall t' : t' \in S \rightarrow M \not\models_{t'} p))$

As a consequence of this definition, K_{ab}^p is a non-normal operator [Chellas, 1980, p. 114]. This means that $K_{ab}^p p \wedge (p \rightarrow q)$ does not imply that $K_{ab}^p q$. This is so, because q could be inevitable. For example, since true holds everywhere, we have $\neg K_{ab}^p true$. This complicates the logical properties of K_{ab}^p. Thus, whereas K_{ab}^p is the intuitively more reasonable sense of ability, K_{rab} is the technically more tractable one. This is one motivation for retaining both. Another motivation for K_{rab} is that in some applications, it is even intuitively the preferred notion (see section 4.9).

The operator K_{ab}^p, can now be axiomatized simply by adding the following axiom:

AX-AB-1. $K_{ab}^p p \equiv (K_{ab}p \wedge \neg AFp)$

Theorem 4.9 $\neg K_{ab}^p true$

Proof. We trivially have AFtrue, which by axiom AX-AB-1 entails $\neg K_{ab}^p true$. $\square$

Therefore, despite Theorem 4.6, the corresponding statement for K_{ab}^p fails. Indeed, we have

Theorem 4.10 $p \to \neg K_{ab}^p p$

Proof. Trivially again, since $p \to AFp$. $\square$

Theorem 4.10 states that if p already holds then the agent cannot be felicitously said to be able to achieve it. By a simple substitution, we obtain $K_{ab}^p p \to \neg K_{ab}^p K_{ab}^p p$, whose contrapositive is $K_{ab}^p K_{ab}^p p \to \neg K_{ab}^p p$. This is in direct opposition to Theorem 4.8 for K_{ab}, and is surprising, if not counterintuitive. It says that an agent who is able to become able to achieve p is not able to achieve p. This too agrees with our intuitions about K_{ab}^p since we explicitly wish to exclude the ability to achieve inevitable propositions. The explanation for this unexpected observation is that when we speak of nested ability, which we do not do often in natural language, we use two different senses of ability: K_{ab}^p for the inner one and K_{ab} for the outer one. Thus the correct translation is $K_{ab}K_{ab}^p p$, which entails $K_{ab}p$, as desired.

Theorem 4.11 $K_{ab}K_{ab}^p p \to K_{ab}p$

Proof. $K_{ab}K_{ab}^p p \equiv K_{ab}(K_{ab}p \wedge \neg AFp)$, by definition of K_{ab}^p. Since $AG((r \wedge q) \to r)$, we can apply Theorem 4.6. Thus the left hand side implies $K_{ab}K_{ab}p$, which by Theorem 4.8 implies $K_{ab}p$. $\square$

We can sometimes do better than this. For example, if p describes a condition that persists over time, as many p's in natural language examples do, then we also have $K_{ab}^p p$. Briefly, the persistence of a condition p can be described by the formula $AG(p \to AGp)$, which says that once p holds, it persists forever on all scenarios. For example, if p denotes that the carpet has an indelible stain, then once it holds it will continue to hold forever.

Theorem 4.12 $(K_{ab}K_{ab}^p p \wedge AG(p \to AGp)) \to K_{ab}^p p$

Proof. Using the definition of K_{ab}^p, we can see that the left hand side expression is equivalent to $K_{ab}(K_{ab}p \wedge \neg AFp) \wedge AG(p \to AGp)$. By Theorem 4.6, this implies $K_{ab}K_{ab}p \wedge K_{ab}\neg AFp \wedge AG(p \to AGp)$. Using Theorem 4.8 on the first conjunct and Theorem 4.5 on the second conjunct, we obtain $K_{ab}p \wedge EF\neg AFp \wedge AG(p \to AGp)$. Now assume AFp. Combining this with the last conjunct of the previous expression, we get $AFAGp$. Note that $EF\neg AFp \equiv EFEG\neg p$. This contradicts $AFAGp$. Hence by reductio ad absurdum, $\neg AFp$. Thus the left hand side of the statement of this theorem implies $K_{ab}p \wedge \neg AFp$, which is equivalent to $K_{ab}^p p$. $\square$

Theorem 4.12 can be weakened to apply even in the case of conditions that occur infinitely often, but do not persist forever. For example, the condition that a certain switch is on would not persist forever, simply because any agent could toggle it. However, it might reasonable to assume that the switch becomes on infinitely often. $AG(p \rightarrow A(\bigvee a : \langle a \rangle Fp))$ means that at all moments in the future if p holds, then for every scenario, there is a moment in its strict future at which Fp holds (this is so because, as required in section 2.1.2, all actions take time). Thus for every occurrence of p, there is another occurrence of p in its strict future.

Theorem 4.13 $(K_{ab}K_{ab}^p p \land AG(p \rightarrow A(\bigvee a : \langle a \rangle Fp))) \rightarrow K_{ab}^p p$

Proof. As before, using the definition of K_{ab}^p, we can see that the left hand side expression is equivalent to $K_{ab}(K_{ab}p \land \neg AFp) \land AG(p \rightarrow A(\bigvee a : \langle a \rangle Fp))$. By Theorem 4.6, this implies $K_{ab}K_{ab}p \land K_{ab}\neg AFp \land AG(p \rightarrow A(\bigvee a : \langle a \rangle Fp))$. Using Theorem 4.8 on the first conjunct and Theorem 4.5 on the second conjunct, we obtain $K_{ab}p \land EF\neg AFp \land AG(p \rightarrow A(\bigvee a : \langle a \rangle Fp))$. But $EF\neg AFp \equiv EFEG\neg p$. In other words, there is a scenario, S, on which there is a moment, after which there are no more occurrences of p. Now assume AFp. This implies that there is at least one occurrence of p on every scenario, hence there is an occurrence of p on S. Consider the last occurrence of p (this could be at the present time). Combining this with $AG(p \rightarrow A(\bigvee a : \langle a \rangle Fp))$, we conclude that there is an occurrence of p on S in the future of the given occurrence. This contradicts the assumption of a last occurrence of p. Hence we obtain $\neg AFp$. Thus we have $K_{ab}p \land \neg AFp$, which is equivalent to $K_{ab}^p p$. $\square$

4.5 Incorporating Action Selection: Reactive Know-How

Ability as defined above considers the choices that an agent can exercise in principle. However, it finesses the problem with regard to the agent knowing enough to actually be in a position to make those choices. I now seek to complete this part of the picture, by explicitly considering an agent's beliefs, which influence the choices that he, in fact, makes. For example, if an agent is able to dial all possible combinations of a safe, then by the above definition he is able to open that safe: for, surely, the correct combination is among those that he can dial. On the other hand, for an agent to really know how to open a safe, he must not only have the basic skills to dial different combinations on it, but also know which combination to dial.

I introduce the following notation into $\mathcal{L}^h$.

SYN-25. $p \in \mathcal{L}_s^h$ and $x \in \mathcal{A}$ implies that $(x K_{hr} p), (x K_{hs} p) \in \mathcal{L}^h$

SYN-26. $p \in \mathcal{L}_s^h$, $Y, Y' \in \mathcal{L}_y^h$, and $x \in \mathcal{A}$ implies that $(x[(Y)]p), (x[Y]Y')$, $(x[Y]Y') \in \mathcal{L}^h$

SYN-27. $\tau \in \Upsilon$, $x \in \mathcal{A}$, and $p \in \mathcal{L}^h$ implies that $x[(\tau)]p \in \mathcal{L}^h$

    $x[(\tau)]p$ denotes that agent x knows how to achieve p relative to tree τ. As usual, the agent symbol can be omitted, since it is obvious from the context. It reduces notational complexity to extend $\vee$ to apply to a given range of trees. Since distinct trees in each such range have distinct radix actions, the extension of $\vee$ from actions to trees is not a major step.

SEM-29. $M \models_t [(\emptyset)]p$ iff $M \models_t \mathsf{K}_t p$

SEM-30. $M \models_t [(a)]p$ iff $M \models_t \mathsf{K}_t(\mathsf{E}\langle a\rangle\mathsf{true} \wedge \mathsf{A}[a]\mathsf{K}_t p)$

SEM-31. $M \models_t [(a; \tau_1, \ldots, \tau_m)]p$ iff $M \models_t \mathsf{K}_t(\mathsf{E}\langle a\rangle\mathsf{true} \wedge \mathsf{A}[a](\vee_{1 \leq i \leq m} \tau_i : ([(\tau_i)]p)))$

Thus an agent knows how to achieve p by following the empty tree, i.e., by doing nothing, if he knows that p already holds. As a consequence of his knowledge, the agent will undertake no particular action to achieve p. The nontrivial base case is when the agent knows how to achieve p by doing a single action: this would be the last action that the agent performs to achieve p. In this case, the agent has to know that he will know p at some moment during or immediately after the given action.

    It is important to require knowledge in the state in which the agent finally achieves the given condition, because it helps limit the actions selected by the agent. If p holds, but the agent does not know this, then he might select still more actions in order to achieve p.

    Lastly, an agent knows how to achieve p by following a nested tree if he knows that he must choose the radix of this tree first and, when it is done, that he would know how to achieve p by following one of its subtrees. Thus know-how presupposes knowledge to choose the next action and confidence that one would know what to do when that action has been performed, provided one has the necessary skills, i.e., the necessary actions, available.

SEM-32. $M \models_t x\mathsf{K}_{hr}p$ iff $(\exists \tau : M \models_t x[(\tau)]p)$

    Consider Figure 4.2 for an example. Let x be the agent whose actions are written first there. Assume for simplicity that each moment is its own unique alternative for x. Then, by the above definitions, $x\mathsf{K}_t p$ holds at t_3 and

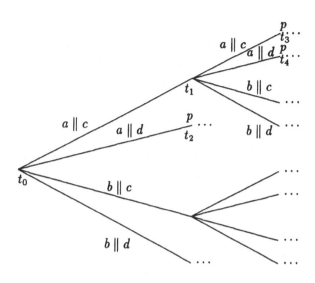

Figure 4.2: Know-how

t_4. Also, $x\mathsf{K}_{hr}p$ holds at t_1 (using a tree with the single action, a) and at t_2 (using the empty tree). As a result, at moment t_0, x knows that if he performs a, then he will know how to achieve p at each moment where a ends. In other words, we can define a tree, $\langle a; a, \emptyset \rangle$, such that x can achieve p by properly executing that tree. Therefore, x knows how to achieve p at t_0.

I now propose the following axioms for K_{hr}. These axioms are motivated by analogy with the axioms for K_{rab} given previously.

Ax-Kh-React-1. $\mathsf{K}_t p \rightarrow \mathsf{K}_{hr}p$

Ax-Kh-React-2. $(\bigvee a : \mathsf{K}_t(\mathsf{E}\langle a \rangle \mathsf{true} \wedge \mathsf{A}[a]\mathsf{K}_{hr}p)) \rightarrow \mathsf{K}_{hr}p$

Ax-Kh-React-3. All substitution instances of the validities of the underlying logic.

Theorem 4.14 Axioms Ax-Ab-React-1 through Ax-Kh-React-3 yield a sound and complete axiomatization for K_{hr}.

    Proof.

Construct a branching-time model, M. The moments of M are notated as t and are maximally consistent sets of formulae that contain all the substitution instances of the validities of the underlying logic. The other components of the model, especially, $<$, **B**, **R**, and **[]**, are constrained by the formulae that are true at the different moments. Furthermore, these sets are closed under the above two axioms for K_{hr}. We can ignore the agent symbol in the following discussion.

Soundness: For axiom Ax-KH-REACT-1 above, soundness is trivial from the definition of $[\![\emptyset]\!]p$. For axiom Ax-KH-REACT-2, let $(\bigvee a : K_t(E\langle a\rangle\text{true} \wedge A[a]K_{hr}p))$ hold at t. Then, by semantic condition SEM-30, $[\![a]\!]p$ holds, which, by semantic condition SEM-32, entails $K_{hr}p$. Hence, axiom Ax-KH-REACT-2 is sound.

Completeness: The proof is by induction on the structure of formulae. Only the case of formulae of the form $K_{hr}p$ is described below. Completeness means that $M \models_t K_{hr}p$ entails $K_{hr}p \in t$. $M \models_t K_{hr}p$ iff $(\exists \tau : M \models_t [\![\tau]\!]p)$. This proof is by induction inside the induction on the structure of formulae. This induction is on the structure of trees with which a formula of the form $K_{hr}p$ is satisfied. One base case is the empty tree $\emptyset$. And $M \models_t [\![\emptyset]\!]p$ iff $M \models_t K_t p$. By Ax-KH-REACT-3, $K_t p \in t$. By axiom Ax-KH-REACT-1 above, $K_{hr}p \in t$, as desired.

The other base case is for single-action trees. $M \models_t [\![a]\!]p$ iff $M \models_t K_t(E\langle a\rangle\text{true} \wedge A[a]K_t p)$. This is equivalent to the following expression: $(\forall t_b : (t, t_b) \in \mathbf{B} \Rightarrow (\exists S_b, t' : [S_b; t_b, t'] \in [\![a]\!])$ and $(\forall S_b : (\forall t' \in S_b : [S_b; t_b, t'] \in [\![a]\!] \Rightarrow (\exists t'' : t_b < t'' \leq t' \text{ and } M \models_{t''} K_t p)))$. But, by axiom Ax-KH-REACT-1, $K_t p \rightarrow K_{hr}p$. And, by axiom Ax-KH-REACT-3, we have that $(\forall t_b : (t, t_b) \in \mathbf{B} \Rightarrow (E\langle a\rangle\text{true} \wedge A[a]K_{hr}p))$. That is, $K_t(E\langle a\rangle\text{true} \wedge A[a]K_{hr}p) \in t$, which trivially entails $(\bigvee a : K_t(E\langle a\rangle\text{true} \wedge A[a]K_{hr}p)) \in t$. Thus by axiom Ax-KH-REACT-2, we have $K_{hr}p \in t$.

For the inductive case, $M \models_t [\![\langle a; \tau_1, \ldots, \tau_m\rangle]\!]p$ iff $M \models_t K_t(E\langle a\rangle\text{true} \wedge A[a](\bigvee_{1\leq i\leq m} \tau_i : ([\![\tau_i]\!]p)))$. This requires that , for some index i, $[\![\tau_i]\!]p$ holds at some appropriate moments. Let t_e be one such moment. Therefore, $M \models_{t_e} K_{hr}p$. Further, by the inductive hypothesis, we have that $K_{hr}p \in t_e$. Consequently, by axiom Ax-KH-REACT-2, we obtain that $K_{hr}p \in t$. Hence we have completeness of the above axiomatization. $\square$

4.6 Strategic Know-How

The above formalization gives a reactive definition of know-how. It considers the beliefs of agents and their influence on the selection of actions by them. However, it still remains to be seen if we can incorporate strategies into the picture to give an abstract definition of know-how. I introduce an operator, $\langle\!\langle\ \rangle\!\rangle$, to denote an agent's know-how relative to a strategy. $x\langle\!\langle Y\rangle\!\rangle p$ means that x knows how to follow strategy Y and thereby to achieve p. Knowing how to follow a strategy presupposes knowing the right actions to perform in order to satisfy it.

Just as for the case of ability, I aim to show that the strategic definition of know-how builds on top of the reactive definition given previously. To this end, I define the *know-how-intension* of a tree, relative to a strategy, in analogy with the *ability-intension* of a tree defined in section 4.3. Let the *know-how-intension* of a tree, τ, relative to a strategy, Y, for an agent, x, be notated as $\langle\!\langle\tau\rangle\!\rangle^x_Y$. This is the set of periods on which the given agent knows how to achieve Y by following τ. Precisely those periods are included on which the agent has the requisite knowledge to force the success of the given strategy; mere ability is not sufficient. Just as for the ability-intension of trees, the know-how-intension of trees needs to be defined only for the $\downarrow$ of strategies, which are always of one of the forms, **skip** or **do**(q). Formally, we have the following cases in the definition of $\langle\!\langle\tau\rangle\!\rangle^x_Y$.

Aux-10. The agent knows how to satisfy the empty strategy, **skip**, by doing nothing, i.e., by following the empty tree.

$$[S;t,t'] \in \langle\!\langle\emptyset\rangle\!\rangle^x_{\textbf{skip}} \text{ iff } t = t'$$

Aux-11. The agent may know how to satisfy the strategy **do**(q) in one of three ways: (a) by doing nothing, if he knows that q holds; (b) by following a single action tree, if he knows that it will force q; or, (c) by following a general tree, if doing the radix of that tree will result in a state in which he knows how to satisfy **do**(q) by following one of its subtrees. Thus we have:

$$[S;t,t'] \in \langle\!\langle\tau\rangle\!\rangle^x_{\textbf{do}(q)} \text{ iff}$$

Aux-1. $\tau = \emptyset$ and $t = t'$ and $M \models_t xK_t q$;

Aux-2. $\tau = a$ and $M \models_{t'} \langle\!\langle\tau\rangle\!\rangle q$ and $M \models_{t'} xK_t q$ and $(\exists t_1 : t < t' \leq t_1$ and $[S;t,t_1] \in [a]$ and $(\forall t_2 : t \leq t_2 < t'$ implies $M \not\models_{t_2} q))$; or,

Aux-3. $\tau = \langle a;\tau_1,\ldots,\tau_m\rangle$ and $M \models_{t'} xK_t q$ and $M \models_t \langle\!\langle\tau\rangle\!\rangle q$ and $(\exists t_1 : [S;t,t_1] \in [a]$ and $(\exists t_2, i : 1 \leq i \leq m$ and $[S;t_1,t_2] \in [\tau_i]_{\textbf{do}(q)}$ and $t_1 \leq t' \leq t_2)$ and $(\forall t_3 : t \leq t_3 < t'$ implies $M \not\models_{t_3} q)$

By the above definition, $[S; t, t'] \in \{\!\{\tau\}\!\}^x_{\mathbf{do}(q)}$ means that starting at moment t, moment t' is the earliest moment at which x knows how to make q happen by following it. As a result, for a scenario, S, and moments $t', t'' \in S$, we have that $[S; t, t'] \in \{\!\{\tau\}\!\}^x_{\mathbf{do}(q)}$ and $[S; t, t''] \in \{\!\{\tau\}\!\}^x_{\mathbf{do}(q)}$ implies that $t' = t''$. This agrees with the intuition behind constraint COH-1 of section 2.3 that an action begun at a moment can end at most one moment on each scenario. In other words, $\{\!\{\tau\}\!\}^x_{\mathbf{do}(q)}$ denotes the intension of the abstract action performed by agent x. This is x's abstract action of achieving q by exercising his know-how.

The above is an important intuition about strategies as they have been used throughout here. In order 'to make it explicit, I extend the formal language by adding two operators on strategies: $\langle\,\rangle_h$ and $[\,]_h$. These operators are defined in analogy with the operators $\langle\,\rangle$ and $[\,]$, which were defined for basic actions in section 2.1.3. However, unlike those operators, $\langle\,\rangle_h$ and $[\,]_h$ involve the evaluation of the given condition at the final moment of the relevant period. Consequently, $\langle\,\rangle_h$ and $[\,]_h$ are duals of each other. Formally, I add the following rule to the syntax of $\mathcal{L}^h$.

SYN-28. $p \in \mathcal{L}^h_s$, $x \in \mathcal{A}$, and $Y \in \mathcal{L}^h_y$ implies that $x[Y]_h p, x\langle Y \rangle_h p \in \mathcal{L}^h_s$

Now I give the semantic conditions for the new operators.

SEM-33. $M \models_{S,t} x \langle \mathbf{do}(q) \rangle_h p$ iff $(\exists \tau, t' \in S : [S; t, t'] \in \{\!\{\tau\}\!\}^x_{\mathbf{do}(q)}$ and $M \models_{S,t'} p)$

> This means that the abstract action $\mathbf{do}(q)$ can be knowingly and forcibly performed on the given scenario and, at the moment at which it is over, condition p holds.

SEM-34. $M \models_{S,t} x[\mathbf{do}(q)]_h p$ iff $(\forall \tau, t' \in S : [S; t, t'] \in \{\!\{\tau\}\!\}^x_{\mathbf{do}(q)} \Rightarrow M \models_{S,t'} p)$

> This means that if the abstract action $\mathbf{do}(q)$ is knowingly and forcibly performed on the given scenario, then at the moment at which it is over, condition p holds. It is all right to quantify over all t''s here, since, as remarked above, there can be at most one t' (on the given scenario) at which the action has been completed. More importantly, we must quantify over all trees with which $\mathbf{do}(q)$ can be performed, because those trees are equally legitimate as ways to perform $\mathbf{do}(q)$. If only some of the ways of performing $\mathbf{do}(q)$ were acceptable, then $\mathbf{do}(q)$ would not be a reasonable abstraction to use in a strategy: one should, instead, have specified $\mathbf{do}(q')$, for an appropriately strong q'. In other words, all that is relevant about acceptable scenarios is specified in $\mathbf{do}(q)$ itself.

The notion of know-how relative to a strategy can now be formalized to explicitly reflect the idea that strategies are abstractions over basic actions. That is, the definition of know-how relative to a strategy should parallel the previous, reactive, definition of know-how. The only difference lies in the fact that the strategic definition employs the operators on abstract actions defined above. An agent knows how to achieve p by following the empty strategy, skip, if he knows that p. The justification for this is the same as the one for the case of the empty tree, i.e., SEM-29, considered in section 4.5.

The case of a general strategy is more interesting. Not only must the agent know how to perform the relevant substrategies of a given strategy, he must know what they are when he has to perform them. I introduce two new operators to capture what the agent does now and what he will need to do later. The formula $x\lfloor Y \rfloor Y'$ means that for the agent x to follow Y at the given moment, he must begin by following Y'. In light of the previous discussion, Y' must be of one of the forms, skip or do(q). Since we have stipulated that the agents' beliefs are true, $x\lfloor Y \rfloor Y'$ holds only if $Y' = \downarrow_t Y$. However, since the agents' beliefs may be incomplete, $x\lfloor Y \rfloor Y'$ may be false for all Y'. Assuming $x\lfloor Y \rfloor Y'$ as above, the formula $x\lceil Y \rceil Y''$ means that for the agent x to follow Y at the given moment, he must follow Y'' after he has followed Y'. As above, $x\lceil Y \rceil Y''$ holds only if $Y'' = \uparrow_t Y$. In other words, $\lfloor \rfloor$ and $\lceil \rceil$ capture knowledge on the agent's part of the $\downarrow$ and $\uparrow$ of a strategy.

SEM-35. $M \models_t x\lfloor\text{skip}\rfloor\text{skip}$

SEM-36. $M \models_t x\lfloor\text{do}(q)\rfloor\text{do}(q)$ iff $M \models_t \neg q$

SEM-37. $M \models_t x\lfloor\text{do}(q)\rfloor\text{skip}$ iff $M \models_t x\mathsf{K}_t q$

SEM-38. $M \models_t x\lfloor\text{if } r \text{ then } Y_1 \text{ else } Y_2\rfloor Y'$ iff $M \models_t (x\mathsf{K}_t r \wedge x\lfloor Y_1 \rfloor Y') \vee (x\mathsf{K}_t \neg r \wedge x\lfloor Y_2 \rfloor Y')$

SEM-39. $M \models_t x\lfloor Y_1; Y_2 \rfloor Y'$ iff
    (a) $Y' \neq \text{skip}$ and $M \models_t x\lfloor Y_1 \rfloor Y'$, or
    (b) $M \models_t (x\lfloor Y_1 \rfloor\text{skip} \wedge x\lfloor Y_2 \rfloor Y')$

SEM-40. $M \models_t x\lfloor\text{while } r \text{ do } Y_1 \rfloor Y'$ iff
    (a) $M \models_t (x\mathsf{K}_t r \wedge x\lfloor Y_1 \rfloor Y')$, or
    (b) $Y' = \text{skip}$ and $M \models_t x\mathsf{K}_t \neg r$

SEM-41. $M \models_t x\lceil\text{skip}\rceil\text{skip}$

SEM-42. $M \models_t x\lceil\text{do}(q)\rceil\text{skip}$

SEM-43. $M \models_t x\text{[if } r \text{ then } Y_1 \text{ else } Y_2]Y'$ iff $M \models_t (x\mathsf{K}_t r \wedge x[Y_1]Y') \vee (x\mathsf{K}_t \neg r \wedge x[Y_2]Y')$

SEM-44. $M \models_t x[Y_1; Y_2]Y'$ iff
(a) $M \models_t (x[Y_1]\text{skip} \wedge x[Y_2]Y')$, or
(b) $(\exists Y'', Y_0 : Y_0 \neq \text{skip and } Y' = Y''; Y_2 \text{ and } M \models_t (x[Y_1]Y_0 \wedge x[Y_1]Y''))$

SEM-45. $M \models_t x\text{[while } r \text{ do } Y_1]\text{skip}$ iff $M \models_t (x\mathsf{K}_t \neg r \vee x[Y_1]\text{skip})$

SEM-46. $M \models_t x\text{[while } r \text{ do } Y_1]Y'$ iff $(\exists Y_0 : Y_0 \neq \text{skip and } Y' = Y_0; (\text{while } r \text{ do } Y_1)$ and $M \models_t (x\mathsf{K}_t r \wedge x[Y_1]Y_0))$

A consequence of these definitions is Lemma 4.15, which states that an agent can have at most one substrategy to perform at a given moment and at most one substrategy to perform on doing the first one. Another consequence is Lemma 4.16, which states that, if x knows what substrategy to follow at a given moment, he knows what substrategy to follow after the first substrategy is over. In analogy with Lemma 2.28, which states that $\downarrow_t Y = \text{skip}$ entails that $\uparrow_t Y = \text{skip}$, we have Lemma 4.17, which states that $x[Y]\text{skip}$ entails $x[Y]\text{skip}$. None of the lemmas mentioned above require the agent's beliefs to be true; they all just require them to be mutually consistent. Also, since true is valid, by the semantic definition of B (or K_t), i.e., SEM-16 in section 2.6, we have that $x\mathsf{K}_t\text{true}$ is valid. The only clause in the definition of $x[Y]Y'$ that allows $Y' = \text{do}(q)$, i.e., SEM-36, requires that $\neg q$ hold in the model, which cannot be the case for true. Therefore, $x[Y]Y'$ entails that $Y' \neq \text{do}(\text{true})$.

Lemma 4.15 $(\forall Y', Y'' : M \models_t x[Y]Y' \wedge x[Y]Y'' \text{ implies } Y' = Y'')$ and $(\forall Y', Y'' : M \models_t x[Y]Y' \wedge x[Y]Y'' \text{ implies } Y' = Y'')$

Proof. It is easily seen that this claim holds for the base cases, i.e., for Y of one of the forms, skip and $\text{do}(q)$. The conditions in the other semantic clauses are also mutually exclusive, so that at most one recursive invocation of $\lfloor \rfloor$ and $\lceil \rceil$, respectively, is possible in each case. $\square$

Lemma 4.16 $(\exists Y' : M \models_t x[Y]Y')$ implies that $(\exists Y'' : M \models_t x[Y]Y'')$

Proof. The semantic clauses given above give the conditions that determine whether $(\exists Y' : M \models_t x[Y]Y')$ holds. Some of these conditions involve the knowledge of agent x at moment t. It can be seen by inspection that, except for the case where Y is of the form $\text{do}(q)$, whenever $M \models_t x[Y]Y'$ holds, so does $M \models_t x[Y]Y''$, for some Y''. When Y is of the form $\text{do}(q)$, then $M \models_t x[Y]\text{skip}$ holds in all cases. This proves the above claim.

The converse of the above claim fails because $M \models_t x[\text{do}(q)]\text{skip}$ may be true even when $M \models_t q \wedge \neg x K_t q$. In that case, neither condition SEM-36, nor condition SEM-37 applies and, therefore, $(\exists Y' : M \models_t x[\text{do}(q)]Y')$ is false. $\square$

Lemma 4.17 $x[Y]\text{skip}$ entails $x[Y]\text{skip}$

Proof. By inspection of the semantic conditions for $\lfloor \rfloor$ and $\lceil \rceil$. The lemma holds for the cases of **skip** and $\text{do}(q)$ trivially. It can be proved for the other cases by checking their semantic conditions pairwise. $\square$

4.7 Strategic Know-How Defined

An agent, x, knows how to achieve a proposition p by following a strategy Y, if there is a strategy Y' such that (a) $x[Y]Y'$ holds; (b) he knows how to perform Y'; and, (c) he knows that, in each of the states where Y' is completed, he would know how to achieve p relative to $\uparrow_t Y$. Since Y' is always of one of the forms, **skip** or $\text{do}(q)$, Y is progressively unraveled into a sequence of substrategies of those forms. Formally, we have

SEM-47. $M \models_t x \langle\!\langle \text{skip} \rangle\!\rangle p$ iff $M \models_t x K_t p$

SEM-48. $M \models_t x \langle\!\langle Y \rangle\!\rangle p$ iff $M \models_t x K_t (Ex \langle \downarrow_t Y \rangle_h \text{true} \wedge Ax[\downarrow_t Y]_h x \langle\!\langle \uparrow_t Y \rangle\!\rangle p)$ and $M \models_t x[Y] \downarrow_t Y$

An interesting observation about the above definition is that it requires an agent to know what substrategy he must perform only when he has to begin acting on it. The knowledge prerequisites for executing different strategies can be read off from the above semantic definitions. For example, a conditional or iterative strategy can be executed only if the truth-value of the relevant condition is known.

In rough analogy with the axioms for ability, and with the knowledge of agents explicitly considered, we can come up with the following axioms for know-how.

AX-KH-STRAT-1. $x \langle\!\langle \text{skip} \rangle\!\rangle p \equiv x K_t p$

AX-KH-STRAT-2. $x \langle\!\langle Y_1; Y_2 \rangle\!\rangle p \equiv x \langle\!\langle Y_1 \rangle\!\rangle x \langle\!\langle Y_2 \rangle\!\rangle p$

AX-KH-STRAT-3. $x \langle\!\langle \text{if } q \text{ then } Y_1 \text{ else } Y_2 \rangle\!\rangle p \equiv$
$\qquad (x K_t q \wedge x \langle\!\langle Y_1 \rangle\!\rangle p) \vee (x K_t \neg q \wedge x \langle\!\langle Y_2 \rangle\!\rangle p)$

AX-KH-STRAT-4. $x\langle\!\langle\mathbf{while}\ q\ \mathbf{do}\ Y_1\rangle\!\rangle p \equiv (x\mathsf{K}_t q \wedge x\langle\!\langle Y_1\rangle\!\rangle x\langle\!\langle\mathbf{while}\ q\ \mathbf{do}\ Y_1\rangle\!\rangle p) \vee (x\mathsf{K}_t\neg q \wedge x\mathsf{K}_t p)$

AX-KH-STRAT-5. $x\langle\!\langle\mathbf{do}(q)\rangle\!\rangle p \equiv (\neg q \wedge (\bigvee a : x\mathsf{K}_t(Ex\langle a\rangle\mathsf{true} \wedge Ax[a]\langle\!\langle\mathbf{do}(q)\rangle\!\rangle p))) \vee x\mathsf{K}_t(q \wedge p)$

AX-KH-STRAT-6. All substitution instances of the validities of the underlying logic

Theorem 4.18 Axioms AX-KH-STRAT-1 through AX-KH-STRAT-6 yield a sound and complete axiomatization of $x\langle\!\langle Y\rangle\!\rangle p$.

Proof.

Soundness and Completeness: The proofs of soundness and completeness are developed together. Only formulae of the form $x\langle\!\langle Y\rangle\!\rangle p$ are considered here. As before, construct a model whose indices are maximally consistent sets of sentences of the language. Completeness means that $M \models_t x\langle\!\langle Y\rangle\!\rangle p$ entails $x\langle\!\langle Y\rangle\!\rangle p \in t$ and soundness means that $x\langle\!\langle Y\rangle\!\rangle p \in t$ entails $M \models_t x\langle\!\langle Y\rangle\!\rangle p$. The proof is by induction on the structure of strategies.

$M \models_t x\langle\!\langle\mathbf{skip}\rangle\!\rangle p$ iff $M \models_t x\mathsf{K}_t p$. But, by axiom AX-KH-STRAT-1, $x\langle\!\langle\mathbf{skip}\rangle\!\rangle p \in t$ iff $x\mathsf{K}_t p \in t$. Thus, we simultaneously have soundness for axiom AX-KH-STRAT-1, and completeness for strategies of the form **skip**.

Let $Y = \mathbf{if}\ q\ \mathbf{then}\ Y_1\ \mathbf{else}\ Y_2$. Then, $M \models_t x\langle\!\langle Y\rangle\!\rangle p$ iff x first performs Y' and then Y'', where $M \models_t (x[Y]Y' \wedge x[Y]Y'')$. But this holds only if $x\mathsf{K}_t q$ or $x\mathsf{K}_t\neg q$ holds at t. By the definitions SEM-38 and SEM-43, $M \models_t (x\mathsf{K}_t q \wedge x[Y_1]Y' \wedge x[Y_1]Y'') \vee (x\mathsf{K}_t\neg q \wedge x[Y_2]Y' \wedge x[Y_2]Y'')$. Therefore, using the definition of $\langle\!\langle\ \rangle\!\rangle$, we obtain $M \models_t x\langle\!\langle Y\rangle\!\rangle p$ iff $M \models_t (x\mathsf{K}_t q \wedge x\langle\!\langle Y_1\rangle\!\rangle p) \vee (x\mathsf{K}_t\neg q \wedge x\langle\!\langle Y_2\rangle\!\rangle p)$. Thus, we simultaneously have soundness for axiom AX-KH-STRAT-3, and completeness for conditional strategies.

Let $Y = \mathbf{do}(q)$. Using definitions SEM-37, SEM-36, and SEM-42 and the definition of $\langle\!\langle\mathbf{skip}\rangle\!\rangle p$ (SEM-47), we have that $M \models_t x\langle\!\langle\mathbf{do}(q)\rangle\!\rangle p$ iff $M \models_t (x\mathsf{K}_t q \wedge x\mathsf{K}_t p)$ or $M \models_t \neg q \wedge x\mathsf{K}_t(Ex\langle\mathbf{do}(q)\rangle_h\mathsf{true} \wedge x[\mathbf{do}(q)]_h x\mathsf{K}_t p)$. The first case is taken care of by one disjunct of axiom AX-KH-STRAT-5. Let t_b be a moment such that $(t, t_b) \in \mathbf{B}(x)$. Let τ be a tree that makes $Ex\langle\mathbf{do}(q)\rangle_h\mathsf{true}$ hold at t_b. Consider the same tree in the definition of $[\ ]_h$.

The rest of the proof of this case is by induction on the structure of trees. Initially, since $\neg q$ holds, $\tau \neq \emptyset$. However, $\tau = \emptyset$ is considered as a base case of the induction. At any moment, t', if $\tau = \emptyset$ satisfies $Ex\langle\mathbf{do}(q)\rangle_h\mathsf{true}$, then $Ex\langle\mathbf{do}(q)\rangle_h\mathsf{true} \wedge x[\mathbf{do}(q)]_h x\mathsf{K}_t p$ implies that $x\mathsf{K}_t(q \wedge p)$ which, by axiom AX-KH-STRAT-5, entails $x\langle\!\langle\mathbf{do}(q)\rangle\!\rangle p$ holds at t'. If $\tau = a$ then, since the first occurrence of q is relevant, $\neg q$ must hold at the given moment. Also, $Ex\langle\mathbf{do}(q)\rangle_h\mathsf{true} \wedge$

$x[\mathbf{do}(q)]_h x\mathsf{K}_t p$ entails $\mathsf{E}x\langle a\rangle$true $\wedge\ x[a]x\mathsf{K}_t(q\wedge p)$. By the definition of K_t, we obtain $x\mathsf{K}_t(\mathsf{E}x\langle a\rangle$true $\wedge\ x[a]x\mathsf{K}_t(q\wedge p))$ at moment t. This trivially entails $(\bigvee a : x\mathsf{K}_t(\mathsf{E}x\langle a\rangle$true $\wedge\ x[a]x\mathsf{K}_t(q\wedge p)))$. By axiom Ax-Kh-Strat-5, $x\mathsf{K}_t(q\wedge p)$ entails $x\langle\!\langle\mathbf{do}(q)\rangle\!\rangle p$. Thus the previous expression yields $(\bigvee a : x\mathsf{K}_t(\mathsf{E}x\langle a\rangle$true $\wedge\ x[a]x\langle\!\langle\mathbf{do}(q)\rangle\!\rangle p))$. Since $\neg q$ also holds at t, we have $x\langle\!\langle\mathbf{do}(q)\rangle\!\rangle p$ by axiom Ax-Kh-Strat-5.

The case when $\tau = \langle a; \tau_1, \ldots, \tau_m\rangle$ follows quite simply by induction. The tree τ follows $\mathbf{do}(q)$ over a period iff (a) the period ends at the first occurrence of q and $x\mathsf{K}_t q$ also holds at that moment; and (b) the radix, a, is done in a prefix of the period and one of the τ_i follows $\mathbf{do}(q)$ over the rest of the period. By the inductive hypothesis applied to τ_i, $x\langle\!\langle\mathbf{do}(q)\rangle\!\rangle p$ holds at each of the moments at which a is performed. Axiom Ax-Kh-Strat-5, then, entails that $x\langle\!\langle\mathbf{do}(q)\rangle\!\rangle p$ holds at the moment at which τ was begun. The rest of the argument is the same as for single-action trees. This proves completeness for strategies of the form, $\mathbf{do}(q)$. It also proves soundness of axiom Ax-Kh-Strat-5 in the left to right direction.

For soundness of axiom Ax-Kh-Strat-5 in the right to left direction, note that for the second disjunct of axiom Ax-Kh-Strat-5, the empty tree makes $x\langle\!\langle\mathbf{do}(q)\rangle\!\rangle p$ hold wherever $x\mathsf{K}_t(q\wedge p)$ holds. For the first disjunct, let t be the given moment. Using the action for which the quantified expression holds and the trees corresponding to the occurrences of $x\langle\!\langle\mathbf{do}(q)\rangle\!\rangle p$ at the moments that action has been done, we can construct a tree at each alternative moment of t that makes $x\langle\!\langle\mathbf{do}(q)\rangle\!\rangle p$ true at t. This parallels the construction given in the proof of Theorem 4.1 in section 4.2, and is not repeated here.

Now let $Y = Y_1; Y_2$. If $\downarrow_t Y_1 = \mathbf{skip}$, the desired condition for axiom Ax-Kh-Strat-2 follows trivially. But, if $\downarrow_t Y_1 \neq \mathbf{skip}$, the satisfaction condition for $x\langle\!\langle Y_1; Y_2\rangle\!\rangle p$ recursively depends on that for $x\langle\!\langle\uparrow_t Y_1; Y_2\rangle\!\rangle p$. Therefore, as in the proof of Theorem 4.3 in section 4.3, we use the fact that strategies are finitary. That is, they have a finite depth or, in other words, require only a finite number of applications of $\downarrow$ when performed at any time. Thus we can assume that for any moment t and strategy Y, such that $\downarrow_t Y \neq \mathbf{skip}$, the fragment of the model restricted to the execution of Y has a finite *depth*. If Y is followed at t, then the $\uparrow_t Y$ is followed at those moments where $\downarrow_t Y$ has just been performed. The depth of $\uparrow_t Y$ equals (depth of Y) $- 1$. The depth of $\mathbf{skip}$ is 0. Thus the depth is a metric to do the necessary induction on. The remainder of the proof is quite simple.

Finally, let $Y = \mathbf{while}\ q\ \mathbf{do}\ Y_1$. Axiom Ax-Kh-Strat-4 captures the conditions for the $\lfloor\rfloor$ and $\lceil\rceil$ of Y. Using the above result for sequencing, and the fact that iterative strategies are finitary, we can perform induction on the depth of the strategy. This yields the desired result.

Thus for all cases in the definition of a strategy, $M \models_t x \langle\!\langle Y \rangle\!\rangle p$ iff $x \langle\!\langle Y \rangle\!\rangle p \in t$. This proves soundness and completeness of the proposed axiomatization. $\square$

SEM-49. $M \models_t x \mathsf{K}_{\mathsf{hs}} p$ iff $(\exists Y : M \models_t x \langle\!\langle Y \rangle\!\rangle p)$

4.8   Results on Know-How

Just as for the case of ability, the strategic definition of know-how exploits its previous, reactive, definition. The following theorem states that strategic and reactive know-how are logically identical.

Theorem 4.19 $\mathsf{K}_{\mathsf{hr}} p \equiv \mathsf{K}_{\mathsf{hs}} p$

    Proof.

    The left to right direction is trivial. In the other direction, associate with $\langle\!\langle Y \rangle\!\rangle p$ a fragment of the model whose root satisfies $\langle\!\langle Y \rangle\!\rangle p$ and whose leaves satisfy the first occurrence of $\mathsf{K}_t p$ since the root. From this, construct a tree as required for $\mathsf{K}_{\mathsf{hr}} p$. The details of this construction are identical to those in the proof of Theorem 4.4. $\square$

It is often convenient to refer to reactive and strategic know-how jointly as K_{h}. Below, we state and prove some results about know-how and its interaction with time and knowledge. These properties help us better delineate the concept of know-how as captured by the formalization presented above.

Theorem 4.20 $\mathsf{K}_{\mathsf{h}} p \rightarrow \mathsf{K}_t \mathsf{K}_{\mathsf{h}} p$

    Proof.

    Consider the two axioms for reactive know-how one by one. $\mathsf{K}_t p$ entails $\mathsf{K}_t \mathsf{K}_t p$. Thus, by the base axiom, we get $\mathsf{K}_t \mathsf{K}_{\mathsf{h}} p$. For the inductive axiom, $(\bigvee a : \mathsf{K}_t (\mathsf{E}\langle a \rangle \mathsf{true} \wedge \mathsf{A}[a]\mathsf{K}_{\mathsf{h}} p))$ entails $(\bigvee a : \mathsf{K}_t \mathsf{K}_t (\mathsf{E}\langle a \rangle \mathsf{true} \wedge \mathsf{A}[a]\mathsf{K}_{\mathsf{h}} p))$ by introspection. And, that entails $\mathsf{K}_t (\bigvee a : \mathsf{K}_t (\mathsf{E}\langle a \rangle \mathsf{true} \wedge \mathsf{A}[a]\mathsf{K}_{\mathsf{h}} p))$. Thus we obtain $\mathsf{K}_t \mathsf{K}_{\mathsf{h}} p$. $\square$

Theorem 4.21 $\mathsf{K}_{\mathsf{h}} p \rightarrow \mathsf{K}_t \mathsf{EF} p$; consequently, $\neg \mathsf{K}_{\mathsf{h}} \mathsf{false}$

    Proof.

    It sufficient to consider the two axioms for reactive know-how. Since $p \rightarrow \mathsf{EF} p$ is valid, we have $\mathsf{K}_t p \rightarrow \mathsf{K}_t \mathsf{EF} p$ by axioms Ax-BEL-3 and Ax-BEL-4. This takes care of the base case. Also, $(\bigvee a : K_t(E\langle a\rangle\text{true} \wedge A[a]K_tEFp))$ entails $K_tE\langle a\rangle EFp$, which entails K_tEFp: this takes care of the inductive case.

It is a trivial consequence of the definitions of E and F that $\neg EF\text{false}$ is valid. Hence, by definition of K_t, $\neg K_tEF\text{false}$ is valid. Thus, $\neg K_h\text{false}$ holds. $\square$

Theorem 4.22 $K_hp \wedge K_tAGK_t(p{\to} q){\to} K_hq$

Proof. It sufficient to consider the two axioms for reactive know-how. From axiom Ax-Kh-React-1, $K_{hr}p$ holds if K_tp holds. $K_tAGK_t(p{\to} q)$ entails $K_t(p{\to} q)$. Thus, by axiom Ax-Bel-4, we have K_tq, which by axiom Ax-Kh-React-1 entails K_hq. From axiom Ax-Kh-React-2, $K_{hr}p$ holds if $(\bigvee a : K_t(E\langle a\rangle\text{true} \wedge A[a]K_{hr}p))$. But, as a consequence of the definitions of A and G, we have that for all actions, a, $K_tAGK_t(p{\to} q){\to} K_tA[a]AGK_t(p{\to} q)$. Therefore, we have $(\bigvee a : K_t(E\langle a\rangle\text{true} \wedge A[a](K_{hr}p \wedge AGK_t(p{\to} q))))$. By the inductive hypothesis, we can conclude $(\bigvee a : K_t(E\langle a\rangle\text{true} \wedge A[a]K_{hr}q))$ which, by axiom Ax-Kh-React-2, entails $K_{hr}q$, as desired. $\square$

For the next theorem, we need to add an assumption about knowledge. The relations, $\mathbf{B}(x)$, which were assumed to be reflexive and transitive in section 2.6, are now additionally assumed to be symmetric. This validates the following axiom of negative introspection [Chellas, 1980].

Ax-Bel-5. $\neg xK_tp{\to} xK_t\neg xK_tp$

I shall assume this axiom in the rest of this section.

Theorem 4.23 $K_hK_hp{\to} K_hp$

Proof. Using the definition of reactive know-how, construct a single tree out of the trees for $K_{hr}K_{hr}p$. For the base case, simply use axiom Ax-Kh-React-1. $K_{hr}K_{hr}p$ holds if $K_{hr}p$ does, which trivially implies $K_{hr}p$. For the inductive case, $K_{hr}K_{hr}p$ holds if $(\bigvee a : K_t(E\langle a\rangle\text{true} \wedge A[a]K_{hr}K_{hr}p))$. By the inductive hypothesis, we obtain $(\bigvee a : K_t(E\langle a\rangle\text{true} \wedge A[a]K_{hr}p))$ which, by axiom-Ax-Kh-React-2 implies $K_{hr}p$, as desired. $\square$

This seems intuitively quite obvious: if an agent can ensure that he will be able to ensure p, then he can already ensure p. But see the discussion following Theorem 4.25.

If p is "returns(Halley's comet)," then assuming the agent knows that he will come to know that it has returned, K_hp holds. The condition here is stronger than for ability, but is perhaps too weak relative to our pretheoretic intuitions. For this reason, it is useful to consider an alternative notion, *proper know-how*, notated as K_h^p that prevents this inference. Its semantic condition and axiomatization are as follows.

SEM-50. $M \models_t x K_h^p p$ iff $M \models_t (x K_h p) \wedge (\neg x K_t AF x K_t p)$

AX-AB-2. $K_h^p p \equiv (K_h p \wedge \neg K_t AF K_t p)$

Theorem 4.24 $\neg K_h^p \text{true}$

    Proof. We trivially have $K_t \text{true}$, which entails $AF K_t \text{true}$, which entails $K_t AF K_t \text{true}$. By axiom AX-AB-2, that entails $\neg K_h^p \text{true}$. $\square$

Therefore, despite Theorem 4.22, the corresponding statement for K_h^p fails. Indeed, we have

Theorem 4.25 $K_t p \rightarrow \neg K_h^p p$

    Proof. $K_t p$ entails $K_t K_t p$, which entails $K_t AF K_t p$. Hence, $\neg K_h^p p$. $\square$

Theorem 4.25 states that if p is known then the agent does not properly know how to achieve it. By substitution, we obtain $K_h^p p \rightarrow \neg K_h^p K_h^p p$, whose contrapositive is $K_h^p K_h^p p \rightarrow \neg K_h^p p$. This is in direct opposition to Theorem 4.23 for K_h, and is surprising. The explanation for this observation is that when we speak of nested know-how, which we do not do often in natural language, we use two different senses of know-how: K_h^p for the inner one and K_h for the outer one. Thus the correct translation is $K_h K_h^p p$, which entails $K_h p$, as desired.

Theorem 4.26 $K_h K_h^p p \rightarrow K_h p$

    Proof. $K_h K_h^p p \equiv K_h (K_h p \wedge \neg K_t AF K_t p)$, by definition of K_h^p. Since $K_t AG K_t ((r \wedge q) \rightarrow r)$, we can apply Theorem 4.22. Thus the left hand side implies $K_h K_h p$, which by Theorem 4.23 implies $K_h p$. $\square$

4.9 Conclusions

I presented two sound and complete logics for ability and know-how that were developed in the same framework as used for intentions earlier in this work. This formalization reveals interesting properties of ability and know-how and helps clarify some of our intuitions about them. Capturing these intuitions is an important first step in applying these concepts rigorously in the design and analysis of intelligent agents. The process of formalization helps uncover certain technical nuances that might never have been brought to the fore otherwise. This is a valuable service. Interestingly, many proofs from the proposed axioms turn out to be much simpler than those that might be given using purely model-theoretic reasoning.

For some purposes, the proper notion of know-how may be preferred, since it excludes cases where the given condition holds and is known to hold already. For most purposes, however, the general notion of know-how is preferred. For example, a household robot should know how to get upstairs when called; in this case, there is no problem if it knows that it is already upstairs.

Of special technical interest are the operators ⟨| |⟩ and [| |], which differ from those in standard dynamic logic. These operators provide a viable formal notion with which to capture the ability and know-how of an agent whose behavior is abstractly characterized in terms of strategies. The differences between the reactive and strategic definitions of these concepts lie mainly in the complexity of the agents to whom they may be attributed. As explained in section 2.5, the strategic definition lets an agent be specified and reasoned about using something akin to macros over reactive actions.

This approach complements previous work on knowledge and action [Moore, 1984; Morgenstern, 1987] in some respects. The details of the conditions that are achieved have been abstracted out, but could be filled in. For example, definite descriptions could be included easily: an agent's strategy can be $do(q)$, where q stands for "dialed(combination of the safe)."

At this point, I have formalized intentions and know-how within the same general framework of actions and time. Now the question arises as to whether we can pull these formalizations together to prove the kinds of results we are most interested in. The next chapter answers this question with a yes. And the chapter after the next reaffirms that for the problem of specifying communications among agents.

Chapter 5

Combining Intentions and Know-How

In the preceding chapters, I developed formalizations of intentions and know-how in a single general framework of actions and time. It is only fair to ask if these formalizations can be technically related in a useful manner. Indeed, they should be and can be. Putting them together makes it possible for us to derive results that are not derivable in other theories. As remarked in section 1.2, we need to be able to capture at least the following intuition concerning intentions and know-how: if an agent intends to achieve something and knows how to achieve it, then he will in fact bring it about.

This intuition can, in essence, be captured in the formal theory as developed so far, though some further technical restrictions need to be imposed to ensure that the given agent performs the appropriate actions. Note that this is intuitively much more reasonable than requiring, as Cohen & Levesque do [1990, p. 233], that if an agent intends to achieve something fanatically, he will succeed in bringing it about. Fanaticism is no cure for incompetence.

5.1 Some Basic Technical Results

In many ways, the definitions of intentions, ability, and know-how given in the preceding chapters paralleled each other. Their relationship to strategies and the progressive unraveling of strategies that those definitions involved were intuitively helpful factors in making their similarities obvious. I now consider some further results on the operators defined previously that help explicate their properties and are also helpful later on.

But, first, I define the formal language of this chapter, $\mathcal{L}^c$, by combining the rules for $\mathcal{L}^i$ and $\mathcal{L}^h$. Formally, $\mathcal{L}^c$ is defined as follows.

SYN-29. All the rules for $\mathcal{L}^i$, $\mathcal{L}^i_s$, $\mathcal{L}^i_y$, $\mathcal{L}^h$, $\mathcal{L}^h_s$, and $\mathcal{L}^h_y$, with $\mathcal{L}^c$ substituted for $\mathcal{L}^i$ and $\mathcal{L}^h$, $\mathcal{L}^c_s$ substituted for $\mathcal{L}^i_s$ and $\mathcal{L}^h_s$, and $\mathcal{L}^c_y$ substituted for $\mathcal{L}^i_y$ and $\mathcal{L}^h_y$

Lemma reflem-h-entails-i states the obvious result that if an agent knowingly performs $\mathbf{do}(q)$ on a scenario, then he performs $\mathbf{do}(q)$ on that scenario. Of course, if p holds at the end of the period over which he knowingly performs $\mathbf{do}(q)$, then p holds at the end of the period over which he performs $\mathbf{do}(q)$: indeed, they are the same period. This is because semantic definition 4.6 of $\langle \rangle_h$ requires that x know that q holds at the first moment at which it holds.

Lemma 5.1 $M \models_{S,t} x\langle\mathbf{do}(q)\rangle_h p$ implies $M \models_{S,t} x\langle\mathbf{do}(q)\rangle_i p$

Proof. $x\langle\mathbf{do}(q)\rangle_h p$ holds on a scenario, S, at a moment t iff there is a tree, τ, such that $(\exists t' \in S : [S; t, t'] \in [\![\tau]\!]^x_{\mathbf{do}(q)}$ and $M \models_{S,t'} p)$. The desired proof is by induction on the structure of trees. If τ is the empty tree, then $t = t'$; hence, $x\langle\mathbf{do}(q)\rangle_i p$ holds at S and t. Therefore, $[S; t, t] \in [\![\mathbf{do}(q)]\!]^x$. If τ is a single action, a, then t' is the moment of the first occurrence of q in the execution of a. Thus, $[S; t, t'] \in [\![\mathbf{do}(q)]\!]^x$. And, p holds at t'. Consequently, $M \models_{S,t} x\langle\mathbf{do}(q)\rangle_i p$. For a general tree, $\tau = \langle a; \tau_1, \ldots, \tau_m \rangle$, $[S; t, t'] \in [\![\tau]\!]^x_{\mathbf{do}(q)}$ iff $(\exists t_1, t_2, i : [S; t, t_1] \in [\![a]\!]$ and $[S; t_1, t_2] \in [\![\tau_i]\!]^x_{\mathbf{do}(q)}$ and t' is the first occurrence of q between t and t_2). If a is sufficient to force q, i.e., if $t < t' \leq t_1$, then it is subsumed by the previous case. Otherwise, $[S; t_1, t'] \in [\![\tau_i]\!]^x_{\mathbf{do}(q)}$ holds. Assume, as the inductive hypothesis, that $[S; t_1, t'] \in [\![\mathbf{do}(q)]\!]^x$. Then, since there is no occurrence of q in $[S; t, t_1]$, we have $[S; t, t'] \in [\![\mathbf{do}(q)]\!]^x$. Thus $x\langle\mathbf{do}(q)\rangle_i p$ holds at t. □

It is important to note that $x\langle\!\langle Y \rangle\!\rangle p$ does not entail $x\langle\!\langle Y \rangle\!| p$, because x may not know how to follow strategy Y. For example, every action that leads to p may also occur on a scenario on which p never occurs. More surprisingly, $x\langle\!\langle Y \rangle\!| p$ does not entail $x\langle\!\langle Y \rangle\!\rangle p$. This is because, p might hold only on those scenarios on which the agent can force Y; it might not occur on other scenarios on which Y is (perhaps accidentally) performed. However, $x\langle\!\langle Y \rangle\!| p$ would imply $x\langle\!\langle Y \rangle\!\rangle p$ at those moments are considered from which either Y is not accidentally performed or its accidental performance does not lead to p. But, the agent may not have strategy Y anyway, i.e., $X * Y$ may be false, at even those moments.

In other words, we can show that intentions do not entail know-how, and know-how does not entail intentions. However, we do have the following positive result, which states that if (a) the agent can knowingly perform Y and (b) p holds at all moments at which Y is successfully performed, then the agent knows how to achieve p by performing Y.

Lemma 5.2 $\mathsf{A}(x\langle Y\rangle_i\mathsf{true}\rightarrow x\langle Y\rangle_i p) \wedge x[\![\langle Y\rangle]\!]\mathsf{true}$ entails $x[\![\langle Y\rangle]\!]p$

Proof. By SEM-48, $x[\![\langle Y\rangle]\!]\mathsf{true}$ means that x knows that he can force $\downarrow_t Y$ and at each resulting moment, $x[\![\langle\uparrow_t Y\rangle]\!]\mathsf{true}$ holds. By finitariness, this bottoms out after a finite number of recursive applications of SEM-48. Let t' be a moment at which that happens. Let $S \in \mathbf{S}_t$ be the scenario to which t' belongs. Then $M \models_{S,t} x\langle Y\rangle_i p$ holds. That is, p holds on t'. This is the case for all such moments t'. Therefore, $x[\![\langle Y\rangle]\!]p$ holds at t. $\square$

Note that $\mathsf{A}(x\langle Y\rangle_i\mathsf{true}\rightarrow x\langle Y\rangle_i p)$ is stronger than $x\langle\!\langle Y\rangle\!\rangle p$, which was defined as $\mathsf{A}(x\langle Y\rangle_i\mathsf{true}\rightarrow \mathsf{F}p)$ in Chapter 3.

5.2 Success at Last

The definition of know-how ensures that, if an agent knows how to achieve some condition, then on all scenarios on which he exercises his know-how, he will succeed in achieving the given condition. It might seem that nothing more remains to be said. However, many of our intuitions are about what conditions agents, in fact, bring about by performing their actions. The notion of "in fact" is captured in the model by the component $\mathbf{R}$, which determines the real scenario at each moment.

Agents, at least those who are sufficiently rational, perform actions in order to achieve their intentions. We thus need to consider the actions an agent performs in trying to follow his strategy, since it is his strategy that determines his intentions at a given moment. This is intuitively quite natural: for an agent to succeed, he must have intentions that are commensurate with his know-how and must act so as to exercise his know-how. For example, an agent who intends to cross a river by swimming across it cannot be guaranteed to succeed if he walks away from the bank, i.e., if he does not act on his intention. He would also not be guaranteed to succeed in swimming across the river if the only way he knows how to cross the river is by walking across a bridge, i.e., if he lacks the know-how to swim across the river.

An agent's actual choices depend both on his beliefs and his strategies (which determine his intentions). For this reason, it is useful to define the notion of a strategy causing an action to be selected. A strategy of the form do(q) *selects* an action if the agent knows that he can perform that action starting at the given moment and that on all scenarios on which that action is performed, either (a) the strategy will be successfully completed, or (b) he will know how to achieve it. In other words, a strategy selects an action if that action is the radix of a tree by following which the agent knows how to achieve the given strategy. I extend the notation of Chapter 4 so that $x[Y]a$ is also interpreted to mean that strategy Y selects action a for agent x. Formally,

SYN-30. $p \in \mathcal{L}_s^c$, $Y \in \mathcal{L}_y^c$, $a \in \mathcal{B}$, and $x \in \mathcal{A}$ implies that $(x[Y]a) \in \mathcal{L}^c$

I now give the semantic definition of $x[Y]a$ in two parts.

SEM-51. $M \models_t x[\mathbf{do}(q)]a$ iff $(\exists S, t', \tau_1, \ldots, \tau_m : [S; t, t'] \in \{\!\{(a; \tau_1, \ldots, \tau_m)\}\!\}_{\mathbf{do}(q)}^x)$ and $M \models_t \neg q$

SEM-52. $M \models_t x[Y]a$ iff $\downarrow_t Y \neq \mathbf{skip}$ and $M \models_t x[\downarrow_t Y]a$

Since the above are all the cases in the definition of $x[Y]a$, an obvious consequence is that $M \not\models_t x[\mathbf{skip}]a$. This is only reasonable: the strategy **skip** does not call upon the agent to perform any actions at all. Indeed, actions may cause spurious changes in the state potentially affecting the executability of the strategy the agent might adopt next. The above definition is well-formed since, when $Y = \mathbf{do}(q)$, $Y = \downarrow_t Y$. This is the only possibility in which both cases apply.

By the definition of $\{\!\{\ \}\!\}$, $x[\mathbf{do}(q)]a$ entails that a is doable on some scenario at the given moment. More importantly, a is selected by an agent's strategy only if the agent knows that it is an available and safe choice for achieving the given strategy. In other words, a is selected only if the agent knows that for any outcome of performing a, he will know how to achieve q, i.e., to select his next action, and so on.

We now have the requisite definitions in place to formally state that an agent will in fact perform an action that has been selected by his strategy. This, I-CONS-12, is the action selection constraint that was promised in constraint I-CONS-4 of section 3.3. Constraint I-CONS-12 states that if an agent has a strategy and some action is selected by that strategy, then the agent performs one of the actions selected by that strategy. The fact that some action is selected by a strategy means that the agent has the requisite know-how. Of course, a strategy may select more than one action: there may be several ways to achieve a given strategy. Therefore, all that is required is that the agent perform *one* of the selected actions.

I-Cons-12. **Selecting a sure action:**

$$(x * Y \wedge (\bigvee a : x[Y]a)) \rightarrow (\bigvee a : x[Y]a \wedge Rx\langle a\rangle \text{true})$$

The above constraint is stronger than the one Newell calls the "principle of rationality" [1982, p. 102]. That principle merely requires that an agent select an action that he knows will lead to one of his goals; constraint I-Cons-12, by contrast, requires that an agent select an action only when he can force the success of his strategy by performing that action. I shall assume that this constraint applies throughout the following discussion. In conjunction with the persistence condition formalized in constraint I-Cons-5 of section 3.3, this leads to the following immediate consequences. The first is Lemma 5.3, which states that if an agent has a strategy and knows how to follow it, then he, in fact, succeeds in forcing the $\downarrow$ part of it to be executed. The second consequence is Lemma 5.4, which states that, if an agent has a strategy and knows how to follow it, then he eventually follows the $\downarrow$ part of it and, on doing so, adopts as his strategy the $\uparrow$ of his original strategy.

Lemma 5.3 $(x * Y \wedge x\langle\!\langle Y\rangle\!\rangle\text{true} \wedge x[Y]\text{do}(q)) \rightarrow R\langle\text{do}(q)\rangle_h\text{true}$

Proof. Using the definitions of $\langle\!\langle\rangle\!\rangle$ and $\lfloor\rfloor$, we can infer $x\langle\!\langle\text{do}(q)\rangle\!\rangle\text{true}$ from $x\langle\!\langle Y\rangle\!\rangle\text{true} \wedge x[Y]\text{do}(q)$. And, $x\langle\!\langle\text{do}(q)\rangle\!\rangle\text{true}$ entails that either q holds or it is the case that $(\bigvee a : x[\text{do}(q)]a \wedge A[a]x\langle\!\langle\text{do}(q)\rangle\!\rangle\text{true})$. By the definition of $\lfloor\rfloor$, q cannot hold at the given moment. Therefore, by I-Cons-12, one of the actions, a, such that $x[\text{do}(q)]a \wedge A[a]x\langle\!\langle\text{do}(q)\rangle\!\rangle\text{true}$, occurs on the real scenario. Since $x\langle\!\langle\text{do}(q)\rangle\!\rangle\text{true}$ holds iff there exists a tree with the appropriate properties, we can induce on the structure of trees to obtain the desired result. $\square$

Lemma 5.4 $(x * Y \wedge x\langle\!\langle Y\rangle\!\rangle\text{true} \wedge x[Y]\text{do}(q)) \rightarrow R\langle\text{do}(q)\rangle_i(x * \uparrow_t Y)$

Proof. By Lemma 5.3, we have $R\langle\text{do}(q)\rangle_h\text{true}$, which by Lemma 5.1 entails $R\langle\text{do}(q)\rangle_i\text{true}$. From $x[Y]\text{do}(q)$, we can infer that $\downarrow_t Y \neq \text{skip}$ (in fact, $\downarrow_t Y = \text{do}(q)$). Therefore, constraint I-Cons-5 of section 3.3 applies and we obtain $R[\downarrow_t Y]_i(x * \uparrow_t Y)$, which is the same as $R[\text{do}(q)]_i(x * \uparrow_t Y)$. In the presence of $R\langle\text{do}(q)\rangle_i\text{true}$, this yields the desired result. $\square$

Lemma 5.5 $(x * Y \wedge x\langle\!\langle Y\rangle\!\rangle\text{true}) \rightarrow R\langle Y\rangle_i\text{true}$

Proof. Consider a moment t at which the antecedent holds. If $\downarrow_t Y = \text{skip}$, then $R\langle\downarrow_t Y\rangle_i\text{true}$ holds vacuously. If $\downarrow_t Y = \text{do}(q)$, then $x[Y]\text{do}(q)$ holds because of the semantic definition of $x\langle\!\langle Y\rangle\!\rangle\text{true}$ (Sem-48). Hence, $R\langle\downarrow_t Y\rangle_h\text{true}$ holds by Lemma 5.3, which by Lemma 5.1 entails $R\langle\downarrow_t Y\rangle_i\text{true}$.

By Lemma 5.4, $R\langle\downarrow_t Y\rangle_i(x * \uparrow_t Y)$. Also, by the definition of $x\langle\!\langle Y\rangle\!\rangle$true (i.e., SEM-48), we obtain that $R\langle\downarrow_t Y\rangle_i x\langle\!\langle\uparrow_t Y\rangle\!\rangle$true. Thus, we can apply mathematical induction on the depth of strategies. The depth of a strategy is defined, as before, as the number of recursive applications of $\langle\!\langle\ \rangle\!\rangle$ needed to evaluate $\langle\!\langle Y\rangle\!\rangle$. The strategy $\uparrow_t Y$ has a smaller depth than Y. The base cases of **skip** and **do**(q) were considered above. Therefore, by induction, we have $R\langle\downarrow_t Y\rangle_i$true. Using Lemma 3.5, we obtain the desired result. $\square$

Theorem 5.6 $(x * Y \wedge x\langle\!\langle Y\rangle\!\rangle p \wedge x\langle\!\langle Y\rangle\!\rangle\text{true}) \rightarrow \mathsf{RF}p$

Proof. From the antecedent of this claim and Lemma 5.5, we conclude that $R\langle Y\rangle_i$true holds. By the semantic definition of $x\langle\!\langle Y\rangle\!\rangle p$, we obtain $\mathsf{RF}p$. $\square$

Clearly, several actions may be selected by a given strategy: these are all the actions that are radices of trees with which that strategy may be achieved. All the actions that may be selected by the assigned strategy are treated on par. Thus only those conditions can be considered as forced by a given strategy that occur on all scenarios on which any of the selected actions is performed.

Constraint I-Cons-12 states that if an agent's strategy selects one or more actions, then he performs one such selected action. An important consequence of this is that if an agent knows how to execute his current strategy, then he performs some action to execute it. This prevents the kind of inaction that arises in Buridan's famous example. That example is of a donkey who cannot choose between two equally accessible and equally tempting bales of hay and thus starves to death. Assuming that only the actions of stepping towards one of the bales are selected by the donkey's strategy of obtaining food, constraint I-Cons-12 requires the donkey to choose one bale or the other.

5.3   Normal Models

The above definitions involve all possible scenarios. In particular, for an agent to know how to achieve p, he must have an action that limits the possible scenarios to those in which, perhaps by further actions, he can actually achieve p. Unfortunately, this may be too strong a requirement in real-life, because no action can be guaranteed to succeed. For example, I know how to drive to work, but can actually do so only if my car does not break down, and the bridge I drive over does not collapse, and so on. That is, there is a scenario over which the required condition will not occur. Thus success ought to be required, but only under *normal* conditions.

One way to improve the above definition is by only considering normal models. Explicit reasoning about whether a given model is normal, i.e., whether an agent has the ability to achieve some condition, however, involves nothing less than a solution to the qualification and ramification problems of McCarthy & Hayes [1969]. This is because to infer whether an agent has some ability, we would have to reason about when different basic actions would be doable by him (this is the qualification problem), and what effects they would have if done in a given state (this is the ramification problem). This issue is not addressed here.

This point was discussed in section 1.2 in relation to the distinction between model construction and usage. The definitions given here assume that a reasonable model has been constructed; nonmonotonic reasoning must be used when model construction itself is considered.

5.4 Other Theories of Ability and Know-How

I now briefly review the other formal theories of ability and know-how. I discuss them here rather than in Chapter 4, since it important to compare them with the results of this chapter, as well as those of Chapter 4.

Oddie & Tichy have proposed a nice theory of ability, which I became aware of only during the last stages of completing this manuscript [Oddie & Tichy, 1981; Tichy & Oddie, 1983]. Oddie & Tichy share many of the intuitions of the present approach, though their ultimate goal is to explicate the notions of ability and opportunity as those notions may be used in characterizing freedom and responsibility. They agree with the present approach in postulating branching models to capture the different choices that agents may make. They also agree in considering different possible consequences of an agent's actions in determining whether he has the ability to force something [1983, p. 135].

Oddie & Tichy consider strategies as in classical game theory. They define ability using strategies. They formally define strategies as *trees*, which for them are fragments of the model that include some possible futures [1983, p. 139]. Their trees are thus different from the trees of the present approach. However, their trees resemble, to some extent, the notions of ability-intension and know-how-intension, which were defined here. The key difference is that Oddie & Tichy's agents may not be able to ensure that the world evolves along one of the branches of their trees; by contrast, the definitions of ability-intension and know-how-intension are such that agents can always ensure that the world evolves according to one of their member periods.

After developing a logic of opportunity, which I shall not discuss, Oddie & Tichy define the concept of ability. I simplify their definitions slightly for ease of exposition. A *steadfast* intention is one that the agent will persist with until he succeeds. An agent is able to achieve A if there is a strategy that ensures A and which the agent *commands* with respect to A [1981, p. 243]. An agent commands a strategy with respect to a condition A if a steadfast intention on part of the agent to achieve A is sufficient to *heed* that strategy (i.e., to successfully follow it).

Thus, Oddie & Tichy's technical definition of ability is quite different from the one given above. They define ability in terms of intentions. However, intentions themselves are not formally defined. Constraints between intentions and actions or ability and actions are not stated in their theory. Paradigmatic examples of such constraints are (a) that agents act according to their intentions and (b) that they may exercise their abilities under certain circumstances. Indeed, if such constraints were stated directly, as they are in the present approach, there would be no need to define ability in terms of intentions. Despite these differences, Oddie & Tichy are able to prove a version of the success theorem, which states that ability conjoined with a steadfast intention implies performance [1983, p. 145]. Of course, this theorem would hold in general only in the presence of constraints such as the ones discussed in this chapter.

A theory of ability has also been proposed by Werner [1991]. Some other aspects of that paper were discussed in section 3.5. Werner assigns information states, I, to agents. He defines Alt(I) as the alternatives or choices available to an agent with information I (p. 112). These are the actions that the agent may perform. This assignment seems counterintuitive in that one would expect the choices available to an agent to be independent of the information he has. Of course, how the agent actually exercises those choices would depend on his information. But that process would also depend on the agent's intentions at that time. Werner defines the intentional state of an agent, but only uses the agent's information state in determining the agent's choices: either both should be considered (to capture the options an agent is focusing on), or neither (to capture all physical options).

Strategies are defined as in game theory. A strategy, δ, is a function from information states to choices (p. 113). $\delta(I) \subseteq$ Alt(I). That is, the choices picked by a strategy are the ones available given the agent's information state. Ability is defined as follows: an agent *can* achieve p iff he has a strategy for p. A strategy is for p iff p is realized in all histories compatible with that strategy. The distinction between past, present, and future is never clearly delineated.

Thus agents may have the ability to achieve past conditions, just as well as future conditions. This seems problematic for any useful notion of ability.

Actions and time are not a part of Werner's formal language. Few logical inferences are given and there is no axiomatization. The only logical property of his definition of ability that Werner notes is the obvious claim that it lies somewhere between necessity and possibility (p. 114).

Independently of, and prior to, the present approach, Segerberg proposed a logic of achievements in the framework of dynamic logic [Segerberg, 1989]. Thus, in spirit, his work is similar to the theory developed here. He defines an operator δ, which takes a condition and converts it into an action, namely, the action of bringing about that condition. This is intuitively quite close to strategies of the form, $do(q)$, as defined here. Segerberg uses actions of the form δq as the primitive actions in his variant of dynamic logic. This too is similar to the present approach: the only difference is that I have considered a deterministic version of dynamic logic.

However, there are some important dissimilarities. Segerberg gives the semantics of actions of the form δq in terms of all paths (i.e., computations) that result from any program α, such that α terminates only in states where q holds (p. 328). In the present approach, the corresponding notion is that of ability-intensions, which also end with an occurrence of the relevant condition. But there are two major differences. First, ability-intensions require that the given agent be able to *force* the relevant condition. Fortuitous occurrences of the condition and the paths over which they occur are simply eliminated from ability-intensions. Indeed, Segerberg's semantics seems to agree more with the definition of [] for strategies that was used to give a semantics of intentions in Chapter 3. Segerberg does not define intentions in his paper, but it is not clear how he would separate the concept of intentions from the concepts of ability and know-how. It is obvious, however, that we should not require that intentions entail ability or know-how.

Second, Segerberg does not consider the knowledge of agents. Thus the effects of agents' knowledge on their choices cannot be considered. Such choices arise in Segerberg's logic as tests on conditions and in the present approach in conditional and iterative strategies. Third, ability-intensions end at the first occurrence of the relevant condition, not an arbitrary one: this is important in considering executions of abstract strategies and in relating know-how with intentions, because it tells us just how far the current substrategy of a strategy will be executed before the rest of it kicks in. This is crucial for unambiguous definitions in the present approach.

Cohen & Levesque's success theorem [1990, p. 233] is one of the counterintuitive consequences of their theory. It allows an agent to succeed with an intention merely through persistence. The agent simply has to be able to correctly identify the intended condition; he does not need to know how to achieve it. Clearly, this requirement is not sufficient: one can come up with several natural conditions that an agent may be able to identify, but would not be able to achieve. A similar, and equally unsatisfactory, result is proved by Rao & Georgeff [1991a, section 4].

Both the abovementioned theories require an additional assumption to prove their respective success theorems. This is the assumption that agents will eventually drop their goals or intentions. If the dropping of a goal or intention is conditioned on the agent's obtaining certain true knowledge, success can easily be guaranteed. However, this is backwards from our pretheoretic intuitions. Agents may drop their intentions eventually, but we cannot force external events to occur on the basis of this change in internal state. In the present approach, an agent may drop an intention at any time, but success is not guaranteed unless he applies his know-how. Assuming that an agent will drop an intention upon success, it can be shown that an agent who meets the conditions of Theorem 5.6, will eventually drop his intention. Thus, under appropriate circumstances, a primitive assumption of the abovementioned theories becomes a consequence of the present approach.

I have shown how to formalize intentions and know-how and to combine them to characterize the behavior of an intelligent agent. However, the main goal of this monograph is to apply these abstractions to multiagent systems. This can be achieved in at least two ways. The agents' intentions, knowledge, and know-how can be used to succinctly describe their expected behavior and constrain it to capture various system properties. For instance, restrictions on how an agent may revise his intentions would be in this category. They can go a long way in specifying the behavior of an agent who is rational enough to act on his intentions. Similarly, constraints may be stated among the intentions, knowledge, and know-how of different agents in a multiagent system. This can, of course, be done directly in our formal language.

However, an extremely important class of interactions among agents pertains specifically to communications among them. The next chapter discusses how to formalize communications in a manner that focuses on their content, and not their form. It also provides a semantics for communications using intentions and know-how and shows how communication protocols can be specified in our approach.

Chapter 6

Communications

Communication among agents in multiagent systems may be fruitfully studied from the point of view of speech act theory. In order for multiagent systems to be formally and rigorously designed and analyzed, a semantics of speech acts that gives their objective model-theoretic conditions of satisfaction is needed. However, most research into multiagent systems that deals with communication provides only informal descriptions of the different message types used. And this problem is not addressed at all by traditional speech act theory or by research into discourse understanding. I provide a formal semantics for the major kinds of speech acts using the definitions of intentions and know-how that were developed in previous chapters. This connection to other theories is reason to be reassured that this theory is not *ad hoc*, and will coherently fit in a bigger picture. The resulting theory applies uniformly to a wide range of multiagent systems. Some applications of this theory are outlined and it is used to analyze the contract net protocol.

6.1 Protocols Among Agents

The behavior of a multiagent system depends not just on its component agents, but also on how they interact. Therefore, in a multiagent system of sufficient complexity, each agent would not only need to be able to do the tasks that arise locally, but would also need to interact effectively with other agents. I take *protocols* to be the specifications of these interactions. Protocols, when seen in this way, are a nice way of enforcing modularity in the design of a multiagent system. They help in separating the interface between agents from their internal design. These protocols are meant to be rather high-level; in the classical seven-layer ISO/OSI framework, they would lie in the application layer. Some of these protocols may, in practice, precede "real" applications-level communication by facilitating the setting up of another protocol. This distinction is not crucial for our purposes.

A formal theory of the kinds of communication that may take place among agents is crucial to the design and analysis of complex multiagent systems. Unfortunately, no theory is currently available that provides the *objective semantics* of the messages exchanged. I propose to develop such a theory by building on work in speech act theory. Before getting to the technical details, I briefly describe what speech act theory is and how it may be applied to multiagent systems.

6.1.1   Speech Act Theory

Speech Act Theory deals primarily with natural language utterances. Initially, it was developed to deal with utterances, e.g., "I declare you man and wife," that are not easily classified as being true or false, but rather are actions themselves. Later it was extended to deal with all utterances, with the primary understanding that all utterances are *actions* of some sort or the other [Austin, 1962; Bach & Harnish, 1979; Searle, 1969]. A speech act is associated with at least three distinct actions:

1. a *locution*, or the corresponding physical utterance,

2. an *illocution*, or the conveying of the speaker's intent to the hearer, and

3. any number of *perlocutions*, or actions that occur as a result of the illocution.

For example, "shut the door" is a locution, which might be the illocution of a command to shut the door, and might lead to the perlocution of the listener getting up to shut the door. All locutions do not also count as illocutions, since some of them may occur in an inappropriate state of the world, e.g., when no receiver is available. At the same time, all perlocutions are not caused by appropriate illocutions, since some of them may occur because of other contextual features. For this reason, a speech act *per se* is usually identified with its associated illocution [Searle, 1969]. I adopt this practice in this chapter.

A speech act is usually seen to have two parts: an *illocutionary force* and a *proposition* [Searle, 1969]. The illocutionary force distinguishes, e.g., a command from a promise; the proposition describes the state of the world that is, respectively, commanded or promised. The propositional part of an

Force	Example
Assertive	The door is shut
Directive	Shut the door
Commissive	I will shut the door
Permissive	You may shut the door
Prohibitive	You may not shut the door
Declarative	I name this door the Golden Gate

Table 6.1: Classification of Speech Acts

illocution specifies the state of the world that it is, in some sense, about. For example, an assertive asserts of that state that it holds currently (though the proposition could be temporal); a directive asks the hearer to bring that state about; a commissive commits the speaker to bringing it about, and so on. Paradigmatic examples of speech acts of different illocutionary forces are given in Table 6.1. The satisfaction of a speech act depends both on its illocutionary force and on its proposition.

The classification of speech acts given above is necessarily coarse. Speech acts of varying strengths, and of differing pragmatic effects are lumped together here. For example, assertives include statements, tellings, claims, and so on; and, directives include commands, entreaties, requests, advice, and so on. This should not be taken to mean that the proposed theory cannot accommodate different kinds of speech acts, or that it cannot capture the distinctions between, e.g., requests and commands. It just means that the distinctions between them are not seen to be *semantic*. The conditions of satisfaction of different speech acts in the same class are identical. Their differences lie in pragmatic factors, e.g., relative social stature of the agents involved and matters of cultural convention. For example, a command can be successfully issued only to subordinates; however, one can request almost anyone. Further constraints on when requests and commands are issued and satisfied may be stated that capture their non-semantic aspects properly.

6.1.2 Speech Act Theory in Multiagent Systems

There are two kinds of applications of Speech Act Theory in multiagent systems. The first, and by far the more common one, uses it to motivate different *message types* for interactions among agents. The idea is that since agents can perform different kinds of speech acts, the language used for communication must allow different types of messages [Chang, 1991; Thomas *et al.*, 1990]. This is quite standard, and something I shall do myself. However, the traditional proposals are informal: even when they are part of a formal theory, e.g., [Thomas *et al.*, 1990], they rely on one's understanding of the labels used to assign meanings to the different message types. The true meanings are embedded in the procedures that manipulate messages of different types.

The second kind of application of Speech Act Theory involves approaches, which treat illocutions as linguistic actions and aim to describe the interactions of agents in terms of what they say to each other. They attempt to generalize linguistic theories designed for human communication to artificial systems [Cohen & Levesque, 1988b]. These theories suffer from being based on traditional formalizations of speech acts [Allen & Perrault, 1980]. Such formalizations are primarily concerned with identifying different kinds of illocutions. Thus these theories give the conditions under which saying "can you pass the salt?" is not a question, but rather a request; it is then an *indirect* speech act [Grice, 1969; Searle, 1975]. An example of a condition for requests might be that the speaker and hearer mutually believe that the speaker has certain intentions and beliefs. The phenomenon of indirect speech acts is, no doubt, of great importance in understanding natural language. But it is of no use in an artificial system other than for interaction with humans: multiagent systems can function quite well with just an artificial language that can be simply designed to be free of the ambiguities that these theories have been created to detect.

At least as a first approximation, we can assume that the illocutionary force of a message transmitted be just the one that is obvious from its syntax. Thus the interesting part of the semantics of speech acts, as they may be applied in multiagent systems, concerns what they cause to be done rather than whether they are interpreted to be of one kind or another.

6.1.3 The Need for a Semantics

The formalization undertaken here concerns the objective conditions of satisfaction for different kinds of messages. Not only is this useful from the point of view of design, it also helps clarify our intuitions about the process of deliberation, since ideally the agents should act so as to "satisfy" some appropriate subset of the messages communicated in their system. The main original contributions of this chapter are described by the postulates given below.

- There is a level of formal semantics of speech acts that is distinct from both (a) what is traditionally considered their semantics, namely, the conditions under which they may be said to have occurred, and (b) their pragmatics, namely, the effects they may or ought to have on the speaker's and hearer's cognitive states. That is, the proposed semantics differs from both the illocutionary and the perlocutionary aspects of speech acts.

- The semantics of speech acts roughly corresponds to the conditions under which we would affirm that the given speech act had been satisfied.

- This semantics can be captured in the usual model-theoretic framework by introducing an operator that distinguishes the satisfaction of a speech act from its mere occurrence.

- The definitions be given in terms of the intentions and know-how of the participants and the state of the world (at some salient time or times).

The conditions of satisfaction for most kinds of speech acts differ significantly from those of assertives that are ordinarily considered in logic. Assertives, being claims of fact, are true or false; other speech acts call for a more complex notion of success. In the context of imperatives, Hamblin distinguishes between what he calls *extensional* and *whole-hearted* satisfaction [Hamblin, 1987, pp. 153–157]. Briefly, the former notion admits accidental success, while the latter does not. Hamblin's aim was simply to be able to state prescriptive conditions on when what kind of imperatives ought to be issued, and the philosophical problems that arise when one is in a "quandary." That is, his focus was pragmatic. I take advantage of some of his ideas, but make a finer distinction and extend it to other important kinds of speech acts here, formally relating them to intentions and know-how in the process.

In section 6.2, I formalize the notion of satisfaction that I argue is appropriate for multiagent systems. In section 6.3, I show how this framework may be used in the design of multiagent systems by using it to state constraints on communication and to formalize the contract net protocol.

6.2 Formal Model and Language

6.2.1 Speech Acts as Actions

Speech acts are, first of all, actions. I take them to be the actions of their speakers, and as occurring over periods (the same as actions in general). The reader may think of the receiver as listening over a part of the period during which the sender is speaking. This is not used in the formalization, however.

Let **says-to** be a parametrized speech act, to be used as in **says-to**(y, m). $[S; t_b, t_e] \in [\![$**says-to**$(y, m)]\!]^x$ means that, on scenario S, agent x performed the speech act of saying m to agent y in the time from t_b (the moment of beginning) to t_e (the moment of ending). This means that the illocution was successfully made. There is no commitment at this stage as to whether it was satisfied or not. Recall that $[S; t, t']$ presupposes that $t \leq t'$.

The semantics of speech acts is captured in the theory of this chapter by means of a modal operator, **W**. It is convenient to have a special predicate in the language that allows us to talk of the performance of a speech act. This allows us to apply the modal operators to formulae that denote propositions, rather than to those that denote actions. Besides allowing us to follow the usual way of defining a modal operator, the definition of **comm** also allows speech acts to be nested as in "I tell you that he pleaded guilty."

Let the new predicate be **comm** that applies to two agents, and an illocution. Since actions take place over scenarios, it is most convenient to evaluate **comm**(x, y, m) at scenarios and moments. **comm**(x, y, m) is true at S, t just if y said (or started to say) m to x then. A performed illocution may, of course, not be satisfiable. For example, some commands may be issued that are impossible to obey. The operator **W**, then, applies on formulae of the form **comm**(x, y, m). It denotes the whole-hearted satisfaction of the given speech act.

Whole-Hearted satisfaction is defined relative to a scenario and a moment. A performative is taken to be in force as soon as it is completed (and not sooner). This is done to allow the possibility of a communication being aborted midway. That is, a speaker's failed attempts to say something, i.e., to get his point across, do not count as communications.

6.2.2 Formal Language

The formal language of this chapter, $\mathcal{L}^m$ is $\mathcal{L}^c$ augmented with the operator, **W**. In the following, $\mathcal{F} = \{$assertive, directive, commissive, permissive, prohibitive, declarative$\}$ is the set of illocutionary forces. $\mathcal{M}$ is the set of *messages* as defined below. The set of basic actions, $\mathcal{B}$, is extended with illocutionary actions, which are generated from the messages and are formally treated as the actions of the sending agent. The resulting set is called $\mathcal{B}^m$.

SYN-31. All the rules for $\mathcal{L}^c$ with $\mathcal{L}^m$ substituted for $\mathcal{L}^c$ and $\mathcal{B}^m$ substituted for $\mathcal{B}$

SYN-32. All the rules for $\mathcal{L}_s^c$ with $\mathcal{L}_s^m$ substituted for substituted for $\mathcal{L}_s^c$ and $\mathcal{B}^m$ substituted for $\mathcal{B}$

SYN-33. All the rules for $\mathcal{L}_y^c$ with $\mathcal{L}_y^m$ substituted for substituted for $\mathcal{L}_y^c$

SYN-34. $p \in \mathcal{L}_s^m$ implies that $\mathsf{W}p \in \mathcal{L}_s^m$

SYN-35. $p \in \mathcal{L}^m$ and $i \in \mathcal{F}$ implies that $\langle i, p \rangle \in \mathcal{M}$

SYN-36. $x, y \in \mathcal{A}$ and $m \in \mathcal{M}$ implies that $\mathbf{comm}(x, y, m) \in \mathcal{L}_s^m$

SYN-37. $x, y \in \mathcal{A}$ and $m \in \mathcal{M}$ implies that $\mathbf{says\text{-}to}(x, y, m) \in \mathcal{B}^m$

6.2.3 Whole-Hearted Satisfaction

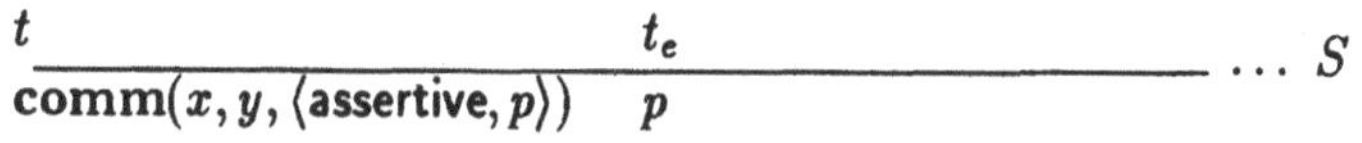

Figure 6.1: The Satisfaction Condition for Assertives

SEM-53. **Assertives:**

$M \models_{S,t} \mathsf{W}(\mathbf{comm}(x, y, \langle\text{assertive}, p\rangle))$ iff
$(\exists t_e : [S; t, t_e] \in [\![\mathbf{says\text{-}to}(x, y, \langle\text{assertive}, p\rangle)]\!]^x$ and $M \models_{S,t_e} p)$

An assertive is satisfied simply if its proposition is true at the moment the utterance is made. Thus the assertive, "The door is shut," is satisfied on all scenarios where the door is, in fact, shut. The satisfaction conditions for the other kinds of speech acts are more interesting than this.

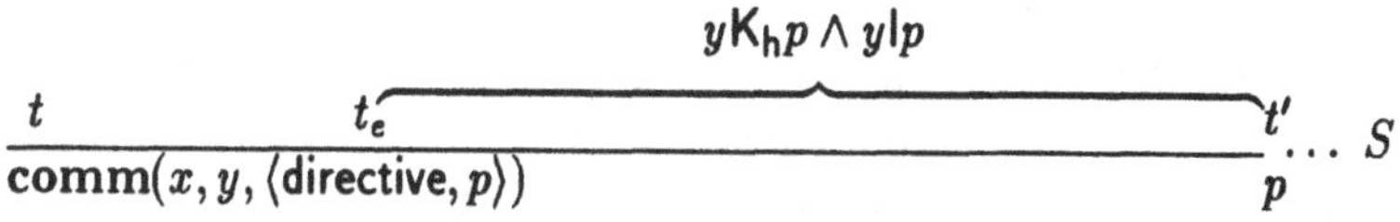

Figure 6.2: The Satisfaction Condition for Directives

SEM-54. **Directives:**

$M \models_{S,t} W(\text{comm}(x, y, \langle \text{directive}, p \rangle))$ iff
$(\exists t_e : [S; t, t_e] \in [\![\text{says-to}(x, y, \langle \text{directive}, p \rangle)]\!]^x$ and $M \models_{S,t_e} (y K_h p \wedge y | p) U p)$

A directive is satisfied just if (a) its proposition, p, becomes true at a moment in the future of its being said, and (b) all along the scenario from now to then, the hearer has the know-how, as well as the intention to achieve it. For example, a directive to open the door is satisfied if the door ends up open (within some salient period of time, perhaps), and furthermore the hearer continuously planned to open the door and was in a position to be able to execute the plan to open it. Note that this definition does not finally require that the door open because of the hearer's actions. This would not be an important requirement to impose in my view, and would only cause action-theoretic complications about the matter of when an agent can be said to have performed a certain action, especially when that action is not a single-step basic action.

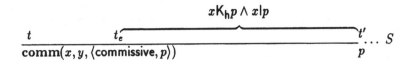

Figure 6.3: The Satisfaction Condition for Commissives

SEM-55. **Commissives:**

$M \models_{S,t} W(\text{comm}(x, y, \langle \text{commissive}, p \rangle))$ iff
$(\exists t_e : [S; t, t_e] \in [\![\text{says-to}(x, y, \langle \text{commissive}, p \rangle)]\!]^x$ and $M \models_{S,t_e} (x K_h p \wedge x | p) U p)$

Similarly, a commissive is satisfied just if (a) its proposition becomes true at a moment in the future of its being said, and (b) all along the scenario from now to then, the *speaker* has the know-how, as well as the intention to achieve it. Technically, a commissive is just like a directive except that the role of the hearer is taken over by the speaker. For example, the commissive, "I promise to shut the door," is satisfied on all scenarios on which the door eventually gets shut and until it does, the speaker intends and knows how to shut it.

A difference with directives that is of significance in some applications is that the satisfaction condition of a commissive depends on the actions, intentions, and know-how of just one agent. This can make the satisfaction of commissives easier to enforce in artificial systems. A related observation that is also interesting is that there seem to be fewer forms of commissives in natural languages than directives. This seems to be related to the fact that the satisfaction of directives involves actions by agents other than the speaker, and so different kinds of social considerations come into play. One may request or command or beseech or advise someone to do something, but one can just do it on one's own (though threats can express commitments conditional on the hearer's actions).

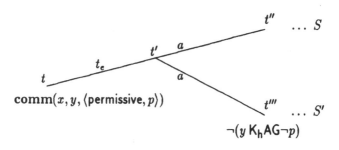

Figure 6.4: The Satisfaction Condition for Permissives

SEM-56. **Permissives:**

$M \models_{S,t} W(\mathrm{comm}(x, y, \langle \mathrm{permissive}, p \rangle))$ iff
$(\exists t_e : [S; t, t_e] \in [\![\mathbf{says\text{-}to}(x, y, \langle \mathrm{permissive}, p \rangle)]\!]^x$ and $(\exists t' : t_e \leq t'$ and $(\forall a : M \models_{S,t'} y \langle a \rangle \mathrm{true} \Rightarrow M \models_{t'} Ey \langle a \rangle \neg y K_h (AG \neg p))))$

A permissive is satisfied at a scenario and a moment just if it is taken advantage of by the hearer at a future moment on that scenario. But when a permissive is taken advantage of, it allows the hearer to do actions at certain times that he could not have done before, because they might possibly have led to the condition becoming true. Thus a permissive is satisfied on a scenario on which the hearer does at least one action whose performance can lead to a state where he is unable to prevent that condition from occurring. That is, the hearer can now risk letting that condition hold. For example, a permissive allowing a hearer to let the door be open is satisfied on a scenario, if (as a result of the given permissive, as it were), the hearer can, e.g., risk opening the window, even though the breeze may open the door. Without this permissive, the hearer would have to take some precaution, e.g., latch the door, before opening the window. The satisfaction of a permissive tends to increase the know-how of the hearer by giving him more options. Unfortunately, no closed-form characterization of this increase in know-how is available at present.

The notion of prevention is captured here using the previous definition of know-how: an agent, x, can prevent p iff he knows how to achieve $\mathsf{AG}\neg p$. This is perhaps too strong in that it requires the agent to arrive at a state where p becomes impossible on every scenario. An alternative definition would let p be possible on scenario, but ensure that is always avoidable through some action on part of the agent. However, the present definition has the advantage of permitting only a finite number of actions. I expect some variation in this component of the semantics depending on what notion of prevention is actually plugged in. The present version appears good enough, but may eventually need to be refined to use the more general notion of prevention where the agent continually prevents the given condition.

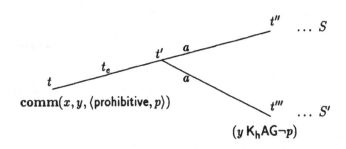

Figure 6.5: The Satisfaction Condition for Prohibitives

SEM-57. **Prohibitives:**

$M \models_{S,t} \mathsf{W}(\mathsf{comm}(x, y, \langle \text{prohibitive}, p \rangle))$ iff
$(\exists t_e : [S; t, t_e] \in [\mathsf{says\text{-}to}(x, y, \langle \text{prohibitive}, p \rangle)]^x$ and $(\forall t_e \leq t' : (\forall a : M \models_{S,t'} y\langle a \rangle \text{true} \Rightarrow M \models_{t'} \mathsf{A}y\langle a \rangle y\mathsf{K_h}(\mathsf{AG}\neg p))))$

A prohibitive is satisfied at a scenario and moment just if none of the actions done by the hearer on that scenario (in the future), can lead to a state where the hearer would be unable to prevent the condition from occurring. That is, the hearer cannot risk violating the prohibition. In other words, the hearer should always (on the given scenario) know how to prevent the prohibited condition and the prohibited condition should not occur on the given scenario. For example, a prohibitive to not let the door be open can be satisfied only if the hearer does not let the window be open, where the opening of the window may lead to the door being opened.

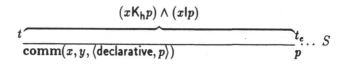

Figure 6.6: The Satisfaction Condition for Declaratives

SEM-58. **Declaratives:**

$M \models_{S,t} W(comm(x, y, \langle declarative, p \rangle))$ iff
$(\exists t_e : [S; t, t_e] \in [\![says\text{-}to(x, y, \langle declarative, p \rangle))]\!]^x$ and $M \models_{S,t_e} p$ and
$(\forall t' : t \leq t' < t_e \Rightarrow M \not\models_{S,t'} p)$ and $M \models_{S,t} (xK_hp \wedge xlp)Up)$

A declarative is satisfied just if (a) its proposition, p, becomes true for the first time at the moment that it is said, and (b) all along while the speaker is saying it, he intends that condition to occur and knows how to make it occur. For example, a declarative to name a certain door the Golden Gate is satisfied if the door ends up named thus, and the speaker intended it to be so named and knew how to name it. The door has its new name as soon as the declarative is completed. The condition about the know-how is included to ensure that, at each moment, the speaker is able to force the completion of the declarative and thereby force the occurrence of the appropriate condition. This helps eliminate cases where the speaker has the intention, but is not in the right social or conventional position to make the declarative succeed. In our example, the naming should succeed, but not because of some contingent features of the given scenario. According to some traditional theories, e.g., that of Vanderveken [1990], the occurrence of declaratives coincides with their success. This seems too weak since it allows a declarative to succeed even if the speaker did not have full control over its occurrence, i.e., even if the speaker could not have forced the given condition to occur.

6.2.4   Interrogatives

The theory as developed so far must be extended to account for interrogatives (and replies). This extension is needed so that this theory may be used for applications where agents interact by querying and replying to one another. What distinguishes interrogatives from other speech acts is the fact that their satisfaction necessarily requires the hearer to perform some speech act. In particular, questions are satisfied when their (true) answer is supplied by the hearer to the speaker.

In order for answers to be coherently defined, I need to extend the definition of the proposition contained in a message to allow for structures to which answers may be specified. The obvious extension is to allow lambda expressions. For a question of this form, the answer is naturally defined as the set of objects (of some sort or from some set) for which the lambda expression evaluates to true. For lambda expressions with more than one argument, the answer is the set of tuples over which it evaluates to true. This definition of an answer is not only a natural one in cases where knowledge-bases are used, but is also compatible with research about the semantics of natural language questions [Groenendijk & Stokhof, 1984].

Thus a question is interpreted in the semantics as if it were a directive to perform an assertive speech act (back to the speaker of the question) that provides the answer to the question. Therefore, a question is satisfied when a true answer to it is given, i.e., when the assertive containing the answer is itself satisfied. This derives from an intuition about treating interrogatives as imperatives of the form 'Tell me Truly' [Harrah, 1984, pp. 747–748]. Let a message be a pair, $\langle\text{interrogative},(\lambda\vec{a}p)\rangle$; since answers are assertives, we just need a new predicate $\text{answer}((\lambda\vec{a}p), \textbf{Ans})$, where $|\textbf{Ans}|$ is finite and $(\forall\vec{b} : (\vec{b} \in \textbf{Ans})\leftrightarrow (p|_{\vec{b}}^{\vec{a}}))$, i.e., **Ans** is the answer. The know-how to produce an answer that is required of the hearer would involve not just the physical capabilities needed to make an assertive utterance, but also the knowledge needed to compute the answer. Let r abbreviate $\text{W}(\textbf{comm}(y, x, \langle\textbf{assertive}, \text{answer}((\lambda\vec{a}p), \textbf{Ans})\rangle))$.

In order to capture this in the formal language, we need to introduce a set of constants, $\mathcal{D}$, and a set of predicates, $\mathcal{PRED}$. $\mathcal{L}_q^q$ denotes the set of query expressions. We have the following syntax, where $\mathcal{L}^q$ is the version of the formal language that includes interrogatives.

SYN-38.   All the rules for $\mathcal{L}^m$ with $\mathcal{L}^q$ substituted for $\mathcal{L}^m$

SYN-39.   All the rules for $\mathcal{L}_s^m$ with $\mathcal{L}_s^q$ substituted for $\mathcal{L}_s^q$

SYN-40. All the rules for $\mathcal{L}_y^m$ with $\mathcal{L}_y^q$ substituted for $\mathcal{L}_y^m$

SYN-41. $\vec{b} \in (\mathcal{D} \cup \mathcal{X})^n$ and $P \in \mathcal{PRED}$ implies that $P(\vec{b}) \in \mathcal{L}^q$

SYN-42. $u \in \mathcal{X}$ and $p \in \mathcal{L}^q$ implies that $(\exists u : p) \in \mathcal{L}^q$

SYN-43. $\vec{a} \in \mathcal{X}^n$, $p \in \mathcal{L}^q$ implies that $(\lambda \vec{a} : p) \in \mathcal{L}_q^q$

SYN-44. $p \in \mathcal{L}_q^q$ implies that $\langle \text{interrogative}, p \rangle \in \mathcal{M}$

SYN-45. $\langle \text{interrogative}, p \rangle \in \mathcal{M}$ and $\mathbf{Ans} \in \mathcal{D}^n$ implies that $\mathbf{answer}(p, \mathbf{Ans})$
$\in \mathcal{L}^q$

SEM-59. $M \models_{S,t} \mathsf{W}(\mathbf{comm}(x, y, \langle \text{interrogative}, (\lambda \vec{a} p) \rangle)))$ iff
$(\exists t_e : [S; t, t_e] \in [\![\mathbf{says\text{-}to}(x, y, \langle \text{interrogative}, (\lambda \vec{a} p) \rangle)]\!]^x$ and
$M \models_{S,t_e} (y \mathsf{K_h} r \wedge y \mathsf{I} r) \mathsf{U} r)$

This takes care of the so-called Wh-questions; Yes-no questions are analogous. A yes-no question for q is a directive to truthfully assert q or $\neg q$. The details are not included here. In some applications, it is useful to allow questions whose answers are commissives (e.g., when the question is a call for a bid section 6.3) or directives (e.g., when the question is a call for advice). The above definitions can also be extended to allow for questions whose answers are given in a piecemeal manner; e.g., as by Prolog interpreters. This would also allow the answers to be evaluated lazily.

6.3 Applying the Theory

The two main motivations for developing the above theory were to provide a rigorous foundation for the design of multiagent systems and to justify some prescriptive claims about how agents should communicate in such systems. The proposed definitions give objective criteria with which to evaluate the correctness of the different scenarios that are the possible runs or executions of a multiagent system. In design, the problem is to create a system which allows only correct scenarios to be realized. Prescriptive claims for agents tell them what to do given their beliefs and intentions, so that only correct scenarios may emerge.

The definition of W can be used to motivate some correctness conditions for multiagent systems. A scenario may be defined to be correct if all the messages passed on it are satisfied. In general terms, the designer's goal is to ensure that all runs that may be realized are correct. This reduces to the design goal that the intentions and know-how of the agents be such that only correct scenarios are realized. This is the sense of correctness that designers use in practice. They usually achieve this kind of correctness by a number of means, e.g., hard-wiring the intention to cooperate in their agents, or by setting up appropriate hierarchical structures. These structures may ensure different patterns of interaction, e.g., that some directives (commands) are always obeyed, and others (requests) obeyed whenever they do not conflict with the hearer's current intentions.

6.3.1   Normative Constraints on Communication

The ways in which a semantics of speech acts, such as the one developed here, may be applied in multiagent systems are perhaps obvious. A semantics can lead to a clearer understanding of the issues involved in the functioning of multiagent systems and can be used in both their design and analysis. The formal model it supplies can be used to verify that a given design has the desired properties. When a given system does not work as expected, this may be traced to a failure in whole-heartedly satisfying some message that should have been so satisfied. A designer may constrain his designs so that they allow only correct scenarios to be followed. Thus the agents must act so that all messages exchanged in certain conditions be satisfied as time passes. For example, in cooperative systems all requests that are "reasonable" (in an appropriate sense, given the system at hand) ought to be acceded to. Similarly, all assertions ought to be true and all promises ought to be kept.

There are two ways that a designer might go about enforcing these constraints on the design. One is to increase the capabilities of the agents appropriately, e.g., to increase the know-how of the agents involved so that directives are more easily satisfied, to improve their perceptual and reasoning abilities so that their assertives may be true, or to limit what they may intend in different conditions so that their directives and commissives are achievable. The other approach is to treat messages, e.g., commissives, as setting up commitments that are later enforced, and limiting directives so that they occur only when a corresponding commitment has been made.

Once these design decisions have been made, they can be stated declaratively in our formal language. One can then use standard methods in creating or testing designs of distributed intelligent systems. Such methods, which have already been developed for standard temporal logics include checking the satisfiability of sets of formulae (for us, constraints on the design) and for checking whether a given design satisfies a set of constraints (this is called *model checking*). These methods are described in [Emerson, 1990, pp. 1058–

1063] and [Burch *et al.*, 1990]. For the particular logic developed here, such automated methods are not yet available.

It should be clarified that the propositions used in the messages are descriptions of conditions of the world, or of the agents' internal states. That is, they include information about the objects and agents that they involve. The exact predicates and objects involved depend on the domain on which this theory is being applied. For example, the proposition "in(elevator, John)" differs from "in(elevator, Bill)." Thus there is no logical contradiction in Bill's not intending that John ride the elevator, while at the same time intending to ride it himself. In fact, if the elevator can hold only one of them, this might be quite reasonable from Bill's point of view. The propositions are evaluated at moments in the model, and may have different truth values at different such moments. The time of reference (e.g., "6:00 pm") could be specified as part of a proposition, though this is not attempted here.

Another important point is that constraints as stated involve objective conditions, rather than the beliefs of the agents. Of course, some of those objective conditions could be about the beliefs of agent; that is, both p and $x\mathsf{B}p$ may be specified, but they are distinct propositions. This is simply because of the normative force of these constraints. For the agents to act appropriately, they would also need to have the relevant beliefs at the relevant moments. This too is something that the designer must ensure, if the designed system is to function as desired.

I now give some examples of formalizations of design constraints. It is by no means suggested that all these constraints make sense in all applications: they are stated below only to exhibit the power of the theory. In the next section, I discuss an extended example that shows how constraints such as these may be used in multiagent systems.

Comm-1. **Intending One's Directives:**

> The proposition of a directive should be intended by its issuer. For example, if an agent requests another agent to raise a certain voltage (in a system they are jointly controlling), this constraint would require that the first agent should intend that the said voltage be raised.
>
> $\mathrm{comm}(x, y, \langle \mathrm{directive}, p \rangle) \rightarrow x\mathsf{I}p$

Comm-2. **Preference for Local Action:**

> If an agent knows how to achieve a proposition by himself, he should not issue it as a directive. For example, an agent who needs to

raise the voltage on a part of a power network he jointly controls with another agent should do so by himself, rather than request the other agent to do so. This constraint is especially useful when communication is expensive or introduces substantial delays.

$$x\mathsf{K_h}p \rightarrow \neg\text{comm}(x, y, \langle\text{directive}, p\rangle)$$

COMM-3. **Load-Dependent Preference for Local Action:**

In practice, constraint COMM-2 would have to be limited to apply not just when the given agent knows how to achieve the required condition, but knows how to do it, even if he carries out the actions that he has to do to fulfill other commitments. Thus an agent may request another agent to do a task that he would have done himself, had he not been swamped with other tasks.

$$x * Y \wedge x[\![Y]\!]p \Rightarrow \neg\text{comm}(x, y, \langle\text{directive}, p\rangle)$$

In other words, if an agent has a strategy by following which he knows how to achieve p, then he does not request another agent to achieve p. This is because, unless he gives up his strategy, he will in fact succeed in achieving p. This is a consequence of Theorem 5.6.

COMM-4. **Weak Consistency for Directives:**

A directive issued by an agent should not clash with the agent's own intentions. That is, a speaker's intentions and his directives should be compatible, at least in some scenarios. For example, if an agent intends that the voltage V_1 decrease, then he should not even request another agent to raise voltage V_2, if raising voltage V_2 would necessarily raise V_1 as well. This constraint differs significantly from constraint COMM-1. Constraint COMM-1 says that the issuer intends the given directive; this constraint says that all of the issuer's intentions are consistent with the directive.

$$x\mathsf{I}q \wedge \text{comm}(x, y, \langle\text{directive}, p\rangle) \rightarrow$$
$$\mathsf{E}(\mathsf{W}\text{comm}(x, y, \langle\text{directive}, p\rangle) \wedge \mathsf{F}q)$$

COMM-5. **No Loss of Know-How for Issuers of Directives:**

A directive issued by an agent should not clash with the issuer's own intentions and its satisfaction should not reduce the issuer's ability to achieve his intentions. That is, on all scenarios on which the directive is satisfied, the speaker should eventually know how to achieve his intentions. In fact, the formalization given below allows the know-how of the issuer to have increased as a result of the satisfaction of the issued directive. For example, if an agent intends that the voltage, V_1, decrease and requests another agent to raise voltage V_2, then on all scenarios on which this request is whole-heartedly satisfied, the issuer would eventually be able to lower voltage V_1. This could either be because the agent already knew how to lower V_1 and this know-how was preserved, or because the actions of the other agent made it possible for the agent to acquire the relevant know-how.

$x|q\wedge$ **comm**$(x, y, \langle \text{directive}, p \rangle) \rightarrow$
$A(\text{Wcomm}(x, y, \langle \text{directive}, p \rangle) \rightarrow F x K_h q)$

COMM-6. **Weak Consistency for Prohibitives:**

A prohibitive is issued by an agent only if the agent himself does not intend that it be violated. That is, the agent who prohibits another from letting a certain condition occur should not itself try to make it happen. This is a minimal level of cooperation or rationality one expects from the issuers of prohibitions. For example, if an agent prohibits another agent from connecting to a certain power outlet, he could not at that moment intend that the latter connect to it. Recall the discussion on propositions earlier in this section. Thus the agent who prohibited the other from connecting to an outlet might himself intend to connect to that outlet; however, there is no problem here, since the two propositions are distinct.

comm$(x, y, \langle \text{prohibitive}, p \rangle) \rightarrow \neg x|p$

COMM-7. **Weak Consistency for Permissives:**

A permissive is issued by an agent only if the agent himself does not intend that the relevant proposition never occur. That is, the agent who permits another from letting a certain condition occur should not himself intend to prevent it from ever occurring. This is required so that permissives are issued only felicitously. If an agent does not intend that a given condition ever hold, then he should not permit others to let it hold. For example, if an agent intends to keep a certain power outlet available for his own use, he should not permit others to use it, because that could only render it unavailable at certain times in the future.

comm$(x, y, \langle \text{permissive}, p \rangle) \rightarrow \neg x|(\neg AGp)$

Certain examples that may seem to contradict the applicability of this constraint actually do not: they just have to be formalized carefully. One case involves game playing, where an agent seemingly permits another to beat him, but intends to win nonetheless. While

the above constraint is meant only as an example and need not
apply in all cases, in this particular case, the permissive is simply
for playing, i.e., for *trying* to beat the issuing agent. The actions
of the hearer could, on some scenarios, lead to the speaker being
beaten, but the speaker would prevent such scenarios from being
realized. Once a game begins, the two agents are peers and neither
can permit or prohibit actions of the other.

COMM-8. **Consistency of Directives and Prohibitives:**

An agent must not issue a directive and a prohibitive for the same
condition, even to two different agents. That is, there should never
be a scenario on which such a directive and a prohibitive occur. This
is a requirement of felicitous communication, since it prevents the
speaker from playing off two agents against one another. For example, if an agent directs an agent to (take actions to) raise voltage V_1,
he should not require another agent to prevent that very condition.
The latter's success essentially precludes the former from succeeding
with the directive.

$$\neg E(\text{Fcomm}(x, y, \langle \text{directive}, p \rangle) \land \text{Fcomm}(x, z, \langle \text{prohibitive}, p \rangle))$$

Note, however, that the corresponding constraint for permissives and
prohibitives might be counterproductive: in some cases, it would be
a good idea to violate it. For example, if agent y cannot achieve
condition q (say, that the current, I_1, is 500 Amp) for fear of letting
V_1 go above 440 V, then a controller x may ask another agent, z to
ensure that V_1 stays below 440 V, while permitting y to let it rise.
This allows y to do the required action, while preventing the harmful
condition of V_1 going above 440 V. This works since permissives only
allow conditions to be risked: they do not require them to occur.

COMM-9. **Prior Commitment:**

A directive should be issued only after a conditional promise is given
by the intended receiver that he would obey it. This solves for the
issuer the problem of issuing only those directives that would be
satisfied, provided the condition that promises are kept is enforced
by the design. However, this condition is easier to enforce in a
multiagent system, since it depends to a large extent on the actions,
know-how, and intentions of one agent (the issuer of the promise),
rather than on those of several of them. For example, in a banking
application, an agent may request a loan only from the bank that
had given him a pre-approved line of credit. For the commissive to

be satisfied, p must hold at least once in the future of the directive being uttered by x.

$$\text{comm}(x, y, \langle\text{directive}, p\rangle) \rightarrow$$
$$\mathsf{P}[\text{comm}(y, x, \langle\text{commissive}, \mathsf{Pcomm}(x, y, \langle\text{directive}, p\rangle) \rightarrow \mathsf{F}p\rangle)]$$

6.3.2 The Contract Net

The Contract Net Protocol of Davis & Smith is among the most well-known and significant protocols for multiagent systems [Davis & Smith, 1983]. While several variations of it are possible, in its most basic form it may be described as in Figure 6.7. We are given a system with several agents. One of them has a task that he has to perform. He cannot do the task entirely locally and splits it into a number of subtasks. Let us consider one of the subtasks that cannot be performed locally. The agent now takes on the role of the *manager*. He sends out a *call for bids* to a subset of the other agents, describing the relevant subtask. Of the other agents, the ones who can, and are willing to, perform the advertized subtask respond by sending a *bid* to the manager. The manager evaluates the bids received, and selects one of them. He then sends a message *assigning* the subtask to that agent, who then becomes the *contractor*. The contractor performs the assigned task, possibly invoking other agents in the process. Finally, he communicates the *result* of performing the assigned task to the manager. The manager collects the results of all the subtasks of the original task and thus computes its result. If that task was assigned to him by some other agent, he then sends the result to that agent.

The key steps in the contract net protocol from our point of view are the following: (a) the call for bids, (b) the bids, (c) the assignment of the task, and (d) the result of the task. The processes of deciding whether to bid on a task and for evaluating the bids when they arrive can be safely abstracted out. These and other steps are local to each agent and involve knowledge of the domain in which the contract net is being used. I assume here that these processes, howsoever designed and implemented, are available and are correct.

One can see almost instantaneously that the message with the result of the task should be classified as an assertive, because, in effect, it states that "the result is such and such." The message making the task assignment is a directive, since it asks the contractor to "do the task!" The message making the bid is a commissive, since it has the force of a conditional promise: "if asked to do the task, I will do it." Finally, the call for bids may itself be treated as a directive, because it has the effect of a request: "please speak up, if you will do this task."

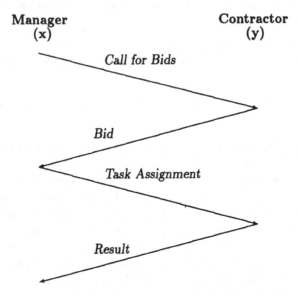

Figure 6.7: Messages Exchanged in the Contract Net

This leads directly to an analysis in which these messages are nested, with the first one to occur being the outermost. Let $\chi(x, y, T)$ capture the conditions under which an agent y will respond to a call for bids sent by x for task, T. Let $r(x, y, T)$ abbreviate comm(y, x, ⟨assertive, result(T)⟩) (*result*); let $a(x, y, T)$ abbreviate comm(x, y, ⟨directive, $r(x, y, T)$⟩) (*assignment*); and let $b(x, y, T)$ abbreviate comm(y, x, ⟨commissive, Pa(x, y, T)→ Fr(x, y, T)⟩) (*bid*).

The initial call for bids has the force of the following schematic message being sent to each of a set of (potential) contractors. The correct performance of the system requires that each instance of this message schema be satisfied by it. Some of them are satisfied vacuously, if $\chi(x, y, T)$ is false.

- ⟨directive, $\chi(x, y, T)$→ $b(x, y, T)$⟩

In other words, the call for bids is a directive asking the hearer to commit to sending the manager the result of the task, if the manager asks him to send him the result. The assertive with the result of the task is satisfied only if the contractor produces the right result. The contractor must commit to producing the result, if assigned the task (the task can be assigned by sending a simpler message than in the above formalization by taking advantage of the context of communication, but it would logically have the same force as above).

Thus the task assignment directive is satisfied if the contractor produces the result when asked to. The call for bids is satisfied if the contractor makes the bid, provided he can perform the given task. As an aside, note that a contractor should not bid on two or more tasks he cannot achieve on some scenarios, i.e., tasks like going North and South simultaneously.

Given that the underlying heuristics, e.g., for selecting one of the bidders, are correct, the above formalization of the contract net can be used to show that it works, provided some additional assumptions are made. Below, x and T are fixed.

- At least one of the agents bids on the task, i.e., $(\exists y : \chi(x, y, T) \cup b(x, y, T))$. This means that at least one of the agents is willing and able to perform task T.

- Of the agents who bid on a task, at least one is selected by the manager to award the task to, i.e., $\bigwedge_{1 \leq i \leq n} b(x, y_i, T) \rightarrow (\exists j : 1 \leq j \leq n \wedge a(x, y_j, T))$. This means that at least one of the bidders meets the manager's criteria for task assignment.

The contract net protocol has been designed the way it has been because of some principles of good design. Since the agents involved have limited knowledge about one another, the only way in which the manager can send a given task to the right contractor (short of assigning the task to every available agent), is by first making an utterance that leads to an utterance that restricts the scenarios that can be realized to those on which the task assignment is guaranteed to be successful. This justifies the sending of the call for bids before making a task assignment and is the canonical motivation for the constraint called *Prior Commitment*, which was introduced in the previous section.

6.4 Conclusions

I now compare the approach discussed above to some semantics of speech acts that others have proposed. One important work is that of Searle & Vanderveken [1985]. However, they do not relate the satisfaction conditions of different sorts of speech acts with the intentions and know-how of the speaker or the hearer. Their greater aim seems to be to derive the possible illocutionary forces from a set of core features, e.g., what they call *illocutionary point* and *direction of fit*.

Searle & Vanderveken's approach has been challenged by Cohen & Levesque who argue that the illocutionary point is theoretically redundant and can be derived from the inferences that a speech act sanctions [Cohen & Levesque, 1988b]. These inferences involve the updating of the beliefs, intentions, and mutual beliefs of the speaker and the hearer. For this reason, Cohen & Levesque's approach is largely of pragmatic interest. Perrault has argued that, despite Cohen & Levesque's attempts, how the participants' cognitive states ought to be updated cannot be monotonically specified [Perrault, 1987]. He proposes that a default mechanism, in his paper Reiter's default logic, be used to characterize the effects of speech acts and, hence, their pragmatic content. The effects of speech acts are related to the processes of deliberation of the agents as they decide how to respond to a message. These processes are highly nonmonotonic and can be accurately understood only with theories of belief-revision and intention-revision, which are still not sufficiently well-developed. In general, these processes depend on issues like the social relationship of the agents or on matters of performance, rather than on the semantics of communication *per se*. Perrault suggests some postulates for such revision using default logic. Thus his focus is not on the semantics as considered here.

In any case, a semantics would help clarify our intuitions even about the pragmatic aspects of communication. As a clarification of my goals, note that the role of the proposed semantics is akin to that of classical semantics for assertives. Classical semantics only tells us when an assertive is objectively satisfied: it makes no claims about when an assertive should actually be uttered or believed.

Werner has proposed a theory of communication based on this theory of intentions, which was discussed in section 3.5 also [Werner, 1989]. Werner considers only directives (besides assertives), and defines their effects on the hearer's "intentional state." A directive forces the hearer's intentional state so that it would be necessarily satisfied no matter what the hearer does (according to the modified intentional state). Werner thus seems to be attacking the problem of the effects of directives in idealized circumstances. A notable weakness of this theory is the lack of compositionality: operators like $\wedge, \vee$, and $\neg$ mean differently in the context of directives than otherwise.

In more recent work than his book with Searle, Vanderveken has independently addressed the problems of the "success and satisfaction" of speech acts [1990; 1991]. Vanderveken's goal is a general illocutionary logic, and a large part of his theory is focused on the conditions of when a performative succeeds, i.e., when a speech act of a particular illocutionary force is made. His goal is to give the semantics of performative verbs in an extension of Montague grammar. He also considers the degree of strength of different speech acts explicitly, and classifies a variety of speech act verbs, as special as the declaratives, "homologate" and "ratify," which differ primarily on their pragmatic aspects. The particular definitions given by Vanderveken are extensional in that no reference is made to the intentions or the know-how of the agents. For example, for him a directive is satisfied if the appropriate condition comes to hold, and a prohibitive, merely a special kind of directive for him, is satisfied if the appropriate condition does not occur. He lumps permissives and prohibitives with directives [Vanderveken, 1990, pp. 189–198], which I have argued should not be done. Vanderveken also does not consider the temporal aspect of speech acts explicitly. In sum, while the results of the theory developed here are more refined than the corresponding results of his theory, they could fruitfully be combined with the pragmatic and other aspects of speech acts that he has studied in much greater detail.

The proposed taxonomy of speech acts is motivated by the semantic definitions given above, which are different for permissives, prohibitives, and directives. This distinguishes the proposed taxonomy from other classifications of speech acts. Since syntactically, permissives, prohibitives, and directives are all imperatives, they are usually classified together, e.g., by Bach & Harnish [1979, pp. 39–54] and Searle & Vanderveken [1985, ch. 9]. This is surprising in the case of Searle & Vanderveken, since their interests are pragmatic, rather than syntactic.

The relationship between the proposed approach and traditional work on speech acts in natural language processing (NLP) is essentially one of complementarity. Traditional theories address the problem of determining when what kind of a speech act occurs. They can thus be used to feed into the proposed theory. One simply has to use the NLP theories under appropriate assumptions to determine the truth of different instances of $\text{comm}(x, y, m)$ and then apply the proposed theory to determine the satisfaction conditions of those expressions. This perspective places the semantics presented here at the natural boundary of deciding what to say, on the one hand, and deciding how to say it, on the other. That is, on the one hand, we have the concerns of deciding what speech act to make, and on the other, the concerns of how to get a point across. This is a useful way to organize a multiagent system that is designed to also communicate with humans: the first aspect mentioned above is a part of distributed computing, the second aspect a part of natural language processing.

An attractive feature of this approach is that it brings the satisfaction conditions for speech acts into the fold of logic. Using definitions of the intentions and know-how of an agent, I was able to give rigorous definitions of the conditions of satisfaction for speech acts of different of illocutionary forces. The theory presented here can yield some normative constraints on communication among agents. An advantage of the model-theoretic approach is that it allows our intuitions to be expressed directly and formally and thus can be used in clarifying and debugging them.

Chapter 7

Conclusions and Future Work

I have presented formalizations of the concepts of know-how and intentions as they are needed in the study of multiagent systems. These formalizations capture many of our pretheoretic intuitions about these concepts. For example, an agent's intending something does not entail that he knows how to achieve it; and, his knowing how to achieve something clearly does not entail that he should intend it. The agents' intentions, along with their knowledge and know-how, constrain the actions they choose to perform. Agents who know how to achieve what they intend can succeed provided they (a) act on their intentions, (b) exercise their know-how, and (c) persist with their intentions long enough.

The formalizations of know-how and intentions were developed in a model of actions and time that is among the more general ones considered in computer science. It unifies temporal and dynamic logics by relating actions and time. Further, it allows several agents to act concurrently and asynchronously. Thus, it admits games with simultaneous moves, i.e., those in which there is no notion of turn-taking. The concept of strategies is revived and formalized as a means for abstractly specifying the behavior of agents. Strategies are then used to unify intentions and know-how and to state constraints on the selection of actions by agents.

Intentions and know-how can be used also to assign a formal semantics to communications among agents. Such a semantics for communications is proposed. This semantics brings to fore the role of communications in influencing the actions of the participating agents. A communication is satisfied only if it has the requisite effects on the intentions of the agents involved and if those agents have the necessary know-how and act appropriately. The unified theory of intentions, know-how, and communications can be used to formalize constraints on the behavior of agents. These constraints are both abstract and in terms closer to the requirements of the ultimate human users of the multiagent system being designed.

Perhaps the key limitation of the approach proposed here results from its being an *intentional stance* or *knowledge level* approach. This causes it to be a "radically incomplete" approximation in Newell's term [1982, p. 111]. In other words, this approach does not faithfully model the limitations of reasoning of real-life systems. As Newell himself argues, there is still much to be said in favor of a knowledge level approach. It provides us with a set of abstractions for artificial systems, a set of abstractions that we use with great success in our daily lives. As long as a designer of multiagent systems is sensitive to the limitations of his agents, he can indeed use the proposed approach effectively.

One way to avoid the abovementioned limitation is to consider one of the representational approaches to beliefs and intentions. Such approaches explicitly consider the representations that agents may have and the computations they may engage in. Many of these approaches, the so-called sentential ones [Konolige, 1986], do not associate any real semantics to the elements of their formal languages. This is a major shortcoming, especially when one wishes to use the resulting theory in developing a methodology for designing distributed systems. Some hybrid approaches exist that seek to avoid the problems of both the proposed framework and the sentential approaches [Fagin & Halpern, 1988; Singh & Asher, 1993]. Such approaches are technically more complex than either. By definition, they require some specification of the representations and the reasoning processes of the agents. Thus they belong in what Newell calls the *symbol level* [1982, p. 95]. Not only are they technically more complex, the hybrid approaches also require a more detailed specification before they can be put to use. Such specifications may not be available when an existing system is being analyzed. And, they may not even be available in the early stages of the design process when the basic behavioral requirements for the desired system are being determined. Thus, while an extension of the present framework to the symbol level would be desirable, the present framework itself may still be needed.

There are also a number of technical problems merit a lot of attention, but which I was not able to properly address in this monograph. Foremost among these is the incredibly hard problem of constructing models. The present work assumes that a model of some sort has been constructed and described, so that further reasoning can proceed in it. It appears likely that good models cannot be automatically generated for all but the most trivial application domains. However, much work is required in developing tools that assist in the formulation of models. Work in the broad area of problem solving in artificial intelligence will be especially pertinent here.

Another problem has to do with how to do with how agents should revise their intentions and beliefs. There has been much work recently on belief revision [Gärdenfors, 1988]. The problem is technically harder when intentions are brought into the fold. However, in an intuitive sense, it might even become simpler because beliefs by themselves give a gloriously incomplete picture of an intelligent agent. Also, the technical results are likelier to be more natural when intentions are included.

Purely qualitative solutions to the revision problem, while possibly of some value, are not likely to be highly accurate. This is because intentions are a matter of what an agent really wants to achieve and reflect the agent's preferences as to how much effort and resources he would assign for what conditions. An instance of this is the problem of how long an agent should persist with an intention: clearly, changing one's intentions extremely frequently or never are both likely to prove inefficient and irrational. Thus, in some sense, the problem is necessarily one of probabilistic or utility-theoretic reasoning. I have studied some of these problems elsewhere, but the solutions are far from complete [1991b; 1991e]. In these works, I also argue that intentions are valuable to limited agents, those who are rational, but are not perfect Bayesian reasoners (and none are). More precise analyses that take the cost of thinking or computation into account are needed.

Another set of related ideas that I mentioned only briefly in this monograph have to do with the structural aspects of multiagent systems. A multiagent system can itself function as a single entity in another, larger, system. This is extremely common in human organizations. If we allow this, we are faced with the problem of defining the know-how and intentions of the system as a whole, so that our approach can apply at the next level up, in terms of the semantics of communications as well as other general constraints. I have explored some of these issues in past research [1991a; 1991c]. That work is not nearly as technically sophisticated as I would like, but it contains some interesting ideas. For example, the structure of a group is seen as embodied in the constraints on the communications among the different members. An open problem is to see how the semantics of communications proposed here would and should interact with the definitions of structured groups.

The theory developed in this monograph provides a framework for specifying multiagent systems, but it is clearly not sufficient in itself. To be practical, any approach to designing multiagent systems must include actual design rules or heuristics that apply in a wide variety of cases. Of course, the theory can be used to formalize the design rules, to show their correctness, and to elucidate the assumptions under which they are most naturally applicable. These are all valuable functions. However, actually coming up the rules is no trivial matter either. A detailed *design theory* is urgently needed.

Besides the uses of intentions and know-how that are of primary interest here, they have some applications in other problem domains. Notable among these are cognitive modeling, plan recognition, and machine learning of how to act. For example, it would be fruitful to design families of algorithms or even instances of them that are phrased directly in terms of the primitives formalized here. Such algorithms could be used for solving any of a variety of problems in multiagent systems, for example, those pertaining to coordination, cooperation, or collective learning. Indeed, the formalization of the contract net protocol present in Chapter 6 can be seen as taking a step in this direction. Other connections, especially those with machine learning, must be explored in greater technical detail, however.

Yet another major piece of remaining work is to develop algorithms for checking the satisfiability of specifications in proposed formal language, or some subset thereof. It is likely to be significantly more tractable to check the satisfiability relative to a given design: this kind of *model checking* has been used to great profit for the case of temporal logics [Burch *et al.*, 1990]. For this reason, the development of efficient model checking algorithms for the proposed framework would be of great use.

One can think of many more challenging research projects in multiagent systems. I only hope that I have convinced the reader that the study of formal methods in multiagent systems is not only of great practical significance, but also promises to be an exciting area for further research.

Appendix A

The Formal Language

The definitions of the syntax of the formal language are collected here.

The Basic Language

$\mathcal{L}$ is the basic formal language; $\mathcal{L}_s$ is the set of "scenario-formulae," which is used as an auxiliary definition. It contains formulae that are evaluated relative to scenarios in the model, rather than relative to moments. In the following,

- Φ is a set of atomic propositional symbols,

- $\mathcal{A}$ is a set of agent symbols,

- $\mathcal{B}$ is a set of basic action symbols, and

- $\mathcal{X}$ is a set of variables.

Time, Actions, and Propositional Logic

SYN-1. $\psi \in \Phi$ implies that $\psi \in \mathcal{L}$

SYN-2. $p, q \in \mathcal{L}$ implies that $p \wedge q \in \mathcal{L}$

SYN-3. $p \in \mathcal{L}$ implies that $\neg p \in \mathcal{L}$

SYN-4. $\mathcal{L} \subseteq \mathcal{L}_s$

SYN-5. $p, q \in \mathcal{L}_s$ implies that $p \wedge q \in \mathcal{L}_s$

SYN-6. $p \in \mathcal{L}_s$ implies that $\neg p \in \mathcal{L}_s$

SYN-7. $p \in \mathcal{L}_s$ implies that $Ap, Rp \in \mathcal{L}$

SYN-8. $p \in \mathcal{L}$ implies that $Pp \in \mathcal{L}$

SYN-9. $p \in \mathcal{L}$ and $a \in \mathcal{X}$ implies that $(\bigvee a : p) \in \mathcal{L}$

SYN-10. $p, q \in \mathcal{L}_s$ implies that $p \mathsf{U} q \in \mathcal{L}_s$

SYN-11. $p \in \mathcal{L}$, $x \in \mathcal{A}$, and $a \in \mathcal{B}$ implies that $x[a]p, x\langle a \rangle p, x\langle a \rangle\!| p \in \mathcal{L}_s$

Strategies

STRAT-1. $\mathbf{skip} \in \mathcal{L}_y$

STRAT-2. $q \in \mathcal{L}$ implies that $\mathbf{do}(q) \in \mathcal{L}_y$

STRAT-3. $Y_1, Y_2 \in \mathcal{L}_y$ implies that $Y_1; Y_2 \in \mathcal{L}_y$

STRAT-4. $q \in \mathcal{L}$ and $Y_1, Y_2 \in \mathcal{L}_y$ implies that $\mathbf{if}\ q\ \mathbf{then}\ Y_1\ \mathbf{else}\ Y_2 \in \mathcal{L}_y$

STRAT-5. $q \in \mathcal{L}$ and $Y_1 \in \mathcal{L}_y$ implies that $\mathbf{while}\ q\ \mathbf{do}\ Y_1 \in \mathcal{L}_y$

Intentions

The formal language of Chapter 3, $\mathcal{L}^i$, is $\mathcal{L}$ augmented with four operators, $\langle\ \rangle_i$, $\langle\!\langle\ \rangle\!\rangle$, $*$, and I (which stands for Intends).

SYN-12. All the rules for $\mathcal{L}$, with $\mathcal{L}^i$ substituted for $\mathcal{L}$

SYN-13. All the rules for $\mathcal{L}_s$, with $\mathcal{L}^i_s$ substituted for $\mathcal{L}_s$

SYN-14. All the rules for $\mathcal{L}_y$, with $\mathcal{L}^i_y$ substituted for $\mathcal{L}_y$

SYN-15. $p \in \mathcal{L}^i_s$, $x \in \mathcal{A}$, and $Y \in \mathcal{L}^i_y$ implies that $x\langle Y \rangle_i p$ and $\langle\!\langle Y \rangle\!\rangle p \in \mathcal{L}^i_s$

SYN-16. $p \in \mathcal{L}^i_s$, $x \in \mathcal{A}$, and $Y \in \mathcal{L}^i_y$ implies that $x * Y \in \mathcal{L}^i$

SYN-17. $p \in \mathcal{L}^i_s$ and $x \in \mathcal{A}$ implies that $(x \mathsf{I} p) \in \mathcal{L}^i$

Ability and Know-How

Trees

Let Υ be the set of trees. $\emptyset$ is the empty tree. Then Υ is defined as follows.

TREE-1. $\emptyset \in \Upsilon$

TREE-2. $a \in \mathcal{B}$ implies that $a \in \Upsilon$

TREE-3. $\tau_1, \ldots, \tau_m \in \Upsilon$; $\tau_1, \ldots, \tau_m$ have different radices, and $a \in \mathcal{B}$ implies that $\langle a; \tau_1, \ldots, \tau_m \rangle \in \Upsilon$

Ability and Know-How

The formal language of this chapter, $\mathcal{L}^h$, is an extension of $\mathcal{L}$. The operator $(\!)$ denotes ability relative to trees and the operator $(\!|\!)$ ability relative to strategies. The operators K_{rab} and K_{sab} are, respectively, the reactive and strategic versions of ability.

SYN-18. All the rules for $\mathcal{L}$, with $\mathcal{L}^h$ substituted for $\mathcal{L}$

SYN-19. All the rules for $\mathcal{L}_s$, with $\mathcal{L}_s^h$ substituted for $\mathcal{L}_s$

SYN-20. All the rules for $\mathcal{L}_y$, with $\mathcal{L}_y^h$ substituted for $\mathcal{L}_y$

SYN-21. $p \in \mathcal{L}_s^h$ and $x \in \mathcal{A}$ implies that $(x\mathsf{K}_{rab}p), (x\mathsf{K}_{sab}p) \in \mathcal{L}^h$

SYN-22. $p \in \mathcal{L}_s^h$, $Y \in \mathcal{L}_y^h$, and $x \in \mathcal{A}$ implies that $(x(\!|Y|\!)p) \in \mathcal{L}^h$

SYN-23. $\tau \in \Upsilon$, $x \in \mathcal{A}$, and $p \in \mathcal{L}^h$ implies that $x(\!\tau\!)p \in \mathcal{L}^h$

SYN-24. $p \in \mathcal{L}_s^h$ and $x \in \mathcal{A}$ implies that $(x\mathsf{K}_{hr}p), (x\mathsf{K}_{hs}p) \in \mathcal{L}^h$

SYN-25. $p \in \mathcal{L}_s^h$, $Y, Y' \in \mathcal{L}_y^h$, and $x \in \mathcal{A}$ implies that $(x(\!|Y|\!)p), (x[\!Y|Y'),$ $(x[Y]Y') \in \mathcal{L}^h$

SYN-26. $\tau \in \Upsilon$, $x \in \mathcal{A}$, and $p \in \mathcal{L}^h$ implies that $x(\!\tau\!)p \in \mathcal{L}^h$

SYN-27. $p \in \mathcal{L}_s^h$, $x \in \mathcal{A}$, and $Y \in \mathcal{L}_y^h$ implies that $x[Y]_h p, x\langle Y\rangle p \in \mathcal{L}_s^h$

Combining Intentions and Know-How

The formal language of Chapter 5, $\mathcal{L}^c$, is obtained by combining the rules for $\mathcal{L}^i$ and $\mathcal{L}^h$.

SYN-28. All the rules for $\mathcal{L}^i$, $\mathcal{L}^i_s$, $\mathcal{L}^i_y$, $\mathcal{L}^h$, $\mathcal{L}^h_s$, and $\mathcal{L}^h_y$, with $\mathcal{L}^c$ substituted for $\mathcal{L}^i$ and $\mathcal{L}^h$, $\mathcal{L}^c_s$ substituted for $\mathcal{L}^i_s$ and $\mathcal{L}^h_s$, and $\mathcal{L}^c_y$ substituted for $\mathcal{L}^i_y$ and $\mathcal{L}^h_y$

SYN-29. $p \in \mathcal{L}^c_s$, $Y, Y' \in \mathcal{L}^c_y$, and $x \in \mathcal{A}$ implies that $(x[Y]Y') \in \mathcal{L}^c$

Communications

The formal language of Chapter 6, $\mathcal{L}^m$ is $\mathcal{L}^c$ augmented with the operator, W. In the following, $\mathcal{F} = \{$assertive, directive, commissive, permissive, prohibitive, declarative$\}$ is the set of illocutionary forces. $\mathcal{M}$ is the set of *messages*. The set of basic actions, $\mathcal{B}$, is extended with illocutionary actions, which are generated from the messages and are treated as the actions of the sending agent.

SYN-30. All the rules for $\mathcal{L}^c$ with $\mathcal{L}^m$ substituted for $\mathcal{L}^c$

SYN-31. All the rules for $\mathcal{L}^c_s$ with $\mathcal{L}^m_s$ substituted for substituted for $\mathcal{L}^c_s$

SYN-32. All the rules for $\mathcal{L}^c_y$ with $\mathcal{L}^m_y$ substituted for substituted for $\mathcal{L}^c_y$

SYN-33. $p \in \mathcal{L}^m_s$ implies that $Wp \in \mathcal{L}^m_s$

SYN-34. $p \in \mathcal{L}^m$ and $i \in \mathcal{F}$ implies that $\langle i, p \rangle \in \mathcal{M}$

SYN-35. $x, y \in \mathcal{A}$ and $m \in \mathcal{M}$ implies that $\mathbf{comm}(x, y, m) \in \mathcal{L}^m_s$

SYN-36. $x, y \in \mathcal{A}$ and $m \in \mathcal{M}$ implies that $\mathbf{says\text{-}to}(x, y, m) \in \mathcal{B}$

Interrogatives

In order to include interrogatives in the formal language, I introduce a set of constants, $\mathcal{D}$, and a set of predicates, $\mathcal{PRED}$. $\mathcal{L}^q_q$ denotes the set of query expressions. $\mathcal{L}^q$ is the version of the formal language that includes interrogatives.

SYN-37. All the rules for $\mathcal{L}^m$ with $\mathcal{L}^q$ substituted for $\mathcal{L}^m$

SYN-38. All the rules for $\mathcal{L}_s^m$ with $\mathcal{L}_s^q$ substituted for $\mathcal{L}_s^q$

SYN-39. All the rules for $\mathcal{L}_y^m$ with $\mathcal{L}_y^q$ substituted for $\mathcal{L}_y^m$

SYN-40. $\vec{b} \in (\mathcal{D} \cup \mathcal{X})^n$ and $P \in \mathcal{PRED}$ implies that $P(\vec{b}) \in \mathcal{L}^q$

SYN-41. $u \in \mathcal{X}$ and $p \in \mathcal{L}^q$ implies that $(\exists u : p) \in \mathcal{L}^q$

SYN-42. $\vec{a} \in \mathcal{X}^n$, $p \in \mathcal{L}^q$ implies that $(\lambda \vec{a} : p) \in \mathcal{L}_q^q$

SYN-43. $p \in \mathcal{L}_q^q$ implies that $\langle \text{interrogative}, p \rangle \in \mathcal{M}$

SYN-44. $\langle \text{interrogative}, p \rangle \in \mathcal{M}$ and $\mathbf{Ans} \in \mathcal{D}^n$ implies that $\mathbf{answer}(p, \mathbf{Ans}) \in \mathcal{L}^q$

Bibliography

[Agre & Chapman, 1987] Agre, Philip and Chapman, David; 1987. Pengi: An implementation of a theory of activity. In *AAAI*. 268-272.

[Allen & Perrault, 1980] Allen, James F. and Perrault, C. Raymond; 1980. Analyzing intention in utterances. *Artificial Intelligence* 15:143-178.

[Allen, 1984] Allen, James F.; 1984. Towards a general theory of action and time. *Artificial Intelligence* 23(2):123-154.

[Allen, 1991] Allen, James F.; 1991. Planning as temporal reasoning. In *Principles of Knowledge Representation and Reasoning.*

[Appelt, 1986] Appelt, Douglas; 1986. *Planning English Sentences.* Cambridge University Press, Cambridge, UK.

[Asher, 1986] Asher, Nicholas; 1986. Belief in discourse representation theory. *Journal of Philosophical Logic* 15:127-189.

[Asher, 1992] Asher, Nicholas M.; 1992. *Reference to Abstract Objects.* Kluwer Academic Publishers.

[Austin, 1962] Austin, John L.; 1962. *How to do Things with Words.* Clarendon, Oxford, UK.

[Bacchus et al., 1989] Bacchus, Fahiem; Tenenberg, Josh; and Koomen, Johannes A.; 1989. A non-reified temporal logic. In *First Conference on Knowledge Representation and Reasoning.* 2-10.

[Bach & Harnish, 1979] Bach, Kent and Harnish, Robert M.; 1979. *Linguistic Communication and Speech Acts.* MIT Press, Cambridge, MA.

[Berthet et al., 1992] Berthet, Sabine; Demazeau, Yves; and Boissier, Olivier; 1992. Knowing each other better. In *Proceedings of the 11th Workshop on Distributed Artificial Intelligence.*

[Boyer & Moore, 1979] Boyer, Robert S. and Moore, J. Strother; 1979. *A Computational Logic*. ACM Monograph Series. Academic Press, New York, NY.

[Boyer, 1992] Boyer, Robert S.; 1992. Personal Communication.

[Brand, 1984] Brand, Myles; 1984. *Intending and Acting*. MIT Press, Cambridge, MA.

[Bratman, 1987] Bratman, Michael E.; 1987. *Intention, Plans, and Practical Reason*. Harvard University Press, Cambridge, MA.

[Burch *et al.*, 1990] Burch, J. R.; Clarke, E. C.; McMillan, K. L.; Dill, D. L.; and Hwang, L. J.; 1990. Symbolic model checking: 10^{20} states and beyond. In *LICS*.

[Burmeister *et al.*, 1993] Burmeister, Birgit; Haddadi, Afsaneh; and Sundermeyer, Kurt; 1993. Generic configurable cooperation protocols for multi-agent systems. In *European Workshop on the Modeling of Autonomous Agents in a Multi-Agent World*.

[Bussman & Müller, 1993] Bussman, Stefan and Müller, Jürgen; 1993. A communication architecture for cooperating agents. *Computers and Artificial Intelligence* 12(1):37–53.

[Chandy & Misra, 1986] Chandy, K. M. and Misra, Jayadev; 1986. How processes learn. *Distributed Computing* 1:40–52.

[Chang, 1991] Chang, Man Kit; 1991. SANP: A communication level protocol for supporting machine-to-machine negotiation in organization. Master's thesis, University of British Columbia, Vancouver, B.C., Canada.

[Chellas, 1980] Chellas, Brian F.; 1980. *Modal Logic*. Cambridge University Press, New York, NY.

[Cohen & Levesque, 1988a] Cohen, Philip R. and Levesque, Hector J.; 1988a. On acting together: Joint intentions for intelligent agents. In *Workshop on Distributed Artificial Intelligence*.

[Cohen & Levesque, 1988b] Cohen, Philip R. and Levesque, Hector J.; 1988b. Rational interaction as the basis for communication. Technical Report 433, SRI International, Menlo Park, CA.

[Cohen & Levesque, 1990] Cohen, Philip R. and Levesque, Hector J.; 1990. Intention is choice with commitment. *Artificial Intelligence* 42:213–261.

[Crawford *et al.*, 1990] Crawford, James; Farquhar, Adam; and Kuipers, Benjamin; 1990. QPC: A compiler from physical models into qualitative differential equations. In *AAAI*.

[Davidson, 1980] Davidson, Donald; 1980. *Essays on Actions and Events*. Oxford University Press, Oxford, UK.

[Davis & Smith, 1983] Davis, Randall and Smith, Reid G.; 1983. Negotiation as a metaphor for distributed problem solving. *Artificial Intelligence* 20:63–109. Reprinted in *Readings in Distributed Artificial Intelligence*, A. H. Bond and L. Gasser, eds., Morgan Kaufmann, 1988.

[Demazeau & Müller, 1991] Demazeau, Y. and Müller, J-P., editors. *Decentralized Artificial Intelligence, Volume 2*. Elsevier Science Publishers B.V. / North-Holland, Amsterdam, Holland.

[Dennett, 1987] Dennett, Daniel C.; 1987. *The Intentional Stance*. MIT Press, Cambridge, MA.

[Durfee *et al.*, 1987] Durfee, Edmund H.; Lesser, Victor R.; and Corkill, Daniel D.; 1987. Coherent cooperation among communicating problem solvers. *IEEE Transactions on Computers* C-36(11):1275–1291.

[Emerson & Clarke, 1982] Emerson, E. Allen and Clarke, Edmund C.; 1982. Using branching time temporal logic to synthesize synchronization skeletons. *Science of Computer Programming* 2:241–266.

[Emerson, 1990] Emerson, E. A.; 1990. Temporal and modal logic. In Leeuwen, J.van, editor, *Handbook of Theoretical Computer Science*, volume B. North-Holland Publishing Company, Amsterdam, The Netherlands.

[Emerson, 1992] Emerson, E. Allen; 1992. Personal Communication.

[Fagin & Halpern, 1988] Fagin, Ronald and Halpern, Joseph Y.; 1988. Belief, awareness, and limited reasoning. *Artificial Intelligence* 34:39–76.

[Fikes & Nilsson, 1971] Fikes, R. E. and Nilsson, N. J.; 1971. STRIPS: A new approach to the application of theorem proving to problem solving. *Artificial Intelligence* 2:189–208.

[Fischer & Immerman, 1986] Fischer, Michael J. and Immerman, Neil; 1986. Foundations of knowledge for distributed systems. In Halpern, Joseph Y., editor, *Theoretical Aspects of Reasoning About Knowledge*. 171–185.

[Fischer & Ladner, 1979] Fischer, Michael J. and Ladner, Richard E.; 1979. The propositional dynamic logic of regular programs. *Journal of Computer and System Sciences* 18(2):194-211.

[Gärdenfors, 1988] Gärdenfors, Peter; 1988. *Knowledge in Flux*. MIT Press, Cambridge, MA.

[Gasser & Huhns, 1989] Gasser, Les and Huhns, Michael N., editors. *Distributed Artificial Intelligence, Volume II*. Pitman/Morgan Kaufmann, London.

[Gelfond *et al.*, 1991] Gelfond, M.; Lifschitz, V.; and Rabinov, A.; 1991. What are the limitations of the situation calculus? In Boyer, Robert, editor, *Automated Reasoning: Essays in the Honor of Woody Bledsoe*. Kluwer Academic Publishers, Dordrecht, The Netherlands.

[Georgeff, 1987] Georgeff, Michael P.; 1987. Planning. In Traub, J. F., editor, *Annual Review of Computer Science, Vol 2*. Annual Reviews Inc., Palo Alto, CA.

[Goldman, 1970] Goldman, Alvin I.; 1970. *A Theory of Human Action*. Prentice-Hall, Inc., Englewood Cliffs, NJ.

[Grice, 1969] Grice, Paul; 1969. Utterer's meaning and intentions. *Philosophical Review*. Reprinted in [Martinich, 1985].

[Groenendijk & Stokhof, 1984] Groenendijk, J. and Stokhof, M.; 1984. On the semantics of questions and the pragmatics of answers. In Landman, F. and Veltman, F., editors, *Varieties of Formal Semantics*. Foris Publications, Dordrecht, The Netherlands. 143-170.

[Grosz & Sidner, 1988] Grosz, Barbara and Sidner, Candace; 1988. Distributed know-how and acting: Research on collaborative planning. In *Workshop on Distributed Artificial Intelligence*.

[Halpern & Moses, 1987] Halpern, Joseph Y. and Moses, Yoram O.; 1987. Knowledge and common knowledge in a distributed environment (revised version). Technical Report RJ 4421, IBM.

[Hamblin, 1987] Hamblin, C. L.; 1987. *Imperatives*. Basil Blackwell Ltd., Oxford, UK.

[Harman, 1986] Harman, Gilbert; 1986. *Change in View*. MIT Press, Cambridge, MA.

[Harper *et al.*, 1981] Harper, William L.; Stalnaker, Robert; and Pearce, Glenn, editors. *IFS: Conditionals, Belief, Decision, Chance, and Time*. D. Reidel, Dordrecht, Netherlands.

[Harrah, 1984] Harrah, David; 1984. The logic of questions. In Gabbay, D. and Guenthner, F., editors, *Handbook of Philosophical Logic*. D. Reidel Publishing Company, Dordrecht, The Netherlands. 715–764.

[Hintikka, 1962] Hintikka, Jaakko; 1962. *Knowledge and Belief: An Introduction to the Logic of the two Notions*. Cornell University Press, Ithaca, NY.

[Huhns *et al.*, 1987] Huhns, Michael N.; Mukhopadhyay, Uttam; Stephens, Larry M.; and Bonnell, Ronald D.; 1987. DAI for document retrieval: The MINDS project. In Huhns, Michael N., editor, *Distributed Artificial Intelligence*. Pitman/Morgan Kaufmann, London. 249–283.

[Huhns, 1987] Huhns, Michael N., editor. *Distributed Artificial Intelligence*. Pitman/Morgan Kaufmann, London.

[Jennings, 1992] Jennings, Nicholas R.; 1992. Joint intentions as a model of multi-agent cooperation. Technical Report Knowledge Engineering Applications Group: 92/18, Department of Electronic Engineering, Queen Mary and Westfield College, London, UK.

[Kamp, 1984] Kamp, Hans; 1984. A theory of truth and semantic representation. In Groenendijk, J.; Jansenn, T.; and Stokhof, M., editors, *Truth, Interpretation and Information*. Foris Publications, Dordrecht, The Netherlands. 1–41.

[Kochen & Galanter, 1958] Kochen, Manfred and Galanter, Eugene; 1958. The acquisition and utilization of information in problem solving and thinking. *Information and Control* 1:267–288.

[Konolige, 1986] Konolige, Kurt; 1986. *A Deduction Model of Belief*. Morgan Kaufmann, Inc.

[Kozen & Tiurzyn, 1990] Kozen, Dexter and Tiurzyn, Jerzy; 1990. Logics of program. In Leeuwen, J.van, editor, *Handbook of Theoretical Computer Science*. North-Holland Publishing Company, Amsterdam, The Netherlands.

[Krifka, 1989] Krifka, Manfred; 1989. Nominal reference, temporal constitution and quantification in event semantics. In Bartsch, R.; van Benthem, J.; and van Emde Boas, P., editors, *Semantics and Contextual Expressions*. Foris, Dordrecht, Holland.

[Kuipers, 1986] Kuipers, Benjamin J.; 1986. Qualitative simulation. *Artificial Intelligence* 29:289–338.

[Kuroda, 1989] Kuroda, S.-Y.; 1989. An explanatory theory of communicative intentions. *Linguistics and Philosophy* 12:655–681.

[Lansky, 1989] Lansky, Amy L.; 1989. A perspective on multiagent planning. Technical Report 474, SRI International, Menlo Park, CA.

[Link, 1987] Link, Godehard; 1987. Algebraic semantics for event structures. Technical report, Seminar für Philosophie, Logik und Wissenschaftstheorie, Universität München, Munich, Germany.

[Martinich, 1985] Martinich, Aloysius P., editor. *The Philosophy of Language*. Oxford University Press, New York, NY.

[McCarthy & Hayes, 1969] McCarthy, J. and Hayes, P. J.; 1969. Some philosophical problems from the standpoint of artificial intelligence. In *Machine Intelligence 4*. American Elsevier.

[McCarthy, 1979] McCarthy, John; 1979. Ascribing mental qualities to machines. In Ringle, Martin, editor, *Philosophical Perspectives in Artificial Intelligence*. Harvester Press. Page nos. from a revised version, issued as a report in 1987.

[McDermott, 1982] McDermott, Drew; 1982. A temporal logic for reasoning about processes and plans. *Cognitive Science* 6(2):101–155.

[Miller et al., 1960] Miller, George A.; Galanter, Eugene; and Pribram, Karl; 1960. *Plans and the Structure of Behavior*. Henry Holt and Company, New York, NY.

[Mitchell, 1990] Mitchell, Tom; 1990. Becoming increasingly reactive. In *AAAI*.

[Moore, 1984] Moore, Robert C.; 1984. A formal theory of knowledge and action. In Hobbs, Jerry R. and Moore, Robert C., editors, *Formal Theories of the Commonsense World*. Ablex Publishing Company, Norwood, NJ. 319–358.

[Morgenstern, 1987] Morgenstern, Leora; 1987. A theory of knowledge and planning. In *IJCAI*.

[Müller, 1993] Müller, Jürgen; 1993. Negotiation principles. Technical report, Unpublished report, Saarbrücken, Germany.

[Newell, 1982] Newell, Allen; 1982. The knowledge level. *Artificial Intelligence* 18(1):87–127.

[Oddie & Tichy, 1981] Oddie, Graham and Tichy, Pavel; 1981. The logic of ability, freedom and responsibility. *Studia Logica* 2/3:227–248.

[Partee, 1973] Partee, Barbara; 1973. Some structural analogies between tenses and pronouns in English. *Journal of Philosophy* 70:601–609.

[Pednault, 1988] Pednault, Edwin P. D.; 1988. Extending conventional planning techniques to handle actions with context-dependent effects. In *AAAI*.

[Perrault, 1987] Perrault, Raymond; 1987. An application of default logic to speech act theory. Technical Report 90, Center for the Study of Language and Information, Stanford, CA.

[Rao & Georgeff, 1991a] Rao, Anand S. and Georgeff, Michael P.; 1991a. Asymmetry thesis and side-effect problems in linear-time and branching-time intention logics. In *IJCAI*.

[Rao & Georgeff, 1991b] Rao, Anand S. and Georgeff, Michael P.; 1991b. Modeling rational agents within a BDI-architecture. In *Principles of Knowledge Representation and Reasoning*.

[Rosenschein, 1985] Rosenschein, Stanley J.; 1985. Formal theories of knowledge in AI and robotics. *New Generation Computing* 3(4).

[Ryle, 1949] Ryle, Gilbert; 1949. *The Concept of Mind*. Hutchinson's University Library, London, UK.

[Sacerdoti, 1977] Sacerdoti, Earl; 1977. *The Structure of Plans and Behavior*. Elsevier Science Publishers.

[Searle & Vanderveken, 1985] Searle, John R. and Vanderveken, Daniel; 1985. *Foundations of Illocutionary Logic*. Cambridge University Press, Cambridge, UK.

[Searle, 1969] Searle, John R.; 1969. *Speech Acts*. Cambridge University Press, Cambridge, UK.

[Searle, 1975] Searle, John R.; 1975. Indirect speech acts. In Cole, P. and Morgan, J. L., editors, *Syntax and Semantics, Volume 3*. Academic Press, New York, NY. Reprinted in [Martinich, 1985].

[Searle, 1983] Searle, John R.; 1983. *Intentionality: An essay in the Philosophy of Mind*. Cambridge University Press, Cambridge, UK.

[Seel, 1989] Seel, Nigel; 1989. Formalising first-order intentional systems theory. Technical report, STC Technology Ltd., Harlow, Essex, UK.

[Segerberg, 1989] Segerberg, Krister; 1989. Bringing it about. *Journal of Philosophical Logic* 18:327–347.

[Shoham, 1988] Shoham, Yoav; 1988. *Reasoning About Change: Time and Causation from the Standpoint of AI*. MIT Press, Cambridge, MA.

[Singh & Asher, 1993] Singh, Munindar P. and Asher, Nicholas M.; 1993. A logic of intentions and beliefs. *Journal of Philosophical Logic* 22:513–544.

[Singh, 1990a] Singh, Munindar P.; 1990a. Group intentions. In *10th Workshop on Distributed Artificial Intelligence*.

[Singh, 1990b] Singh, Munindar P.; 1990b. Towards a theory of situated know-how. In *9th European Conference on Artificial Intelligence*.

[Singh, 1991a] Singh, Munindar P.; 1991a. Group ability and structure. In Demazeau, Y. and Müller, J.-P., editors, *Decentralized Artificial Intelligence, Volume 2*. Elsevier Science Publishers B.V. / North-Holland, Amsterdam, Holland. 127–145.

[Singh, 1991b] Singh, Munindar P.; 1991b. Intentions, commitments and rationality. In *13th Annual Conference of the Cognitive Science Society*.

[Singh, 1991c] Singh, Munindar P.; 1991c. Intentions for multiagent systems. Extends [Singh, 1990a].

[Singh, 1991d] Singh, Munindar P.; 1991d. A logic of situated know-how. In *National Conference on Artificial Intelligence (AAAI)*.

[Singh, 1991e] Singh, Munindar P.; 1991e. On the commitments and precommitments of limited agents. In *IJCAI Workshop on the Theoretical and Practical Design of Rational Agents*.

[Singh, 1991f] Singh, Munindar P.; 1991f. Towards a formal theory of communication for multiagent systems. In *International Joint Conference on Artificial Intelligence (IJCAI)*.

[Singh, 1992a] Singh, Munindar P.; 1992a. A critical examination of the Cohen-Levesque theory of intentions. In *10th European Conference on Artificial Intelligence*.

[Singh, 1992b] Singh, Munindar P.; 1992b. On the semantics of protocols among distributed intelligent agents. In *IEEE International Phoenix Conference on Computers and Communications*.

[Singh, 1993] Singh, Munindar P.; 1993. A semantics for speech acts. *Annals of Mathematics and Artificial Intelligence* 8(I–II):47–71.

[Spector & Hendler, 1991] Spector, Lee and Hendler, James; 1991. The supervenience architecture. In *IJCAI Workshop on Theoretical and Practical Design of Rational Agents*.

[Stalnaker, 1984] Stalnaker, Robert C.; 1984. *Inquiry*. MIT Press, Cambridge, MA.

[Thomas *et al.*, 1990] Thomas, Becky; Shoham, Yoav; and Schwartz, Anton; 1990. Modalities in agent-oriented programming. Computer Science Department, Stanford University.

[Thomason & Gupta, 1981] Thomason, Richmond H. and Gupta, Anil; 1981. A theory of conditionals in the context of branching time. In *[Harper et al., 1981]*. 299–322.

[Tichy & Oddie, 1983] Tichy, Pavel and Oddie, Graham; 1983. Ability and freedom. *American Philosophical Quarterly* 20(2):135–147.

[Tuomela & Miller, 1988] Tuomela, Raimo and Miller, Kaarlo; 1988. We-intentions. *Philosophical Studies* 53:367–389.

[Tuomela, 1991] Tuomela, Raimo; 1991. We will do it. an analysis of group-intentions. *Philosophy and Phenomenological Research* LI(2):249–277.

[Turner, 1984] Turner, Raymond; 1984. *Logics for Artificial Intelligence*. Ellis Horwood Ltd., Chichester, UK.

[Vanderveken, 1990] Vanderveken, Daniel; 1990. *Meaning and Speech Acts, Volume 1: Principles of Language Use*. Cambridge University Press, Cambridge, UK.

[Vanderveken, 1991] Vanderveken, Daniel; 1991. *Meaning and Speech Acts, Volume 2: Formal Semantics of Success and Satisfaction*. Cambridge University Press, Cambridge, UK.

[Vendler, 1967] Vendler, Zeno; 1967. *Linguistics in Philosophy*. Cornell University Press, Ithaca, NY.

[Werner, 1989] Werner, Eric; 1989. Cooperating Agents: A Unified Theory of Communication and Social Structure. In Gasser, L. and Huhns, M. N., editors, *Distributed Artificial Intelligence, Volume II*. Pitman/Morgan Kaufmann, London. 3–36.

[Werner, 1991] Werner, Eric; 1991. A unified view of information, intention and ability. In Demazeau, Y. and Müller, J.-P., editors, *Decentralized Artificial Intelligence, Volume 2*, Amsterdam, Holland. Elsevier Science Publishers B.V. / North-Holland. 109–125.

Springer-Verlag
and the Environment

We at Springer-Verlag firmly believe that an international science publisher has a special obligation to the environment, and our corporate policies consistently reflect this conviction.

We also expect our business partners – paper mills, printers, packaging manufacturers, etc. – to commit themselves to using environmentally friendly materials and production processes.

The paper in this book is made from low- or no-chlorine pulp and is acid free, in conformance with international standards for paper permanency.

Lecture Notes in Computer Science

Lecture Notes in Artificial Intelligence (LNAI)

Printing: Weihert-Druck GmbH, Darmstadt
Binding: Theo Gansert Buchbinderei GmbH, Weinheim